Praise for John L. Young
and *MURDER AT THE AIRPORT INN*

In *Murder at the Airport Inn* John L. Young has the gift of
sharing history in a way that the natural drama, suspense and
excitement spring to life. I enjoyed reading it, very much.
Robert W. Plyler
Arts Critic, Jamestown *Post-Journal*

Mystery lovers and fans of true crime and local history will
enjoy John Young's thoroughly researched and memorable
account of *Murder at the Airport Inn.*
Penelope Wolboldt
Reference Department Manager
Warren County Library

I really enjoyed your book entitled *Murder at the Airport Inn.*
You have done a marvelous job at extracting the fact and
weaving a story which I could not put down. What a
fascinating story.
Gregory L. Peterson, Esq.
Phillips Lytle LLP

In *Murder at the Airport Inn* Young documents the local history
of a murder prosecution and its many appeals. Young's
thorough research adds color and context to the story's
complex legal proceedings making for a compelling read.
Rene Johnson, Esq.

John's talent for local history research and his luck and
perseverance in gaining first-hand accounts is extraordinary!
Derek B. McKown
YankeeBush Productions

# MURDER
## IN THE
# COURT
# ROOM

**A TRUE STORY OF SEXUAL COMPULSION, JUDICIAL MISCONDUCT AND HOMICIDAL RAGE**

JOHN L. YOUNG

*With an Introduction and Afterword by*
LYLE JAMES SLACK

*Windy Knoll Productions*
Russell, Pennsylvania

# ACKNOWLEDGEMENTS

I want to thank and acknowledge those who helped with this book. First, as always, I thank Debra, my wife, editor, and overall helpmate. Next, much thanks to Michelle Gray and her staff and interns at the Warren County Historical Society for their many fine photos. And many thanks also to Penelope Wolboldt and her staff in the Reference Department at the Warren County Public Library for providing an accessible haven where history lives on. Without the support from organizations such as these two, local history would be lost and books like this one would not exist. And, finally, much thanks goes to my co-author Lyle James Slack, for his meticulous research and his superior interviewing skills, without which, this story would have died a slow death from our collective memory. — J.L.Y.

This story could never have been reconstructed without the generous help of those who had first-hand knowledge of the facts and gave freely of their time and memories. They include Judge Fred C. Adams, Leonora Ward Beebe, Samuel Bonavita, Patricia Borger, Art Cagle, Lorraine Cole, Richard Curtin, Martha Eaton, Mike Evan, Emery Fox, Nell Gustafson, Robert Hampson, Peggy Kifer Harp, Donna Hartley, Marie Hartley, Elizabeth Hunter, Phyllis Grettenberger Hunter, Dr. Robert Israel, Bill and Donna Johnson, Lynn Jordan, Doris Lindell, Nick Merenick, Helen Moon, Melvin Moon, Robert Moon, Jamie Moore, Sam Notoro, Zo-Ann Nicholson, Nick Pillar, Don Rice, Lee Schaeffer, Bob Schwab, Mary Schwab, Chuck Sellin, Quinn Smith, Marcella Flasher Stover, Candace Snyder, Roger Thelin, Rob Thomas. — L.J.S.

# CONTENTS

"What an awful lot of trouble one girl can cause in the world."

# ♦ THE BEGINNING

On January 13th 1954, I was a student in Miss Nelson's second grade class at McClintock Elementary School in Warren, Pennsylvania. Along with most of the other kids in the school, I walked home for lunch. For me that meant two blocks west along Pennsylvania Avenue to Eddy Street, then south three blocks to my home at 215.

On that cold January day I had just turned off the Avenue and was halfway down the first block when I heard the first, faint, frightening wail of a siren. As the seconds passed, it grew closer and louder and more terrifying, until finally I stood rooted in the middle of the sidewalk, staring back up Eddy Street toward the Avenue. At the last possible moment, a new, even more paralyzing sound was added to the siren's scream—the ferocious roar of a car engine revved to its limit.

In a moment a state police car flashed past going probably 80 or 90 miles an hour, certainly faster than I had ever seen a car go. Later, my parents told me what had happened: Someone had shot the judge and the state police were chasing the killer.

Thirty-four years later, in June of 1988, I began to investigate the circumstances surrounding the shooting death of Warren County President Judge Allison Wade. I had begun a screenwriting career following 10 years as a reporter for the daily Canadian newspaper in Hamilton, Ontario, and my writer's instinct told me Judge Wade's murder would interest an American broadcaster.

I was right about that. For a while NBC had my screenplay on its movie development roster with Valerie Bertinelli set to headline the movie-of-the-week, playing Janet Schwab, the wife of Judge Wade's killer. Negotiations between multiple producers dragged out, and eventually the deal with NBC fell apart, as so many deals in Hollywood fall apart. Over the years since, other producers have been intrigued by the story and made their own futile attempts to produce my screenplay.

Here, after all, was a sensational crime: a defendant standing up in court, in broad daylight, and opening fire with a Colt .45 automatic, eventually killing the presiding judge. Even in today's superheated climate of real and video violence, the courtroom shooting of a judge is a dismaying event, as we saw with the wide coverage given to the similar shooting of Superior Court Judge Rowland Barnes in an Atlanta courtroom in March of 2005.

In 1954, the murder of a sitting judge was a national shock. The news was instantly flashed around the country by radio. Former Warren County Sheriff Don Allen, serving with the 82nd Airborne in North Carolina that day, remembered hearing another GI shout to him in the barracks, "Hey Don, aren't you from Warren, Pennsylvania? Good god, what kind of county is that up there? They just shot the judge right off the bench!" The Associated Press and several magazines dispatched reporters to Warren to cover the arrest and trial of Judge Wade's assailant. Newspapers in Los Angeles and London, England, carried stories about the shooting.

For me, moreover, there was a built-in mystery. I eventually learned that 28-year-old Norman Wilfrid Moon, Judge Wade's assailant, was in court that day for refusing to pay his estranged wife $30 a week support. Even granting that $30 was a lot more money in 1954 than it is now, especially to Moon, a construction worker, I couldn't believe $30 was the real motivation for the shooting. There had to be more to it.

There was, of course. That's what my screenplay, and now this book, are about.

Discovering the full story took me on a four-year journey, between other projects, a pilgrimage that began with me sitting at a table in the Warren County Historical Society sifting through its files. It ended four years later with me standing before the state's lieutenant governor, attorney general and other members of Pennsylvania State Board of Pardons. In between, I interviewed 50 or 60 people, every living person I could track down who knew either Allison Wade or Norman Moon or Janet Schwab, the three principals in the drama. Thirty four years after the shooting, simply locating witnesses, jurors, family members and friends of the three was itself a project.

Many I found in Warren County, of course. Attorney Sam Bonavita, the only living witness to at least some of the events at the courthouse on January 13, 1954, was still practicing law in 1988. I found him in his office in the Penn Bank Building, looking every bit the distinguished barrister in gray suit, red tie and silver-rim glasses. I tracked down the four living jurors from Norman Moon's murder trial. Dick Curtin, the jury foreman, talked with me in the paneled family room of his home in Barnes as we ate quarter-cut sandwiches his wife had brought in. Nick Merenick, a friend of Allison Wade, both before and after Wade was elected judge, had become the court tipstaff by the 80s, so we sat on a park bench across the street from the courthouse one sunny fall day and talked for a long time. Scattered around the county were a number of women who had been waitresses at the Carver House Hotel in Warren where Janet Schwab had also worked as a waitress—and was observed sharing drinks with Judge Wade.

I sat with Mike Evan, police chief at the time of the shooting, in the kitchen of his home on Prospect Street. He had retrieved from his basement a thick black three-ring binder, which turned out to be what he called the "evidence book" for Norman Moon's murder trial. It contained, Chief Evan told me, every sworn statement, every piece of forensic evidence involved in the case. "If it ain't in here, it wasn't worth having," he said. The Chief had apparently taken the evidence book as a souvenir when he retired from the department, which tells you something about his sense of entitlement. I eventually asked to read it. Chief Evan spit some tobacco juice into a can and said he didn't think so. By that time I had asked some less than flattering questions about Judge Wade, and the Chief said he didn't like the "direction" my thinking was going.

Many other witnesses, however, were scattered around the country. Ardelle Aldrich, Janet Schwab's sister, was living in Phoenix. When I phoned her in September of 1991, a bad thunderstorm cut short our conversation—but not before she threatened to sue me for invasion of privacy if I ever wrote anything about her family. I found Phyllis Grettenberger Hunter, a girlhood friend of Janet Schwab's, hiking around a small mobile home park in north central Florida one frigid January morning. Mary Schwab, who had married Janet's older brother Joe, was wintering farther south, in Englewood, Florida. One of Norman Moon's older brothers, Melvin, had moved from the family home in Connellsville, Pa., across the state border to Oakland, Maryland. Robert

Moon, the oldest of the brothers, I traced to a mobile home park—it was more like a city—on the outskirts of Mesa, Arizona. Leonora Ward Beebe, yet another Carver House waitress, was living in Las Vegas.

The recollections of these and many others often corroborated each another, and just as often they contradicted one another. My co-author and I have attempted as best we can to make sense of their conflicting testimony. Where we couldn't, we've left it to the reader to draw his own conclusions.

And there was Norman Moon himself. In 1988, he was still alive, having spent 34 years in either state prisons or mental institutions. I wrote to him and asked if I could come and interview him. "There are always two sides to a story," I told him. "This could be a chance to let the public know your side." 10 days later I received a reply. He would put my name on his visitor's list. At the end of August I drove to the State Correctional Institute at Rockview just outside Bellefonte in the central part of the state and sat for several hours in a large visitors' room talking with Norman Moon.

"He was quite nervous but very cooperative," I wrote afterwards to a Warren businessman who was interested in producing the play I had proposed to write based on the case at Warren's historic Struthers Library Theater. Moon seemed, I added, "the least likely human being on the face of the earth to have committed murder—timid, polite, a simple man, a little beaten even." At age 64 Norman was tall and gangly, almost boyish-looking. His eyes stared out at you questioningly like two saucers, and I drove home from Bellefonte with a profound sadness, believing that in all probability one man had died and another had spent most of his life in prison because of a tragic series of miscalculations.

Afterwards I wrote to the superintendent of Rockview, requesting permission to interview Norman Moon's counselors and to use a tape recorder in the future when interviewing either them or Norman. As a journalist I always used a tape recorder and had attempted to take one into the prison for my initial interview with Moon. The prison guard who searched me on entry confiscated the recorder, informing me that advance permission was required. In my letter to the Superintendent, I indicated that Norman was prepared to waive confidentiality in order to allow me to interview his counselors. I also listed my media credentials which included my 10 years as a newspaper reporter, numerous magazine assignments and, most recently, teleplays for CBS, the Fox Channel and the Disney Channel.

The Superintendent's reply was prompt, and blunt. He would not give me permission to use a tape recorder in the prison or to interview any member of the Corrections Department. Furthermore, if Moon had not already added me to his visitor's list, he would make sure I never got to speak with him again. The letter was signed, "J. F. Mazurkiewicz, Ph.D." This was the beginning of my education about our state and federal corrections system and their attitude toward journalists. Despite the fact that Norman Moon and everyone else in prison is there by virtue of a public trial and placed there in the name of the public welfare, the press and public are regularly and rigorously denied access to information about them. Why? My impression is that corrections officials detest seeing convicted criminals have any kind of public platform where they can suggest they received something less than justice.

Over Mazurkiewicz's objections, I visited Norman Moon half a dozen times over the next four years and we corresponded regularly. Norman had engaged yet another attorney, Fred C. Adams, a retired judge in Uniontown, Pa., in an attempt to obtain his release, and in the beginning Norman often wrote about that.

Eventually I went to Uniontown and spoke with Adams in his downtown office. He was in his 60s then, impressive in a gray suit and subdued purple tie with thinning white hair. Adams had met with Moon at Rockview and come away in disbelief. "Who in the world could have believed Norman the kind of man who could walk into a courtroom and start shooting the place up?" he remarked to me. "I thought he was a very sympathetic person and constituted a threat to no one."

However, Adams had encountered a stone wall in his very first step, a request sent through channels for copies of Moon's medical and mental records. Norman had, of course, given Adams permission to seek those records, but Adams told me Rockview's superintendent claimed Moon's records were "confidential," even, apparently, from Norman himself. Adams told me he then petitioned Judge Robert Wolfe in Warren asking that the Court direct the superintendent of Rockview to produce the records. Wolfe initially directed Rockview to yield the records, Adams said, then reversed himself and sided with the warden. The message was clear to Adams. The judicial and correctional system would block any attempt to secure Moon's release, even to the extent of denying him his obvious rights. Having been a judge himself, Adams was not without understanding. "Anytime a public servant is killed—policeman, fireman, judge—it's a special case."

Judge Wolfe declined comment through a Courthouse spokesperson.

Don Allen, at the time Warren County Sheriff, sat behind his desk at the courthouse complex one day and put it a little differently. "I think if you check," Allen told me, amused, "Norman's been in prison longer than anyone else in Pennsylvania." Why do you think that is, I asked. "He shot a judge. Our system frowns on that."

Even a generally unhelpful Clerk of the Warren Courts, from whom I had requested a copy of Norman's murder trial transcript, couldn't help remarking to me in passing, "I think this is one of those cases where he'll never get out. If it had been me or you he'd shot, why...." The Clerk laughed. "Which isn't very comforting, is it? There are probably a lot of people who get let out who are a lot more of a potential danger than Moon."

Judge Adams returned the retainer fee Norman had sent and told Norman that, regrettably, he didn't believe there was anything he could do for him.

In our first meeting I had told Norman in passing that I was to be married the following September, so in several subsequent letters, he would ask, "How's marriage been?" Invariably he would go on to mention his ex-wife, Janet Schwab, for whom, all those years later and despite her role in the train of events that led to his lifelong imprisonment, Norman still had obvious great affection. "I'd been married 40 years July 1," he wrote in a letter dated July 13, 1989. "Was married by Rev. Stevenson at his home. His mother was witness. Paid him $10 and he gave each of us a small glass of wine. Don't know if anyone else paid him."

The local businessman who had been so enthusiastic about the idea of producing a play about the case suddenly lost interest. He didn't say why, but I got the impression he had talked with some of Warren establishment figures and discovered they were not pleased with the idea. I'd been contemplating adapting the story as a TV movie anyway, so in October of 1989, Norman and I signed an option agreement giving me the exclusive right to develop a movie about the circumstances surrounding his shooting of Judge Wade. In the event a movie were made, he was to be paid

$25,000, which would go into a fund to cover his legal expenses.

Afterward, I went to the Warren County Courthouse to request a copy of the transcript of Norman's murder trial from the Clerk of Courts. The Clerk kept me waiting half an hour, only to tell me the transcript was in storage on the third floor and the Clerk didn't know when there would be time to look for it.

I returned six weeks later, informing the Clerk in writing beforehand that I would be coming. When I again arrived in the office, the Clerk again told me there hadn't been time to look for it. I walked down the hall to the office of a County Commissioner I knew slightly to make my case, namely, that the Moon trial transcript was a matter of public record, that I, like any citizen, was entitled to see a copy, and that six weeks seemed sufficient time to make it available. The Commissioner phoned the Clerk, who showed up a minute later, and I was thinking finally I'd get some action. Instead, the Commissioner began lecturing me, saying he had absolute faith in the Clerk's integrity and was sure that everything that could be done was being done

All this was instructive, if frustrating. Earlier, while waiting in the Clerk's office, I had watched two young men come in, separately, minutes apart, with the same angry complaint. They were apparently in arrears in, I think, child support and under a court order to pay both the child support and a fine. Each told a clerk the same story, that they had given their probation officer one lump sum and the probation officer had promised he would send half of it to the Clerk's office to pay down the fine. Now, each man complained, he had received notice that they were delinquent and the matter would go before the judge for costs and a fine.

In each case the clerk behind the long counter replied in a monotone. The Clerk's office had not received any money from the probation officer, nor did they know about any agreement to split the money given to the probation officer. The issue would be going up before the judge again, period. The clerk hardly bothered to look at the young men as she brushed them off, and the two had left red-faced and angry. Within minutes I overheard the same clerk on the phone with someone who obviously had exactly the same complaint. For a third time she brushed him off and said the matter would again go up before the judge.

This, I realized, is how Norman Moon was probably treated decades earlier, rudely, without any attempt to understand his complaint, with arrogant disregard for due process or, ultimately, justice. You can see it again later in this book at Moon's murder trial when a deputy attorney general prosecuting the case ridicules Moon, makes sarcastic comments to goad him and puts damning words in his mouth. This kind of courtroom "justice" is not about trying to determine the truth and make fair judgments but about trying to nail a defendant anyway you can. None of this is justification, of course, for taking a gun into a courtroom and opening fire. But I began to understand the rage which must have built in Norman over the many months he was repeatedly dragged back into court.

I refused to go away, and the Clerk eventually produced a copy of the transcript, slapping it down on the counter in the office without a word and walking away. When I asked for a photocopy of the nearly 800 page document, I was told the charge would be one dollar a page. I replied that that was extortionate when every copy shop in town was charging 10 cents a page. The Clerk eventually agreed to 25 cents a page in return for my promise never to show my face in the office again.

In August of 1991 reporter Chuck Hayes wrote a story that ran on the front page of the Warren *Times Observer*. It gave an overview of my research into the shooting of Judge Wade and my plans to fashion a television movie from the material. I had asked Hayes to include my address in the article, hoping people unknown to me but with knowledge about the case would contact me. Two dozen did. Many of the letters were written anonymously, which is what I had expected. But about half were signed, which surprised me. Most people are reluctant to become personally involved in a sensational crime case. Apparently, those who signed their names felt deeply about the case, as the content of their letters verified. Out of respect for their privacy, and their courage, I have withheld their names here.

One anonymous correspondent wrote to say "I am very appalled at what you are doing to relatives who are trying to go on with their lives to forget hurt & heartaches." That was the only disapproving letter I received. All the others were sympathetic to Norman Moon or critical of Judge Wade and other court officials. Some had no specific knowledge of the case, just an unarticulated sense of outrage. "I have always thought that Moon should have been tried under mitigating circumstances," one anonymous correspondent wrote. "All I have to add," wrote a Weiler Road woman, "is that in our minds, Norman Moon is the victim." A Hinkle Street man recalled that, "Most men said they wished they had the nerve to shoot the judge that would order them to pay support to an unfaithful wife."

But others wrote with specific, if unverifiable, information. One woman said Judge Wade's gardener had told her about seeing Janet Schwab coming and going from the judge's Fourth Street home. Another woman wrote, movingly: "I have given a great deal of thought to whether I should write to you, and I have decided that perhaps this is the open door I have been praying for sometime now." She went on to recall having seen Norman Moon only once in her life, on his honeymoon in Atlantic City where she happened to be vacationing. "I remember thinking what a clean cut, good looking boy, and I have never changed my mind about that." What this woman felt compelled to reveal, she eventually said in the letter, was that she had once overheard Norman Moon's then attorney, Henry Nicholson, tell another individual that he, Nicholson, had been told to be out-of-town on January 13th, 1954 and thus not available to speak for Norman when his case was called that day. "Now can you tell me," she asked, "who would have the authority to instruct a man's attorney to be out of town on the day that he was scheduled for a hearing?"

Others had very specific information and offered to meet with me and be interviewed. Lynn Jordan and Lorraine Cole were second cousins of Judge Wade's wife, Ruth Tillotson. Sitting around the kitchen table in Lynn's Sugar Grove home, they recounted their many visits to Ruth and Allison's home in the old Mansion House on Fourth Avenue in Warren—along with their darkest suspicions about how Ruth Wade had died. In Tidioute where Janet Schwab grew up, Janet's childhood friend, Doris Lindell, invited me into her neat little mobile home and, sitting in a rocking chair, remembered one telling detail after another about young Janet, the little girl who had everything, except perhaps love. Nick Pillar, living in Erie at the time, had been engaged to Janet Schwab and helped me understand what the grown-up Janet was like in the months just prior to meeting Norman Moon at the Tidioute Hotel in 1949.

Finally, a Sugar Grove woman met with me to relate a story of unbelievable coincidence. As a child she had lived directly behind a house off Fifth Avenue where

Judge Wade lived at the time. Mr. and Mrs. Moon, she told me, lived in a house nearby. When Norman would go out of town, which he did frequently, Mrs. Moon would often go over to the Judge's house on nearby Beaty Street. The Sugar Grove woman told me she had sometimes spied on the two of them having dinner through the windows of Judge Wade's house, along with Mrs. Moon's two daughters. Abruptly I realized there was some misunderstanding, because I knew Norman and Janet Moon had never had any children together. Other irreconcilable facts began to come out: Mr. Moon was a truck driver, again something I knew for a fact Norman had never been. In disbelief I found a copy of an early '50s Warren phone directory—and verified that, in fact, a different family named Moon had lived on Fifth Avenue during the same period.

I completed my research in late 1991 and spent several months organizing and dramatizing the material into the screenplay for a four-hour television miniseries. I conceived of the piece as a kind of *Appointment in Sumarra*—three complex characters moving toward a fateful appointment none of them knew about. In January of 1993, I moved from Toronto to Los Angeles where I reworked the story into a two-hour movie-of-the-week, because of the extreme difficulty of selling a miniseries. Within a few months Stuart Benjamin—most recently executive producer of *Ray*, the Academy Award-winning musical biography of Ray Charles—optioned my screenplay and convinced NBC to put it on the network's movie roster. That deal, as I said earlier, eventually fell apart because of internal political problems, and my screenplay has never been produced.

In April of 2005 I got a phone call from John Young, a resident of Russell and a local author. He had recently published a true crime book titled *Murder at the Airport Inn*, about a Warren County murder case from the 1930s.

He told me that, in the course of book signings around the county, someone would invariably suggest that his next book be about the shooting of Judge Wade. Doing some preliminary research into the idea, he came across a *Times Observer* article about me, found my phone number on the internet and called with the idea of interviewing me for the book. I eventually suggested that we instead collaborate on a book. Many of those I interviewed in the late 80s and early 90s had since died and would no longer be available to him, so I would be able to offer him a great deal of material he would have no way of duplicating. John readily agreed.

Beyond that, I wanted the public to learn what I had learned. I had collected more information about the crime than anyone else possessed by virtue of having brought together the recollections of many people who individually possessed only part of the story.

Murder stories fascinate us, I'm not sure why. It may be that, sociologically, murder is a deep-seated taboo bred into our genes for the sake of preservation of the species, like the taboos against incest and cannibalism. When someone violates that taboo, we react with collective, genetic shock. Beyond that, for me the train of events that led a gentle, previously nonviolent man to open fire in a courtroom exemplifies the many ways in which the powerful in our society often thoughtlessly abuse the weak. Worse, the betrayal that Norman Moon suffered transpired on two incendiary planes: within a marriage where emotional and sexual abuse take a terrible toll; and within our justice system, which I believe should be the ordinary citizen's last, best protection against governmental oppression.

Both those institutions, I think, failed Norman Moon.

Lyle James Slack
*Los Angeles, August, 2005*

# ◆ PROLOGUE

N orman Moon sat in his car and looked out the window at The Swap Shop, a sporting goods store, across the street. It had been a house once, you see that. It was almost a carbon copy of all the other single family homes up and down East Street, an old neighborhood on the north side of the city. The owner probably lived upstairs, in the room with the bay window and the lace curtains. At some point, however, the façade of the first floor had been replaced with plate glass and two large doors that opened from the center.

Moon got out of blue '50 Dodge sedan and crossed the street. He was a tall man with an ungainly lope, a florid face and a full head of reddish-brown hair, and even at 28 there remained something boyish about him. In conversation he had a way of staring blankly at you, as if he didn't quite comprehend what you were saying. But he comprehended. He had a real mind for details.

Inside the store a middle-aged man looked up from the sports section of the Pittsburgh Gazette and asked jovially, "What can I do for you?" Moon looked directly at him and said, "I'd like to buy a Colt .45 automatic."

Back in his Dodge Moon drove down the descending grade of Union Street and parked under a suspension bridge that catapulted across the Allegheny River. The view of Pittsburgh, especially in winter, was not inspiring. The cold gray water moved slowly past a shoreline of dreary factories and working class homes. Though it was not yet three in the afternoon, the sky was slate gray and lights were on in all the buildings.

Moon looked down at the large brown envelope lying on the seat beside him. Printed in heavy block letters in the upper left-hand corner was "Superior Court, Commonwealth of Pennsylvania." He pulled out a three-page document and stared at it morosely a moment. Then he put the Superior Court appeals ruling aside, reached inside his jacket and pulled out the Colt .45 automatic. Methodically, he released the clip, broke open a box of shells lying on the seat beside him, loaded the clip and jammed it back into the handle of the pistol. The Colt was standard Army issue, and Moon could do this blind-folded. Not that he'd ever had a chance to use the gun during his three years in the Army Air Corps. As a tail-gunner in a B-17, he had flown 24 missions over Europe, never getting closer than 15,000 feet, straight up, from a German soldier.

Now, sitting in the Dodge, he stared at the Pittsburgh skyline. His face looked as blank as it always did, except for his mouth which was drawn down at the edges. He raised the Colt and placed the muzzle just under his right ear at the end of the jawbone. He held it there for an infinity of time. He seemed to stop breathing. The air crackled with silence. And then his arm and the gun with it collapsed into his lap, and Moon sucked in air spasmodically.

As darkness fell, he drove along U.S. route 22 through southern Ohio passing through one small town after another: Wintersville, Bloomingdale, Cadiz. He'd head for Colorado, he thought. Maybe get his old job back at the smelter in Leadville. Then he began thinking maybe that wasn't such a good idea. When the authorities discovered he was gone, Janet would be sure to give the police information about every place they had ever lived. They'd be sure to look for him in Leadville.

By the time he got to Piedmont, he was thinking he'd go to Alaska instead. He'd known a guy from Alaska in the Army. The fellow had said it was all right there. People left you alone. And what Moon wanted more than anything right now was to be left alone. He had a certified check for $1,500 in his wallet, the amount the Court said he owed Janet in back support. He could use that to make a new start.

On the outskirts of Cambridge, Ohio, where U.S. 22 and U.S. 40 headed off across the belly of America, Moon sat in his car at the side of the road. Alaska was a long way from everything he'd ever known: Connellsville, the town of 11,000 southeast of Pittsburgh, where he'd grown up; his mother and father and three brothers, who still lived there; Randall Shearer, who ran a gas station in Connellsville and was just about Moon's only buddy. Maybe—maybe if he went back to court and explained one last time how unjust all this was, maybe Judge Wade would listen to him. It was so clear to Moon. Why couldn't the judge understand? He seemed like a reasonable man. Maybe he'd listen this time.

Moon wheeled his car around and headed back up U.S. 22.

Warren sits along the Allegheny River in the northwestern part of the state. It is a town of about 15,000 but this part of the state is rural and sparsely populated—the county itself has a population of 42,000—and so despite its size, Warren was the county seat.

The town also lies 60 miles directly south of Lake Erie. In the winter heavy gray clouds lumber off the lake day after day, covering the sky for as far as you can see. So it was typically overcast when Moon woke the next morning and stared out the window of the Annex Tourist Home. Looking at the heavy sky, he felt defeated all over again. He had been driving to this town on-and-off for nearly 18 months, pleading his case before Judge Wade in the grand, French Renaissance courthouse at the intersection of Fourth Avenue and Market Street. Nothing was likely to change, Moon now realized. He began to feel again as he had in Pittsburgh the previous afternoon. He couldn't see any road ahead of him.

Moon got into his Dodge and drove out Market Street Extension. At Big Joe's Fruit and Vegetable market just outside of town, he bore right onto the old river road. About two miles farther on he pulled off and parked under one of the stately maples that lined the road. The Conewango Creek flowed by peacefully in front of him. Across the road was a high black wrought iron fence and beyond that the sweeping grounds of the Warren State Hospital, a mental institution, impressive red brick Victorian buildings dotting the grounds. Moon pulled the Colt. .45 from his waistband and stared at it. He flicked the safety off. Looked out the window at the creek. For a long time he just stared at the muddy water.

He just couldn't do it.

It was 10 o'clock when Moon walked through the rear doors of the second floor courtroom. Judge Wade was on the bench, listening to an attorney. At 57, Allison Wade was a homespun looking man, slender with thinning white hair and a quiet manner. He'd served as President Judge of the 37th Judicial District for 12 years. Two years earlier his wife had died, leaving him to care for their nine-year-old adopted daughter. Moon removed his fedora, slipped off his heavy wool coat and sat down at the corner of a bench right next to the aisle. Immediately in front of him was a low wooden railing separating the spectator gallery from the lawyers' tables.

A few minutes later Samuel Bonavita, a young local lawyer, came down the aisle and stopped to whisper to a witness sitting on the opposite side of the aisle from Moon. Bonavita recognized Moon from his numerous previous appearances in the court and said hello to him. Moon nodded. A half hour later District Attorney Meyer Kornreich came into the courtroom and immediately noticed Moon. "Hello, Norman," Kornreich said, offering his hand. Moon stared at Kornreich stonily. When Janet's own attorney had been unable to attend the hearing on Moon's appeal in Superior Court, it was Kornreich who had driven to Pittsburgh and argued against Moon's appeal. Moon was not about to shake hands with Kornreich.

"Listen," the DA told Moon, "I saw Nicholson yesterday and he told me he won't be able to be here this morning." Henry Nicholson, a local attorney, had been retained by Moon the previous summer to represent him. Judge Wade, exasperated by Moon's refusal to comply with his support order, had jailed Moon on the spot. Moon spent 20 days in jail before he found Nicholson's name in the phone book and the attorney managed to get him out on bail pending an appeal to the state Superior Court. "So if you like," Kornreich now told Moon, "we can defer your case until this afternoon." Moon shook his head. "No, I want to get it over with now."

Kornreich shrugged, crossed the room and whispered to Bernice Seavy, the court stenographer. Then he continued out of the courtroom through a side door. Judge Wade came out from behind the long judge's bench, stepped down off the dais on which it sat and left the courtroom, followed by a lawyer, the court clerk, Ralph Sires, and stenographer Seavy.

Moon sat and waited. Twenty minutes later Judge Wade and the others returned through the side door, followed by Harold Hampson, Janet's lawyer. Hampson—56, well-dressed, upper-crust—saw Moon immediately and crossed to him, asking him what he wanted to do. "You'll be told in due course," Moon replied.

Kornreich stood up at the prosecution table and addressed Judge Wade. "Your honor, Norman Moon is present." Kornreich continued, explaining that Moon's attorney could not be present until the afternoon but that Moon had indicated he wanted to proceed anyway. Kornreich went on to review the case in brief, noting that it had been more than a year since Wade had ordered Moon to pay his estranged wife $30 a week in support; that Moon had refused, claiming he was being subjected to "double jeopardy" inasmuch as his wife had first filed a claim for support in Moon's home town of Connellsville and that the court there had continued to pursue the matter; but that the state's Superior Court had three weeks earlier affirmed Judge Wade's support order.

Moon sat silently, listening. He continued to listen silently as Harold Hampson got up from behind another lawyers' table and added to Kornreich's review of the details. He noted that, after separating from Moon, Janet Schwab had moved back to Tidioute to live with her parents and that the Warren County Court was the reasonable place for her to pursue her claim for support; further, that everyone had been quite patient with Moon even as he refused to abide by the support order and continued to argue against its legitimacy. Kornreich turned to Moon and said, "Do I understand that you still refuse to comply with the court order?"

Moon stared back at him with a blank expression. "Absolutely, that is correct."

Judge Wade studied Norman Moon for a moment. Then he turned to the court's chief clerk and directed him to make a note of the question that had just been put to Moon and of Moon's reply. Wade turned back to Moon. "Mr. Moon, come forward for sentencing."

Moon stood up and took a few steps toward the judge's bench. As he did, he shoved back one flap of his unzipped jacket and pulled the Colt .45 from his waistband. Kornreich, seeing the gun, shouted, "He's got a gun!" and ran for an exit.

♦

# ♦ JANET

Janet wanted to be a movie star. From as far back as anyone could remember, even as a little girl, Janet always felt that she was a little bit better, a little bit prettier, than the other girls in Tidioute in the 1930s, and she belonged in Hollywood. Her mother spent hours curling Janet's long blond hair and using lemon juice on it to keep it blond so she could become a blond Shirley Temple.

Later, when Janet was older and she had the figure to go with the hair, she was going to be the next Carole Lombard, the next blond sex goddess.

Janet's mother Helena was one of those mothers who seemed to live vicariously through their children. In Helena's case it was as if she had given up on her life and her chance to ever be happy and she expended all her energy pushing little Janet in the direction that she might have chosen for her own life.

But Helena's and Janet's dreams never seemed to materialize into anything that lasted. One big dream was for Janet to take voice lessons in Erie, 75 miles northwest of Tidioute. Helena got on the phone and made all the arrangements and Janet made sure all her girlfriends knew about it, and that they understood that this was the necessary first step for anyone who is bound for stardom. But after three 150-mile roundtrips to the instructor's studio, the pair decided to call it quits.

Another time Helena enrolled Janet in dance lessons in Jamestown, New York, 60 miles to the northeast. But it wasn't enough for Janet to take lessons and learn the fundamentals like other children. No, her mother wanted her to be perfect in everything she did, and if she couldn't be perfect, they would quit and blame the instructors or the long drive, or the price of tea in China.

"Janet was spoiled," a girlhood friend, Phyllis Grettenberger Hunter, recalled years later. "I would be with her mother when she'd put curlers in Janet's hair. And of course it took hours to put all the little curlers in her hair to be just right. As I recall, it was a real pain for her, she just wanted to get out. She wasn't very reverent to her mother, yelling at her, calling her names."

"'Shut your trap,' that was what she used to say to her mother," Janet's sister-in-law, Mary, recalled. "'Shut your trap,' stuff like that."

"Her mother was a little Casper Milquetoast, shy and retiring," continued Phyllis Hunter, "so Janet could run all over her. Her mother idolized her, I mean, she was a pretty little girl and her mother spoiled her rotten, she had anything she wanted."

Helena wanted Janet to be the prettiest and the smartest little girl in Tidioute, with her fluffy pink dress just so and her shiny new Mary Janes sparkling and her curly blond hair shining as if God himself had spent a little extra time on her and had gotten her just right. But as mother and daughter found out after year upon agonizing year of Janet's childhood, it would take more than piano and dancing and singing lessons to make Janet the number one sweetheart of Tidioute.

As one of her childhood friends and schoolmates, Doris Lindell put it, "She wasn't overly bright or talented or anything. I'd say she was pushing it to be average."

In grade school and throughout her early high school years at Hunter Memorial, Janet got mostly Bs and Cs, with the occasional A offset by the occasional D. But as she grew older, her grades slid down the scale until by her senior years she received D's in English, French, American History, Problems of Democracy, Biology, Typewriting, and Home Economics. She received Cs in Health and Physical Education, and B's in Music and Chorus. Out of twenty students in her graduating class of 1945, Janet ranked 18th.

To her credit during her high school years, she did graduate from the Warren Conservatory of Music, which was located at 13 Market Street in Warren, 25 miles east. Its director was Dr. Leroy S. Campbell, who was in the habit of writing letters to school district officials asking that one of his pupils be given a credit or two for his or her time spent studying musical instruments in his institution. He wrote such a letter for Janet pointing out that she "has had, at the least, enough music to warrant two points on a high school course."

It appears that Helena also taught Janet how to rationalize. If Janet didn't get a part in the school play or a dance recital, it was because people were jealous of her—not because she wasn't good enough. If Janet got a bad grade, she was sure the teachers were picking on her.

"Janet thought she was going to be the greatest," Doris Lindell recalled. "It got to the place where you couldn't stand her. She'd say, 'You think I look like such-and-such a movie star? Do you think my hair's a good color?' She was so clothes conscious. And she wasn't nice about it either: 'Oh that looks like a hand-me-down that so-

and-so wore.' She would say this to the other girls. She was a nasty little brat."

For Janet's ninth birthday party Helena had invited all the neighborhood kids to the Schwab home at Kinear and Sheridan streets, on a hillside overlooking the town and the Allegheny River. When they got there, Helena had them sit on the floor while Janet sat in a chair wearing a cape she had made her and looking like a little princess. In the 1930s most of the working class families in Tidioute were struggling to put food on the table, so when these children were invited to the Schwab household, they went, not because they thought they were Janet's best friends but because they knew there would be ice cream and cake.

"Another time," said Doris Lindell, "I remember we were up there on the sidewalk in front of that house. It must have been Louise Tipton's or Ann Copland's doll. But anyway, there was a bunch of us kids playing around up there on the street, and one of the girls had a new doll and doll buggy she'd gotten. It was summertime. And Janet took that doll out of the carriage and banged its head against the cement steps there and said, 'Oh look at that, it broke. I knew it wasn't any good.'

"And of course, by that time the girl was crying. And one of the other girls took after Janet and she went running into the house for her mother. So we all scattered. She was spiteful. I can remember her at school breaking other kids' pencils and stuff, just for meanness. Pick their pencil up, break it, and walk on and leave it."

Janet and Helena didn't live like the other folks in Tidioute. Their lives were more like one of those fanciful Hollywood movie dreams where the well-to-do husband stays home and tends to his business while his beautiful wife and daughter dash off in their new convertible with the top down and their scarves trailing in the wind.

Sometimes, Janet and Helena would take a summer vacation that lasted most of the entire summer, then return with trunks full of new clothes, country-club suntans, and the latest hairstyles.

Doris Lindell remembered riding out to the country with Janet and her mother to the farm of a family friend who boarded Janet's pony. It could be fun but it could just as easily turn sour. "If Janet was in a good mood, she'd promise you if you go out with her you could ride her pony. But if she was in one of her moods, by the time you got there, why—'You can't ride my pony.'

"There weren't too many of us who put up with Janet. But we used to go to her house because there was always ice cream. And I always liked the piano they had, and I got a chance to ride the horses. And Janet always had lots of coloring books and stuff that we didn't have."

Tidioute neighbor Bill Johnson remembered Janet as a child: "She was a pretty girl, very nice complexion, and beautiful hair. I always thought she had beautiful blond hair." Bill's wife Donna adds "Nice clothes, too. That's one thing I can remember."

But, even neighbors like Bill and Donna knew there was trouble in paradise, and that things just weren't as shiny and wonderful as Janet's fancy clothes and hair would have you believe. For one thing, Helena and her husband had already started their family fourteen years before Janet was born when they had a son named Joe, who was born in 1913, and two years after that they had a daughter named Ardelle.

"It just seemed to me that Janet was so young, and her parents were quite old. She always seemed to me more like a grandchild. There was no family life as far as I could see. Like, you'd see parents and children traveling in the same automobiles, going here, going there. You'd never see Janet with her father going here, going there. You'd never see Janet with her father driving through town. He never attended any activities at school." Art Cagle, who was Janet's third husband, recalled Janet telling him two decades after her high school graduation that Lou Schwab didn't even attend her graduation ceremonies, something Cagle said hurt her deeply.

"So I don't believe she had a really happy life most children experience," remarked Donna Johnson.

Of course none of Janet's childhood friends or neighbors could have known that her life would turn out to be as explosive as it did, but early on they all sensed that when it came to being part of a loving and nurturing family, Janet got shortchanged. As pretty as she was on the outside, Janet really felt like an Ugly Duckling on the inside.

Doris Lindell Observed, "I really think all the way around Janet was never really wanted, and she was a miserable child. She had so many material things, but I never saw any affection between any of them. Not between the older brother and sister, either. They were a lot older than Janet, but I never, ever remember them doing anything with her. And you never saw her mother give Janet a hug or anything. Nothing she did was ever fine or good enough."

If Helena was anything to her family and to her friends and neighbors in Tidioute, she was an enigma. She seemed to be nice and gentle to some yet to others she seemed like a woman possessed with the idea that her child was the best and the brightest, and she would do whatever it took to make people understand this.

Helena's daughter-in-law, Mary Schwab, described Helena years later: "Janet's mother was always—I don't know what you'd call it—stayed a little bit childish. But she was a nice woman, gentle and quiet. Both girls were mean to her." More so than most folks in Tidioute, Mary understood what was going on in the Schwab household. "Janet's mother spoiled her, she really did.

Janet was born quite a few years after the first two, and I think her mother really did spoil her badly. Janet never worked; she never did anything—chores, never did anything that I knew of. She expected people to wait on her and do her bidding.

"Well, look at the father she had. That is the basis of all the unhappiness in that family." Mary Schwab added. It was, moreover, common knowledge in Tidioute that Lou Schwab had not one but two mistresses in town, sisters, incredibly enough, who lived in the same house.

"All his life it affected my Joe, until he died," Mary Schwab observed. "He was sad every Christmas, and I'd say, 'What's the mater, Joe?' He was just sad. He'd say, 'You never had a father like mine. On Christmas day, he wasn't home to play with my toys or show me a train or anything. You know what that means to a child.'

"Lou would eat with them," Mary said, "but then hurry right over there to the two girls. No bones about it, no excuses, anything."

Mary Schwab believed Joe's younger sister, Janet, was also deeply affected by her father's abandonment. "Other kids knew this stuff. They heard their parents talk about it. 'Her dad's this, her dad's that.' I don't think Janet tried to hurt other people's feelings. She was just going to show her father, I think, and the world that she could be a hellion too, or I don't know what.

"She didn't have any scruples in sexual matters or whatever. Janet was just bound that she was going to run with everybody she saw. I can't fathom anybody being attracted to everybody and anybody."

While some people, like Mary, saw Helena and her family in terms that were harrowing yet easy to understand, other people, like Bill Johnson, saw Helena as a little bit peculiar. "Her mother was never seen much in public—practically never. She was a person that remained in the house at home all the time. You would occasionally see her driving her own car."

Bill saw some unusual behavior that he still recalled quite vividly: "I don't think her mother was that well, really. She'd be out roaming the streets at very late hours. For what reason, I don't know. But people in small towns like this don't go out and walk the streets in the late night hours."

Janet's life had begun like a hometown Hailey's Comet. She was like a golden light that lit up the sky over Tidioute. Everyone who saw her in those early years bobbed their heads in agreement—Janet had everything she needed: she was pretty, she had that golden blond hair, a wealthy father, a mother who knew which fork to use, and who dedicated her life to making sure that her lovely little daughter grew up to be a fine young lady.

◆

The Great Depression of the 1930s hit Tidioute just like it hit everywhere else in the United States. It seemed like everyone in Tidioute was poor in those days—that is everyone but Lou Schwab.

Lou was tall and slim and was described by some as having an austere look about him. To others, he looked sophisticated, like he knew how to survive while others were floundering. Lou owned the local Ford dealership, which he had named, appropriately enough, Schwab Ford. The dealership was smack dab in the middle of town, and everyone knew Lou was doing okay.

In those days most women stayed home and took care of the children and ran the household while the men were expected to provide the paycheck. In this scenario Lou was a winner; he was a good provider. Like many successful businessmen, Lou was used to being in charge and he was used to people more or less doing what he said; after all, he was the boss.

Somewhere along the line, the Schwab marriage became less and less about love and more and more about control and manipulation. Lou's message to Helena was simple: you take care of the house and the kids and I'll take care of the money. I won't ask you why you need this or why you need that and you won't ask me why I stay late at the office or who I was with.

Predictably, as the years of Lou and Helena's *faux* marriage mounted up, and their possessions and standing in the community continued to rise, their marriage deteriorated to the point where it resembled that other kind of Hollywood movie where the wealthy husband fools around and the wife stays because she likes the money and the prestige of swimming in a small pond alongside her own big fish.

Janet's teen years and her relationship with her mother started out where her childhood ended. Doris Lindell recalled, "I remember when she was 14 or 15, she was taking dancing lessons with Dick Rapp in Warren. And I went up with them, and I can remember him telling her mother, 'She doesn't have enough rhythm,' for whatever her mother was wanting her to learn. And Janet went home crying, because her mother said to her, 'You've *got* to learn to dance!'"

Janet's childhood had revolved around riding her pony, taking lessons, and learning from her mother how to escape the reality of life by spending money and taking vacations. As a youngster, Janet knew she was special; she was rich and pretty and she made sure her friends never forgot it. But when she stepped across the line between childhood and becoming a teenager, she put away her childhood toys.

Janet had a brand new interest. She discovered that she didn't have to step one pretty little foot outside the village of Tidioute to get what she wanted. She didn't have to go to Hollywood to get attention.

Books could be written about what happened next in Janet's life. Indeed, many books have been written over the years about how teenagers are introduced to the mysteries of sex and what role their parents played in shaping their children's perspectives. Janet's case was no different: her perspective was shaped by a mother, an ineffectual, stay-at-home, submissive who suffered in silence and roamed the streets alone in the early morning hours; and by a father, a dashing man-about-town, who did what he wanted, when he wanted, and with whomever he wanted.

"I'll tell you," Doris Lindell recalled, "her father always ran around, and that always bothered Janet. I can remember going to the house with her. She must have been thirteen maybe. She wanted some money for some reason, and her mother wasn't around. So we went down to the garage to get it. She walked in on her father and this bookkeeper. They were on the couch together, in his office. Janet went tearing out of there. I didn't see what was going on. But she was really broken-hearted. She sobbed all the way up the hill and into the house. She went crying to her mother, 'Daddy and Lucille were on the couch again—going at it. I don't know why you stay with him! I don't know why we stay here?!'

"And her mother said, 'Janet, look around. I have a car. You have all kinds of clothes. You have your horse. I have everything we want at this house. We can go to Florida, we can go to California. If I leave him, I don't have anything.'

"I think Janet resented his affairs and resented that it was so open."

Bill Johnson knew all about Lou's amorous adventures: "There are those who looked upon her father as notorious. I would say that her dad was living a California lifestyle; he had girlfriends, which wasn't common in Tidioute."

It is said that the apple doesn't fall far from the tree. It was also said in Tidioute that Janet was becoming just like her father. She did what she wanted with whomever she wanted and she didn't seem to care who knew. In fact, she was downright boastful at times.

Sometimes, Janet would take a boy up to the loft in the barn where she kept her horse. Doris Lindell recalled, "I can remember her telling about her boys; she'd tell at school in the girls' restroom about how the boys had been up to her hay mow."

Another friend, Phyllis Hunter remembered that "Even in high school she never went out steady with a local boy—because she was used goods. So she tended to take up with out of town men, and older than herself, mostly from road gangs. I mean older men, and this was when we were seventeen."

Doris Lindell recollected a particular incident: "There was somebody working on the road, and I was with her that day. She picked up three of us at school, and the Buckingham girls got out at their house. And she circled around, they were working on the highway over at Route 62, the men were working, and she just pulled right alongside of them. 'Well, what are you doing?' she says. And before we left there she had a date with two of them for that night, and she tried to talk me into going along.

"Ain't no way, I said. In the first place I ain't allowed to date, and in the second place, those guys are old and I don't know them. They were probably in their twenties and I was only fourteen or fifteen."

Besides being pretty and willing, Janet had another advantage over the other girls her age. Being the daughter of the owner of the local Ford dealership, she had what every other teenager coveted.

"Oh yes, she had a car," Doris smiled, "We all liked her when she had that car. We could all jump in that car and go, you know. But then, you had to put up with Janet. I guess it was her mother's car, but she had it all the time. She'd go roller skating or to a movie in Jamestown or Corry. You would have loved to go roller skating or something, but there was no way you'd go with Janet because of her reputation. She'd pick up with older fellows and that."

Janet had arrived. She might have been a poor student, and she might have felt lonely and rejected at home, but when it came to getting attention from the opposite sex, she had no peers.

High school friend Marcella Flasher Stover remembered: "She was wild. Different boys used to say they'd take her out. They'd laugh. Like they'd go out with her and let on they didn't know anything and she would show them how.

"I think she had to be aware of what people thought of her. But I don't think she cared. She had her money. She had her car. And always guys. That was the main topic of conversation."

But, according to Marcella, being the number one sex goddess of Tidioute did have its down side. "One day she came to school and she was mad. Well, her dad got up that morning and went out to the car first. Someone had put a rubber on the gearshift in the car, a condom you know. So she was really provoked at that. But she didn't know who had done it because she'd been out with so many different ones."

Marcella Stover was not from Tidioute. She was boarding with a family in town while she went to high school, where she and Janet were casual friends, someone you knew just to say hi to. But all of that changed one day when the naïve Marcello was used in a ploy for Janet to get a boy into her car. Janet's scheme was for Marcello to go to the boy's door and ask for him.

"Janet came to the house where I was boarding at 281 Main Street on a weekday evening. We drove to this boy's house and I went to the door and asked for him. Next thing I know the boy's old man was there and he let Janet have it, 'I told you stay away from my son, you tramp, you.'

Marcella was thoroughly embarrassed. "I never realized I was being used. But it didn't seem to faze Janet. This boy was younger, kind of homely and not that bright. But he was just some boy Janet thought she could get."

Mary Schwab watched her sister-in-law Janet grow up. "I think Janet never had a close girlfriend. In a town like this, you're ostracized. And I think the name Schwab— people reacted. I pitied the girl. I still do when I think of her. I pitied that family even though they dragged me through one scandal after another. You know you feel like leaving the country, this county I mean. Go somewhere else. Because I don't think the shame ever leaves your name."

Janet never had that many friends to begin with, but when she went boy crazy, she became so driven in her conquests that the few friends she did have started pulling away. High school friend Zo-Ann Nicholson explained: "We had home economics together, but we weren't really friendly. She was the type you don't really want to associate with. I honestly can't say that she had any close friends. She was a loner."

Marcella Stover agreed, "You know I can't recall her having a boyfriend all the time we were in school. I mean a steady boyfriend. They were all just one-night things."

Janet's obsession with picking up boys was steadily building until it went far beyond the antics of giggling, boy-crazy teenaged girls. Once she realized that she could, literally, attract any boy (or man) that she wanted, she became obsessed with her power to the point where she didn't even know why she wanted a boy, or a certain boy. All she knew was that when she did what she did, and got the response that she got, she liked it; in effect she loved it.

"One time Janet and I went to the Chocolate Shop while we waited for her mother to finish shopping," Doris Lindell remembered. "And there was a couple boys. I was too young to go out with fellows and I know my grandmother would have killed me. But we sat there and talked with these boys. Janet was telling everybody about her father was a car dealer, which he was. But she was really pushing it, as if he had a bigger garage than it was. And then she was talking about their summer house on the lake. I *knew* they didn't have a summer house on the lake.

"Then Janet's mother found us, and I got the blame. She says, 'I'm not going to bring you down here anymore, Doris, if you're going to try and pick up boys.' Then Janet yelled at her, 'I did it on my own! And I'm glad! I can get any boy I want; I don't need her help!' Then her mother said, 'I don't want to talk about it. I don't want to talk about it.'"

The closest Janet came to a girlfriend was her relationship with Phyllis Grettenberg Hunter. Phyllis always felt that Janet attached herself to her. Mimicked her. If she took tap-dancing lessons, Janet took tap-dancing.

"She came and asked me what I was going to do after high school and I told her I was going to Villa Maria," Hunter recalled years later, referring to an all-girls' college in Erie, 60 miles away. "So right away she went over and applied, but it only lasted a couple of months. She wasn't into studying. You know, it was a bigger city and more conquests. She was after men and that was all there was to it, and it didn't seem to make any difference what walk of life or marital status or whatever."

"Janet was, I don't know, for lack of a better term, she was boy-crazy,' Phyllis observed. "She liked the men and she liked to go on dates and that was a lot of her problem.'

Janet's exploits at Villa Maria were so transparent, so predictable that it was almost funny. "I had a Spanish or Puerto Rican girlfriend and Janet would come into our room and ask the meaning of a Spanish word," Phyllis continued. "There were crews of men of Spanish descent working on the roads around the college. We soon found out that Janet was more interested in talking to them than in learning the language. Just hello or how are you. Just enough to spark up a conversation with the Mexicans who were working on the road."

Phyllis recalled another incident, probably the last trouble Janet got in before she quit Villa Maria. "We lived in a dormitory and one time Sister Dollareta came into my room and woke me from a sound sleep: 'Miss Grettenberg, where is Miss Schwab?' I said I'm sorry, Sister, I don't know where she is.' Janet left shortly thereafter."

After the Villa Maria disaster, Janet moved back home and it looked like maybe, just maybe, she was going to turn over a new leaf when it came to men. No more one-night stands. This time when she met a man she liked, she was going to keep him, maybe even marry him.

◆

Nick Pillar was a regular at the Polish club in Pittsfield. He liked the dances, and the polkas, but most of all he liked dancing with the girls. In 1946, a 19-year-old blond bombshell walked into the club and into Nick's life.

"We started dating. She wanted to get married," Nick recalled later in life. "I think the reason was she wanted to get married, she wanted to get out of the house. She came out one night—I don't know if we were parked somewhere—and she says, 'Well, if you want to continue this relationship, you're going to have to buy me a ring.'"

Ironically, up to this point in their relationship, Janet had withheld sex, but as soon as she got the ring and Nick proposed, she willingly obliged.

"I liked her," Nick continued. "I mean she was good looking, nice shape. But I don't think she could get that attached to any one guy. I think she just wanted to get out of the house."

Nick, of course, had met Janet's father, but there was something about Janet and her father's relationship that didn't sit right with Nick. "I remember picking her up one night at the house and Janet getting sarcastic with him. He'd asked where she was going and she would retort, 'I don't ask where you're going when you go out.'

"Oh, Lou was all right to me, anyway. But him and her didn't get along too swift. He just didn't like what she was doing. But she knew he had this mistress, and I think it was like a wedge. If he said something, she'd use it against him. And she usually won out."

Almost as quickly as the relationship began, it ended. Aside from all the other problems Janet had, it soon became apparent to Nick that he couldn't spoil Janet with gifts in the way she was used to.

"Well, she liked to be on the go all the time," Nick remembered. "She would have gone out every night if I could have. And she was kind of a jealous type. Well, hell, I couldn't go out every night. I wasn't making that much money. But her father had kind of spoiled her, and so she wanted things from me that, Christ, I couldn't afford to myself.

"Like, if she didn't get her way she'd be—if she wanted to go to Warren to the movie and I said I didn't have the money—why she'd give me the cold shoulder and be quiet the rest of the night, she'd hardly talk. But I couldn't afford all that stuff."

But Janet, as the saying goes, was just too cute to stay home. So if her fiancé wasn't going to take her out, she'd find some other guy who would.

"Well, then I started finding out she was seeing other guys." Nick recalled. "My buddies, they'd tell me, 'Hey Nick, I saw Janet here and there.' So I asked her about it. 'Hey we're engaged and you're running around with these guys!' And her only response was, 'How did you find out about it?'

"I figured she was having sex with these guys. I don't know, maybe she was oversexed. She had to be out every night. That's the way it seemed to me. So I thought I'd better try and break this thing off. I know her dad thought I was a farmer. He was a businessman and you know what they think of farmers. Cause Janet told me he said he didn't want to see her end up on a farm."

After Doris Lindell married, she moved into the house next door to the Schwabs and remembered hearing the screaming match between Janet and her father regarding her engagement to Nick Pillar.

"Our houses were only about fifteen feet apart," Doris recalled, "and we had our windows up and we heard Janet yelling, 'Pillars are just as good as we are. I never heard of their father sleeping all over town.' And my husband said, 'Boy, she's telling it like it is!'"

After her engagement to Nick ended, Janet took up her old ways. Mary Schwab recalled, "She was in Pittsburgh for a while, then. I think her mother tried to get her to go to some school. But she was home in no time. So then she was just around town. No job, she never worked. I'd see her on the streets, somebody would honk a horn. Or she'd go down and sit in her car on the street. Anything at all to get attention. Hunting season, she'd go with a hunter to his cabin, or any stranger in town."

Mary Schwab paused and shook her head. Finally she added, "What an awful lot of trouble one girl can cause in the world."

Doris Lindell remembered, "When I had my first baby, Janet would come over and see the baby. And oh, she wished she could find somebody that would love her and she could have a family. She'd say, 'You really think you'll stay married? Well, how do you know you love somebody?'

"She was so envious to think I had a daughter and a husband. And yet, there she had cars, money, everything, always did. And yet she'd say, 'I don't think I'll ever find someone who will love me.' She was very insecure; I really think she didn't think anybody cared about her. She just put on this big front is what I think.

"I always felt sorry for Janet because she had so much—and yet she was always so miserable. She never was content with anything or anybody. Very miserable. I don't think that girl was ever happy."

♦

# ♦ NORMAN

Dolly and Fred Moon were married in 1912 in Connellsville, Pennsylvania. They set up housekeeping in Dunbar Township, just outside the city limits, and in short order they had five sons: Robert, Melvin, Edward, Earl, and the youngest, Norman, who was born on the third of November in 1925.

Norman started his life out a little differently than his four older brothers. He just wasn't that healthy. Right off, he floundered in grade school where he failed third grade. He got along with his brothers okay but he didn't seem to want to make friends with the neighborhood kids. He was withdrawn. But young Norman never gave his parents any trouble, and in turn they never really concerned themselves with his behavior.

On some occasions Norman did the regular things that boys do. He joined the Boy Scouts. And when Sundays came, he went along with the rest of the family to the United Brethren Church. But he had a peculiar habit of not wanting to go outside and play. He preferred to stay in the house and read or play Monopoly, and on the rare occasions when he did play with a neighbor boy, he tried to get the boy to come into the house and do things.

Norman's oldest brother Bob was 12 years older than Norman, and because of their age difference Bob was able to see things in his brother that younger kids just wouldn't notice. "He was very quiet and I have never known him to be angry at anyone in our family, he may have been with others, that I do not know. He was very nonchalant, very willing to forgive any wrong that was done to him."

In high school Norman brought home library books and he was a regular reader of the *Saturday Evening Post* and *Reader's Digest,* and when he tired of reading, he would play checkers with his father.

Norman continued to stay close to home until he entered his junior year at Connellsville High School. That year he became interested in sports and he was elected by the players to be the manager of the varsity football team his junior and senior year. He liked sports well enough and he even may have thought of playing but he was just too small. For some reason Norman had not grown physically or emotionally like the other boys his age. Norman was small and skinny; when he stood around with the other boys on the team, you could see that he was underdeveloped.

World War II hit the Moon family exactly as it hit all the other families in Connellsville and in every town, city, and hamlet across the country. Before the war was over Dolly and Fred would send four of their five sons into battle; one would not return. Earl was a pilot in the Air Force, and on the first day of the invasion of France, his plane was shot down over the Mediterranean Sea and his body was never found.

The war was in its third year when Norman quit school his senior year in February 1944 to join the Army. He reported for induction in Pittsburgh, was sworn in and then sent home for three weeks. Afterwards he was ordered to report to Fort Mead, Maryland, for his medical exam, to receive his clothing issue and to take a series of aptitude tests. From there he went to Miami Beach, Florida, for basic training. While in Miami Beach, he took the cadet exam but he was rejected. His next stop was gunnery school in Laredo, Texas, and afterwards he went to Lincoln, Nebraska to become part of a flight crew. From there he was sent to Pueblo, Colorado where he met his flight crew members and the group was trained to operate as a crew on a B-17. The crew was then sent to Topeka, Kansas, where the men received their weapons and gear; from there they went to Camp Kilmer in New Jersey, then boarded the Queen Elizabeth for the Atlantic crossing before finally they were assigned to a base in Ipswich, England.

From there Norman and his shipmates were diverted from their flight assignment, in typical Army fashion. Never mind that they were trained as a crew to fly a B-17, they were soldiers and they would be used where the Army needed them most. In short order Norman's crew was loaded onto barges, ferried to France and joined thousands of other GIs in the Battle of the Bulge.

When they returned to base, they were assigned to their first B-17 and, although he had been trained to be a turret gunner, Norman was assigned to be a tail-gunner. In all, Norman flew 24 missions over Germany in six months. His plane was strafed a number of times but he was never hit. When the war in Europe ended in May of 1945, Norman was sent back to the States and told he was to await deployment to the South Pacific where the war against Japan still raged. But in August while en route on a troop train to his new assignment, his unit got the news of the Japanese surrender. World War II was finally over. Norman was discharged at the rank of Staff Sergeant on November 4, 1945, one day after his 19th birthday. He had made rank, earned the respect of his crewmembers, and in the eyes of many, he was a bonafide war hero. But apparently Norman didn't see his exploits during the battle of the Bulge or his sorties over Germany as any big deal; he didn't go out on the town and celebrate for weeks like the other GI's did.

When it came to getting ecstatically excited or going out and partying for weeks on end with his fellow soldiers, the shy teenager seemed to have had a governor on his emotions. He didn't get too high and he didn't get real low. He tended to roll with life's punches.

Certainly being stuck in a plastic bubble in the tail of a B-17 didn't do Norman's mental health any good. The tail-gunner is the hottest place on a bomber; you're in there cramped up, and fighter planes, when they come in, they blast at the tail first. "It's not something easy to look back on—being near death," Norman recalled in later years. "When we came back from those missions, they always gave us a shot of whisky. It wasn't easy."

Robert Moon noticed a difference right away when his teenaged brother came back from the war. Later, after the courtroom shooting, Robert went to Texas and talked to the captain of the plane Norman flew in during the war. "He said they were all shell-shocked and so on. He said, 'I thought we all come out of it all right, but we should all probably have gone for rehabilitation, but we wanted to get home. That's where we made our mistake.' That pilot thought Norman was probably a war casualty, that he just cracked up from the strain."

A few days after Norman was discharged, he signed on to a construction crew in Sioux Falls, South Dakota, where they were building a golf course. He worked there for a week, got his pay, then headed home to Connellsville, arriving in time to celebrate Christmas with his family. He moved back into his parents' home and a few days later went to work for his father at Moon & Sons Construction.

Norman was 19 and picked up his life where he left it when he joined the Army. The only thing that changed was instead of going to high school during the day, he went to work for his family's construction business and spent his nights at home with his parents.

Years later, Norman's mother Dolly would recall that when Norman came back from the war, "He seemed rather nervous; it seemed he wanted to be doing something all the time. He seemed to feel better doing something than not doing anything."

After the war, Moon Construction was busy clearing right of ways and stringing lines for telephone and power companies. Norman drove truck, did labor work, and eventually learned to drive heavy equipment.

In the early months of 1949, the company took on what was known as the "Warren Job." The contract was for Moon Construction to work ahead of the telephone and power companies constructing a tow pole along the right of way that ran from Oil City to Warren, a distance of about 50 miles. Then, using the tow poles, they strung the power and telephone lines that connected the two towns.

Norman and the crew moved along with the line and stayed in different towns as the job stretched northward. The first part of the job they stayed at Oil City; from there they went to Titusville. And in the summer of 1949, they ended up in Tidioute, taking rooms at the Tidioute Hotel. For Moon & Sons Construction the entire job lasted four months.

It was while staying at the Tidioute Hotel that Norman met the girl who would become his wife. "The man who owned the hotel I was staying at introduced me to her," Norman later explained. "He saw these girls on the other side of the street in Tidioute, across the street by the theater, and he took me over and introduced me to her.

"I made a date with her for the next night. I forget where we came up here, to a show or what in Warren. The next night I went to her home and took her out. I can't exactly say where we went, whether to the theatre or where we went."

Less than a month later, on July 1, 1949, 23-year-old Norman Moon was married to 21-year-old Janet Schwab.

♦

# ♦ MARRIAGE

T he trouble with living in a town as small as Tidioute is that everyone knows your business. And even more troubling is the fact that everyone—from the mayor to the butcher to the guy who pumps your gas—has an opinion of how you should conduct your life. After 21 years, everyone had an opinion about Janet Schwab and in a few short weeks everyone had an opinion about her fiancé, Norman Moon.

"I can remember my husband liked Norman," said Janet's girlhood friend, Doris Lindell, long after the event. "My husband probably saw him at the bar or something; he was a part-time bartender down there at the Tidioute hotel. Then one night after work he told me, 'This fellow that Janet has snagged, he's too damn good for her.'"

Doris remembered when Janet met Norman and decided to marry him. "Boy that was fast! She must have been going with him for about two weeks. I remember I was out hanging up clothes on the clothesline when her mother came over and told me Janet's getting married. I was invited to the bridal shower and I met Norman's brother and sister-in-law. Different ones said that Lou thought it was a good match.

"And Norman, he seemed like an awfully nice, quiet person. Well-mannered. I mean he wasn't prissy or anything, but he was clean-cut."

If people in Tidioute were concerned that such a nice young man was going to marry Janet, the reaction in Connellsville was closer to anger.

"I tried to talk him out of marrying Janet," Norman's brother, Melvin, recalled years later. "See, we was working up to Tidioute area when he met her and married her. I was up there in charge of it, and we had Norman running one crew, so I know that he got going with her up there.

"The fellas that was working with us voiced their opinions about it—just basically that she wasn't the right one for him to be messing around with. But Norman just turned a cold shoulder to you."

Another of Norman's brother, Robert, recollected, "My dad was bitterly opposed to the wedding. He wouldn't even go to the wedding because he'd been warned about her promiscuity."

"I didn't know what to do," Norman admitted. "We'd been dating every night for two weeks, and I knew the job was winding down and I'd be leaving Tidioute. I felt a lot of pressure to make a decision. So one night at her house I just came right out and asked her if we should get married. And she said yes. After that, we walked down to the Ford dealership and I asked Lou for his daughter's hand in marriage.

"There was one other thing. We'd been going at it hot and heavy and every time we got to a certain point, she'd say, 'No, Norman. Not until we're engaged.'"

At any rate the wedding date was set for two o'clock on Friday, July 1st, 1949. But at the last minute Janet insisted on moving the time up to one o'clock—and refused to allow her parents to attend the ceremony. Robert Moon drove his mother to Tidioute from Connellsville, and because the time was moved up, the wedding was over before they got there.

Robert Moon had never seen his mother so upset as when they arrived too late for the wedding. There were only four people who attended the wedding, which was held not in the Methodist Church but in the parsonage living room where the pastor, Rev. Stevenson, married the pair with his elderly mother as their witness and only attendee.

After the ceremony Rev. Stevenson gave Janet and Norman a small glass of wine each, and that was that. Mr. and Mrs. Norman Moon were ready to begin their new lives together.

After the wedding Norman and Janet went to Atlantic City for their honeymoon, and after a week or so they returned to Tidioute, where Norman went back to work on the utility right-of-way. By the end of July Norman had finished up the Warren project and the newlyweds moved to Connellsville. Norman drove the company truck with equipment in the back and Janet drove the new Mercury he had bought her as a wedding gift.

Norman was used to driving the 175-mile trip from Tidioute to Connellsville straight through. But Janet complained about being tired, so they stopped at Delmont, a small town on the eastern outskirts of Pittsburgh. Saturday morning they drove the rest of the way, arriving in Connellsville before noon.

It would seem that two adults could figure out how to get their marriage up and running with no more than a modicum of problems, but from their very first day in Connellsville, ordinary situations somehow seemed to overwhelm the pair. They had driven all that way and hadn't bothered to ask a family member in Connellsville to see if he or she could locate an apartment for them.

And it appears that Norman, or more likely Janet, did not want to stay at the Moon household—not even for one night. Couldn't they have checked the classifieds of the local newspaper while they still lived in Tidioute?

Norman and Janet each had specific problems that had hampered them in their earlier lives. Norman's problem was that he never confided in anybody; he never opened up—about anything, not to his brothers nor to his parents. In short, he seldom asked for help. Janet lived on the other side of the equation, was all too glad to ask for help. She had never done any chores growing up and she certainly never had a job or took any interest in cooking or keeping house.

So they found themselves in downtown Connellsville looking for an apartment. After a long and frustrating day, they finally secured an apartment on the second floor of a house owned by Norman's aunt. It was unfurnished, and Janet insisted they immediately buy furniture for the apartment. They did, but the store closed shortly afterward and could not deliver the furniture until the next day. Janet became so upset that Norman borrowed a pick-up truck from the delivery boy and hauled everything to the apartment, unloading it in the dark. That first weekend they ate their meals at restaurants. They had no kitchen utensils and no table and chairs. But then they didn't need much, as it was a simple studio apartment with a bathroom, a kitchen, and large room that served as a living room-bedroom combination.

Then, like it always does for the working man, Monday morning rolled around and Norman got ready for work. But there was one little problem: Janet didn't want him to leave. She didn't know anyone in town; what was she supposed to do?! Each morning Norman tried to get out of the apartment as quickly as he could but invariably when he finally got to work, the crews were waiting for him.

Because of his habitual lateness, Norman was soon transferred from the outside work with the crews to shop work where he took care of the equipment and at least coming in late didn't hold anyone else up. Everything was fine for a few days, but then one day when he went home for his lunch break, Janet was lying in bed holding her stomach.

"I think I have appendicitis," she moaned. Norman called a doctor, who came and examined Janet and said he couldn't find anything wrong with her.

Norman went to work and Janet stayed home, and the boxes of their clothing and possessions remained scattered around their apartment. After a week or so it began to get on Norman's nerves. It seemed to him that Janet stayed in bed as long as she could during the day, just waiting for him to come home so they could go out to the bars and nightclubs and she could have a good time.

Then one night Norman came home late from work, and Janet wasn't there. She came in while Norman was cleaning up from his supper and went into a tirade about his habitually coming home late, then stormed out of the apartment. She came back later with beer and continued to drink and rant until Norman's landlady aunt came up to see what was the matter.

Janet immediately shut up. But as soon as the aunt went downstairs, Janet went into a rage again and tried to hit Norman. It was then that Norman accidentally caught her on the chin with his fist and all hell broke loose. She got even louder and more violent, until the aunt called Norman's mother to come over and see if she could calm Janet down. Dolly Moon recalls that night.

"She said Janet was carrying on in such a terrible way that she was going to have to call the police. She asked me, 'Will you come out and see if you can get her settled down? My husband is sick. She just screams, carries on. I cannot have it.'

"Before I even got in the house, I could hear her fussing and making a noise. But when I got in the room, she didn't say anything. I tried to talk to her and asked her not to cause a disturbance.

"Norman was petting her and coaxing her and trying to keep her quiet, that she didn't make a noise, and I stayed a while. But when I started down the stairs to leave, why, she started again to make a noise, started to scream, hollering and fussing, and I went back up and tried to talk to her. As long as I was in the room, she didn't say anything, but as soon as I would go out, she would start again."

By this time Norman was getting concerned that something was really wrong with his wife, so he tried to get a doctor to come out. None would come, so he drove Janet to the hospital. The doctor at the hospital examined her and said she was all right but that she seemed a little nervous. He asked Norman to follow him to his office, which he did while Janet waited in the car. The doctor gave Norman a bottle of medicine and instructed Norman to give Janet a teaspoon every hour.

When Norman got to the car he tried to hand Janet the bottle. "I'm not taking that crap." She pushed it away.

"What do you mean? The doctor said—"

"I don't care what he said. That stuff is poison."

At an impasse, they drove around with bottle rolling back and forth on the seat between them.

"Norman, I want to leave Connellsville," Janet finally said.

"And go where?"

"I don't know." Janet sat up straight in her seat. "Anywhere away from here. No one in your family likes me. It's just not working."

"But where?"

"Let's just go somewhere and start over. Just the two of us."

Norman hesitated only briefly. "Okay. If that's what you want. If you're sure that's what you want."

"Oh, I'm sure." Janet picked up the bottle of medicine and tossed it out the window of the car, where it shattered. Then she slid over and rested her head on Norman's shoulder.

Like she always had during her growing up years, Janet got her way, and the very next morning they packed up their belongings and left. They had lived in Connellsville a total of six weeks.

◆

The next afternoon Janet and Norman were right back where they started, in Tidioute. They stayed at her parents for a few days while they sorted things out, and before the week was out they were on their way to Colorado. Just where in Colorado they would settle they didn't quite know, but they were going to stop first to see Janet's relatives in a place called Silver Cliff.

They stayed in a motel in Silver Cliff for a week while Norman looked for work and Janet visited her relatives. Norman couldn't get connected with any kind of a job in Silver Cliff and eventually he found his way to a construction job in Leadville, a played-out mining town that had seen better days in the late 1800s as a processing center for lead and zinc ores. By the time Norman and Janet hit Leadville, it was not much more than a modern-day ghost town.

Their first days in Leadville were spent at a motel. Then when Norman got hired on at a construction job, they took a room in a run-down boarding house. Things seemed to settle down for a few days after that as Norman went to work, and Janet got herself acquainted with the town. But, almost as if on cue, Janet got restless again.

"I'm lonely and bored," Janet said as soon as Norman's boots hit the floor of their room. "Maybe I can get a job as a waitress at that place, the Frontier Café."

Norman had mixed feelings about all this. On the one hand he wanted Janet to stay busy and maybe get involved in life in the tiny town, but on the other hand, he didn't feel like the Frontier was such a great place for her to hang out. In the end Janet won out and she got her first job.

Leadville sat at an altitude of over 10,000 feet. It took newcomers a few days or even a few weeks to get used to living and working in the thin air. Norman was no exception. Most days after work, he was just too exhausted to do much of anything but get cleaned up, eat his dinner, and hit the sack. Janet, of course, was working nights.

But after a few days Norman decided he needed to go to the Frontier to see how his wife was doing. What he saw surprised him. First of all, the Frontier was more of a nightclub than a café. Although food was sold at the Frontier, it was clear to Norman that its main business was selling booze to the patrons at the bar and at the tables while they watched floorshows.

When Norman made his way into the bar, he got his second surprise of the night. Instead of running around with a tray full of drinks and serving customers, Janet was sitting at the bar talking and drinking with male customers. Later, back at the boarding house they argued, and Janet couldn't understand why Norman was so upset.

"God, Norman," Janet raged, "I don't know why you're so upset. I wasn't even drinking."

"Janet, I saw you there talking to those guys at the bar. You were drinking."

"God, Norman, Don't you know anything? I wasn't drinking whiskey. It was tea, just plain old tea."

"You telling me they're paying you to sit there and drink tea with the customers?"

"That's right. That's what they want me to do."

It's hard to believe that a man could be as naïve as Norman appeared to be. Is it possible that he didn't know that what Janet was doing was 'hustling' the customers: getting them to buy her drinks that were, as she said, nothing more than tea?

Life went on with Norman working at the construction site and Janet entertaining male customers at the Frontier Café. Then something odd happened after a week or so. Janet complained that she wasn't feeling good again. She said the boarding house was cold and drafty. She just couldn't get herself warm. When Norman said he would get more blankets, she said no that's not good enough.

"I'm getting out of this drafty old room. I can't stand it here anymore."

"So I'm supposed to stay here and you're going to live at the hotel. Is that it?"

"Yes," Janet said, "I suppose that's it."

Janet spent the next two nights at the hotel while Norman went to work and came home too exhausted to do much about it. Late in the afternoon of the third day of Janet's hiatus, Norman was sleeping and his landlord woke him.

"Mr. Moon, I just seen Janet down at the Frontier and she was drinking there at the bar with some fella. I asked her if she was coming home and she just laughed and said they was going to drive down to Salida to have themselves a good time."

Exhausted or not, Norman got dressed and drove the fifty-eight miles to Salida and started searching the bars. In one bar he found the man Janet was supposed to be with, but when Norman asked him about her he just shrugged his shoulders and turned his back. Frustrated and exhausted Norman left Salida and headed back to his room. Along the way he passed a car stopped along the road; the driver beeped the horn at him, and when Norman stopped and walked up to the car his saw the driver, a salesman from Denver, a girl beside him, and next to the window, Janet.

Janet jumped out of the car and got in with Norman. Norman was so tired he didn't say anything; he kept his hands on the wheel and his eyes on the road. By the time they made it back to their room Janet said she wasn't feeling well.

"It's like I'm nervous," Janet said, pacing the length of the small room. Unable to endure the feeling, she called a doctor who came out and gave her a routine examination and talked in private with their landlady, but he could find nothing wrong, except maybe she had a cold.

"He threatened to hit me," Janet screamed at the doctor, pointing her outstretched arm toward Norman.

"Maybe he should," the doctor said as he picked up his bag and left.

The next day Norman went to work and Janet made an appointment with another doctor, who, after examining her, recommended that she be placed in the Mount Airy Sanitarium in Denver. Norman took the following day off work and drove her the one-hundred-and-forty miles to Denver.

After a two-week stay Janet was discharged and the only advice her doctor gave her was that maybe she was reacting to the altitude, maybe the lack of oxygen was affecting her brain. He suggested they move to Denver, which at 5,000 feet above sea level was considerably lower than Leadville.

And so, once again, Norman quit his job and in typical Janet-Norman style, they threw their belongings in their car and set out for a brand new place to live.

When they got to Denver it was a repeat performance of when they first got to Connellsville and Leadville: they couldn't find a place to stay so they ended up the first few nights in a motel.

A few days later when they were out searching for an apartment, they came across a business that was selling what they called house trailers in those days and more often these days "mobile homes." They did not in any way appeal to Janet, but after a few visits—probably because she was tired of living in a motel, they bought one and set it up in a trailer park in Englewood, a suburb of Denver.

A week later, Norman got a job as a salesman at the place where they had purchased the trailer. He worked there for four months and sold one trailer.

A few days after Norman lost his job at the trailer company, he started feeling weak and when he went to a doctor he was diagnosed with viral pneumonia. When he was feeling better he got a job with the borough of Englewood. There had been a heavy snowfall and the borough hired extra workers to clear away tree limbs and clear the snow from the streets. Norman worked for the borough for a month.

But before he could go out and start his job search, he got sick again. Both his mother Dolly and Janet's mother Helena, and Janet's aunt and two nieces had come out to visit for the holidays. On a drive to Echo Lake, Norman started feeling worse and by that night when they were back at the trailer, he felt even worse. The next morning he checked himself into the VA Hospital at nearby Fort Logan, and remained there for two weeks.

When he got out he was feeling well enough to look for a job. He and Janet still had company, but that first Monday morning at breakfast Janet got angry with him.

"I was getting ready to go out and see if I could find a job or something," Norman recalls. She said something at the breakfast table. Her nieces and her mother and my mother and I was there, and I said 'That is enough of that!' and she started to carry on pretty bad and I just got out and left and went and packed my clothes and went looking for work. I found a job that day and stayed at a hotel that night. About the next day or so at work the company I was working for got a phone call. They told me my wife was in the hospital and I was to go see her."

Dolly Moon was shocked when she learned what was going on with Norman and Janet in Colorado. "I remember that morning that they argued about Norman getting a job. She didn't want him to go out looking. He asked her three times if she wouldn't sit down and discuss it and she wouldn't. So he says, 'Well, I guess I will go and see about that job,' and she just let out a scream, took her fingers and made a dive for his face.

"After Norman left, Janet told her mother in my presence that she took a job in this café in Leadville and her job was to sit and drink with men and entice them to go upstairs, and told of her going out with a man.

"She told us that she and another man and another couple had gone in a car while Norman was at work. I believe the town was Salida. She and Norman had trouble that night and she stayed in town at the hotel.

"And then she took one of her ugly hysterical spells like she did when she was at home. She pulled her hair and scratched herself. Then she held out her arm and showed her mother scars and says, 'There are the scars on my arms yet where I scratched myself.'

"The next day while Norman was working, Janet drove me and her mother and aunt and nieces out to Red Rocks. She was moody and sullen and she hollered and had her mother upset all day. After Red Rocks she drove down to Golden to hunt for the man she had gone to Salida with. She would stop in a café and asked for him;

she understood that he was working down around Golden.

"All the while she was trying to find this man, her disposition got worse. And later on, why, she put her mother to the wheel and told her to drive. It was her mother's car and Janet kept hollering at her all the time. That evening when we got back to Janet's, her mother passed out, she was just hanging limp in a chair.

"After that we took her to the doctor and he put her in Rose Memorial Hospital in Denver for a week. They told her there that she had caught a disease from working in Leadville. It almost drove her crazy."

After Janet's weeklong stay at Rose Memorial, just like always, Norman picked her up and brought her back to their trailer, and things were as normal as could be expected. Norman continued working for Hudson-Carey Housing in Englewood and Janet continued to sit around the trailer and make herself unhappy.

Within weeks from her release, Janet went from the chaos of her most recent breakdown to daydreaming about how their life would be better if they moved back home. The two talked about it and agreed maybe it would be best if they did move back home to Pennsylvania, and so in March of 1951 they hitched up their trailer and drove to Janet's parents' home in Tidioute. They visited in Tidioute a week and then drove on to Connellsville.

◆

Norman's brothers, perhaps like Norman, were quiet types and didn't feel the need to go spouting off their opinions of Norman's marriage while he was married to Janet. But years later, when Melvin Moon was asked to recall what he could about Norman and Janet's Colorado escapade, he told what he had been holding in all those years.

"He took Janet to Colorado basically for the reason of getting her away, to a new environment. My mother went with Janet's mother out there one time for a visit. My mother came back and claimed Janet was messing around out there and gave Norman a dose of the clap.

"All I know is what Norman told me. I think he caught her with two different men out at a club or something. The one guy I think he caught her in the act. But as I say, the whole thing was a little embarrassing to him and you never really got too much information out of him."

On their way to Connellsville Janet and Norman stopped to visit Norman's brother Bob and his wife in a suburb of Connellsville named Poplar Grove. There was an empty lot near Bob's house and after considering it, Norman and Bob set up the trailer on that lot. A few days after they got settled, Norman went back to work for his father and brothers on a water line project in Harrison City 25 miles northwest of Connellsville. When that job finished for Moon & Sons, Norman stayed on working for another contractor who wanted to rent the Moon construction equipment.

It looked like Norman was going to be okay as far as work was concerned. There was plenty of construction going on in the area in the 1950s and it seemed like Norman was finally in the right place at the right time. The job at Harrison City had been completed and Norman stayed with that company and drove back and forth to the jobsite in Westmoreland County, spending more and more time away from home.

Norman and Janet had been getting along all right, but Janet just couldn't get used to spending long days at home, cooped up in a trailer far from home and not knowing anybody. Norman's brother Bob remembered those days.

"After they were married, when Norman would be at work, Janet frequented the nearby riding stables. And many a man bragged to us about their scoring. This all came out later. Other times she would drive up to Moon & Sons and call out of the window for Norman. When I would tell her he wasn't there but on a job, she would hit the accelerator and hotrod away, disgusted."

Despite her promiscuous ways, Bob got to know her well enough during the time they lived near him that he could see that she was childlike and didn't really understand life the way other adults did.

"She wanted to plant some flowers, and the ground sloped," Robert Moon recalls. "and she said, 'Well, the flowers will grow crooked won't they?' And then we had a baby and she just insisted that we give her the baby to raise. And there was no way; we hardly wanted her to touch it. She had a child's mentality."

Janet had had a miscarriage the first few months after her wedding and since then she had taken measures so she wouldn't get pregnant again. But here she was, almost three years later, daydreaming about raising a baby.

But domestic bliss in the Moon household ran in cycles and was short-lived. There would be a flare-up, usually about Janet running around with another man; they'd both be angry and silent for a while. Then one would soften and the other would respond until finally they would talk and make up.

But in some marriages, nothing changes but the date. After four months of Norman commuting to and from work and Janet watering her flowers and trying to be a regular housewife, something inside her snapped. Norman was especially late getting home from work that day.

"One day the machinery broke down and I had to go to Connellsville to get parts," Norman later recalled, "and when I come back from there, why things got in a fracas again.

"It was about 10 o'clock in the evening and she got to raising heck and saying where had I been and everything. Then she got in the car and left. She came back after a while and got raising more heck and asked me to take her to the doctor. I took her to the doctor and he recommended sending her to the hospital again."

Norman drove Janet to Pittsburgh and admitted her to the psychiatric ward at St. Francis Hospital, where she stayed for two weeks. After that he picked her up and they returned to the trailer, which was now parked near the construction site in Maymount, where Norman was working. Janet seemed a little better and the two got along for a few months.

Later that year, in December of 1951, Norman took a week off work and the two of them spent a week at the Schwab home in Tidioute while Norman and Janet went hunting. When Norman returned to his job, he learned the subcontractor had hired someone else to operate the Moon & Sons equipment.

Once again the couple decided that life would be better somewhere else. In January of 1952, they moved to a trailer park in Morrell 10 miles southwest between Connellsville and Uniontown. And predictably enough their life went on just as it had: they'd have a few good months, a few so-so months, and then a major explosion.

The explosion this time happened one evening after Norman got home from work and Janet and her mother and nieces, who were visiting from Tidioute, came home from swimming.

"I just asked her where they were swimming that day. She said out at Pennsville and she got pretty sarcastic, and we got in a little fracas there, and I had to go to the bathroom. I had taken off my work clothes. When I came out of the bathroom my wallet was sticking out of my pocket. I looked in. All my money was gone. I had around $50 in it and I asked her whether she had taken it. I said I had to have the money for the next day.

"She said, 'I have it and I am going to spend it, do what I want to with it.' I got pretty mad, slapped her a couple of times, told her I had to have some of it. She wouldn't give me any of it so pretty soon she went over to the neighbors there, and after a while she come back and got dressed up and said she was going out for the evening."

Norman and Janet kept arguing until Janet gave in and gave Norman some of the money. After that she left for the neighbors. Norman got dressed and started to drive into town for milk and to stop at his parents to see if any mail had been delivered there for him. As he left the trailer park, he saw in his rearview mirror Janet pulling out from the neighbor's and driving into town behind him.

Norman figured she was following him so that she could learn where he was going so that she could go somewhere else. Norman pulled off the road and Janet continued toward town. Norman then drove to his parents' house and borrowed one of their cars so that he could check out the bars where she liked to go without her recognizing his truck.

About the third place he went he spotted her car, parked in front of the Club Lido, a nightclub in Scottdale, a village about 10 miles north of Connellsville.

"I went over to it, and Janet and Bill Dye were in the car," Norman later recalled. Bill Dye was a high school classmate. Norman had run into Dye just a few weeks earlier, at the American Legion hall, and had introduced him to Janet at that time. "Bill was in the driver's seat and she was in the passenger's seat," Norman remembered about the night outside the Club Lido. "I said to her, 'Isn't it about time you are getting a divorce or something?' Then I said, "Maybe you should get a divorce and marry Bill. I have taken all I can take.'"

After a short back-and-forth between Norman and Janet—with Bill sitting between them—Norman ended the conversation with, "We might as well get a divorce then."

Norman returned his father's car to his parents' home, drove his truck back to the trailer and went to bed. Janet never came home that night. Norman woke at four in the morning and drove to town for his breakfast before going to work. As he passed his neighbor's trailer, he saw Janet's mother's car in front of it, so he figured Janet had spent the night there.

The rollercoaster ride that was Janet and Norman's marriage continued into the summer of 1952. During this period Janet visited Dolly alone one night and told her that, as far as she was concerned, the sooner she and Norman divorced the better it would be for everybody.

"We have been talking about a divorce and I have about decided we better get it," Janet said one night about eleven o'clock in Dolly's living room. "We have got nothing in common. I like to roller-skate and go dancing and swimming and sports and all and Norman isn't much interested in those things."

On the Sunday night of the last weekend the couple lived as man and wife, Norman came to his parents' home alone. Dolly fixed him his dinner, and after he ate, Norman went out to find Janet. By nine o'clock he had found her and brought her back to his parents' house so that they could talk. But a few minutes later, while Norman was in another room, Janet jumped up, ran out to Norman's pickup truck and took off.

At eleven o'clock that night Janet called Dolly and Fred Moon's house looking for Norman. He was not there. She called again at 12:30 in the morning from the American Legion in Connellsville. She told Dolly that she was with some men and that they were having a good time. Dolly could tell Janet was drunk and became concerned for her. She tried to coax Janet into coming to her house, but Janet said, not now. She got back to the trailer at 3:30 Monday morning.

Norman got up to go to work and discovered Janet had hidden the keys to his truck. Instead of getting into a fight about it, Norman slipped under the dash of the truck and hotwired it.

When she woke up that day, Janet phoned her mother in Tidioute and told her to come to Connellsville because she needed to use her car. Helena arrived in Connellsville the next day, and later that evening she and Janet came to the Moon residence. Dolly Moon remembers that meeting.

"Janet's mother came to the house with Janet and a niece. She came in and put her arms around me and she started to sob and Janet turned around and said, 'Stop that or I will kill you both.' Then she said she was lonely."

Norman was working in the Dunbar Mountains that week. Late one morning he stood and watched the dust fly as his brother Melvin hightailed it up to the site.

"I saw Melvin driving to the site and when he got there I went over to him and he said, 'Norman I understand there's a warrant out for you.'"

♦

# ♦ DIVORCE

By July of 1952 Norman and Janet Moon had been married and had lived together as man and wife for three years. To say that their marriage was rocky would be the same as saying The Great Wall of China had a lot of stones in it.

The warrant against Norman listed the charges that Janet had lodged against him as assault and battery, surety of the peace, desertion, and nonsupport.

After work on the day that Norman was served the warrant, he went to the office of Alderman Prinkey in downtown Connellsville. Janet and her mother and his mother were there waiting for him. Janet's mother Helena was the first to speak. She said that Janet not only didn't have any money of her own but she had no way to support herself and that she would need support from Norman.

After going over the charges and attempting to settle the dispute and realizing that this was one case that was not going to be reconciled in any amicable way, Prinkey asked Norman if he could move out of the trailer so that Janet could live there. Norman agreed, and after Dolly posted a $500 bond, they left and he moved in with his parents later that evening.

Janet never did move back into the trailer. For the next few days while she gathered some of her belongings, she stayed in the neighbor's trailer. But before she left town she went to her favorite ladies' stores in Connellsville and went on a shopping spree. She had the stores send the bills, totaling more than $500, to Dolly Moon. Enraged, Robert Moon gathered the bills and mailed them to Janet's father, Lou Schwab, in Tidioute.

Two days after the meeting with Alderman Prinkey, Norman received a telephone call from an attorney named Brown in Connellsville.

"He asked me if I would like to make a settlement or anything and I said as far as I could see, why, I would like to get a divorce and if he could arrange it I'd pay him for it. The next thing I can remember he called and wanted me to come in to his office. He said Mr. Hampson, an attorney from Warren, was coming down and wanted to talk the thing over and see if there could be any settlement reached.

"We was there waiting for Mr. Hampson, and when he came in, we talked and Mr. Brown asked him what they had in mind. And Mr. Hampson said they'd like to get some support, and he said they wanted about $30 a week. I told him I'd just as soon leave it into the Uniontown court and see what kind of settlement was there, because I couldn't see paying that much under any conditions that existed so far.

"Then Mr. Hampson said, 'Well, we will get $30 a week if we take it into court.' Then we talked some more and Mr. Hampson said, 'Well, you will hear from me in court.'"

A few days later Norman received a letter that directed him to report to his probation officer, Mr. Sparks, in Uniontown in the matter of the warrant that had been lodged against him. Norman's probation officer asked him a number of questions regarding the issue and asked him how much he made a week. The probation officer had sent a 'notice to appear' to attorney Hampson to attend the meeting, but Hampson never appeared. After waiting a half hour, Sparks called Hampson on the phone and Hampson told the probation officer that he, Hampson, didn't need to appear at the meeting.

A short time after the meeting with Sparks, Norman received a second warrant for his arrest in Connellsville. This one charged him with desertion and nonsupport in Warren County. Norman went to Alderman Molinaro this time and posted a second cash bond—this time $300—ensuring that he would appear.

A few weeks later, Norman received a letter from the district attorney's office in Warren directing him to appear in the county courthouse on September 26, 1952, at 10 a.m.

At this point in the proceedings, Norman thought his being arrested in two different counties for the same thing must somehow be a mistake, some sort of an oversight; and besides that, it certainly couldn't be legal that he was charged with the same offenses in two counties. Before he left Connellsville for Warren, he went to the Uniontown Court and got certified copies made of the warrant he was charged with there.

Years later Art Cagle, who was married to Janet briefly, said Janet told him it was her father who pushed her to pursue the support payments in Warren court. To Art, that sounded in character: "To Lou Schwab," Cagle said, "money is what mattered."

At two o'clock that afternoon Norman's case was called before Judge Allison Wade in the Warren County Court, and Norman presented his paperwork. "I told him I didn't think it was legal in this court when it had been in another court previously, the charge, so he said, he'd rule on it."

After Norman presented his papers, Judge Wade called Janet to testify. Janet, who was represented by Hampson, told the court her side of the story—how Norman had punched her and abused her and wouldn't give her any money. When she had finished Hampson informed the court that he had to be someplace to take care of another matter and he asked that the proceedings be carried over.

After some discussion, wherein Judge Wade advised Norman to hire an attorney, the case was postponed to October 13th. Apparently neither Judge Wade nor anyone else involved in the case thought it unfair to ask Norman to make the 386-mile round-trip a second time simply to accommodate attorney Hampson's schedule.

But that was not to be. On October 10th Norman received a letter from Hampson informing him that the case had been heard on October 7th and that the court had ruled in favor of Janet. Norman was to begin making his $30 a week support payments.

Three days after that a discouraged Norman made the drive to Warren to try to find out how his case had been resolved when he wasn't even there. He was angry and he was looking for his day in court.

"Well, we discussed it there." Norman said later, "There was Judge Wade, Mr. Hampson, Mr. Sires (the Prothonotory), and Mr. Kornreich (the district attorney). They all told me that the case was decided and it was up to me to start paying. But finally, they decided to let me take the stand. I attempted to bring some things out of the testimony that I was cross-examined on on September 26th. I was looking for one thing to relate out of it (the testimony), and I couldn't seem to locate it in there. I had read it before but I couldn't seem to find it, and about that time, why, Mr. Hampson stepped up and said I was trying to contradict, to say that the testimony didn't contain it, and I got pretty mad about that time. I guess I walked out of the court, more or less."

♦

In addition to his legal problems, Norman had become depressed and even more withdrawn than before. In October of 1952 Janet and her mother had driven down to Connellsville and picked up the remainder of Janet's belongings. The trailer was closed up and Norman, who had been staying at his parents' home on and off since the separation in August of 1952, officially moved back into his parents' house.

"He became very depressed and moody and despondent," Dolly Moon later said. "Well, he worked pretty hard, and was tired when he come home at night. Occasionally he would go out. But usually he would go to bed." Norman would turn on his radio in his room and listen to country music—a station from Del Rio, Texas, was a favorite. Or he'd lie down and read. He still liked *Reader's Digest* and the *Saturday Evening Post* but would sometimes also look at *Time* and *Business Week*.

"Norman never talked about his troubles," observed Dolly. "Maybe if I would ask him something, he would just answer me and give me a short answer."

As Norman's legal problems became more and more troubling, he sank deeper into depression until he had reached a point where he didn't even want to go to work or even get out of bed.

"Around this time he wasn't feeling well," said Dolly. "He seemed to be in a deep heavy sleep, when he could go to sleep. It wasn't a natural sleep. He couldn't seem to get up in the morning. He was just all tired out or something. He just wasn't himself at all. He would get up in the middle of the forenoon. He wouldn't eat regular meals, would be up part of the day but it seemed like he could hardly go on.

"The one time we did talk, he said he was very discouraged with life, that there wasn't anything in life for him. He said he had gone through so much in the service, and his married life, he just seemed to think there wasn't anything for him. He spoke of taking his life.

"Well, after that I would always look in his room at night before I would go to bed. Quite often he would put the radio on and sometimes he would go to sleep in the evening, and I would go in and turn it off. Other times, why, he would wake in the night and turn the music on to try to go to sleep. That had been going on for quite a while, and it kept getting worse. He seemed to have an unnatural sleep, seemed his nerves were dead or something, that the sleep wasn't natural at all.

"Then one time when he did go out of his room, I went in and searched it and I found a gun in the drawer of the chifforobe. It was just a small pistol but I was afraid he would take his own life so I took it and hid it in a cupboard."

♦

After he walked out of court on October 13th, Norman received a letter from Warren County District Attorney's Office ordering him to appear in court again on December 1st, 1952. But a few days before December 1st, Norman received a telegram from Judge Wade instructing him that his court date had been changed to December 15th and that he was to have his counsel with him when he appeared.

Once again Norman made the 386-mile round trip to Warren. But when he appeared in the courtroom on December 15th, Judge Wade told him that the court was not aware that he was scheduled to appear that day.

Wade told Norman to leave, and that he would get another letter informing when he should next appear.

By July of 1953 the Warren County Court had issued a warrant for Norman's arrest for nonsupport, as he had not made any payments to Janet. The court contacted officers in Connellsville to pick him up. Norman, of course, was still contesting Judge Wade's jurisdiction in the matter. Even so, when he learned there was a warrant out for him, he drove to Warren and turned himself in to the Sheriff's Department and was locked up.

Norman was kept in jail for 20 days. During his stay he opened the phone book, picked out a name and hired attorney Henry Nicholson to represent him. Nicholson turned out to be the perfect Warren attorney for Norman. At 5 ft. 6 inches, he was a kind of bandy rooster, tough and something of a rebel. A few days after he was retained, Nicholson set up a meeting with Hampson to try to work out a settlement for what was owed as back payment. According to Hampson's reckoning, Norman owed Janet $30 a week from August 1952 to July of 1953, about $1,440. Norman, who felt he'd still not had his day in court, at least with an attorney, was not even sure he owed anything but offered $500. An argument ensued, and Hampson stormed out.

Nicholson got Norman settled down and tried to reason with him. "Well, why don't you add a little more to it and see if you can't get it settled up, straightened out, and forget things? Won't you go as high as fifteen-hundred?"

Norman reluctantly agreed, and Nicholson chased after Hampson. But a short while later Nicholson returned to the jail and told Norman Hampson had refused his offer.

At this point Norman laid out his dilemma to Nicholson. He felt that it was unfair—and even illegal—

to prosecute him in Warren County when he was being charged for the same offenses in Fayette County. Nicholson researched the matter, returned the next day and said he agreed, that legally a person couldn't be charged in a second court until the case was dismissed in the first court.

A date was again set for Norman's case to be heard before Judge Wade, on July 20, 1953. Nicholson made his argument, based on two cases he had found wherein an appellate court had ruled that, when a defendant was being tried in two different jurisdictions for the same offense, the second jurisdiction may *not* prosecute the case until the case is resolved in the first jurisdiction. Judge Wade withheld his decision while the court contacted the Fayette County Court to determine if, in fact, Norman's case was still in that court.

Following the hearing before Judge Wade, Norman posted a $200 bond and was released from jail. He was told that he would receive written notice as to the date of his next court appearance.

After he was discharged from jail, Norman returned to the jail bearing gifts. Sheriff Don Allen, Jr., whose father was the warden at the time, explained later: "We hadn't done anything different for him than we had for the other prisoners. But a half hour later, here comes Norman back—with a box of candy for my wife and me, and a large basket of fruit for the other prisoners." It was this sort of unexpected act which frequently endeared Norman to people. Attorney Sam Bonavita remembered getting Christmas cards from Norman year after year.

Nicholson advised Norman to go back to Fayette County, obtain copies of all his legal proceedings there and bring them with him to his next hearing in Warren, which had been set for August. Norman got his paperwork from the court, from the aldermen involved and from his probation officer, then appeared again before Judge Wade in August.

At that hearing Norman and Nicholson learned that someone else was running around in Fayette County getting Norman's records. It seems that District Attorney Kornreich and Sheriff Linder also made the 386-mile round-trip to Fayette County for the purpose of making sure that justice was served.

After both sides handed in their paperwork, Judge Wade said he would study the case and render his decision. A short time later Norman received a letter from the court informing him that Judge Wade had ruled that he was entitled to jurisdiction and that Norman was to begin paying the $30 a week. Norman's attorney, Nicholson, contacted him and asked if he wanted to appeal Wade's decision to the Superior Court in Pittsburgh. Norman said he did and would send Nicholson the money to proceed.

Nicholson argued the case before Superior Court in Pittsburgh in early December. But the appeals court affirmed the Warren court's jurisdiction. Nicholson then sent a letter in December of 1953 to Norman asking him go to the Superior Court building in Pittsburgh and request copies of the proceedings. At which point Norman drove to Pittsburgh, went to the eighth-floor offices of the appeals court and obtained copies of the decision. While there he asked for a copy of the proceedings of the hearing as well but was told that those could not be copied. He could, however, read them on the spot, which he did.

Later in December Norman received a second letter from Nicholson, by registered mail.

Dear Mr. Moon:

Yesterday I received from the District Attorney a letter which reads as follows:

"Since talking with you about the above case I am informed that there is a special session of court on

January 13, 1954. I am therefore giving you this formal notice to have Norman W. Moon in court in Warren the morning of January 13, 1954. Otherwise a petition will be filed for an attachment to issue to have him brought before the court. Yours very truly, M.A. Kornreich, District Attorney."

Inasmuch as I must be in Jamestown, New York, on January 13, at 10 A.M. in connection with a public sale of real estate, I wrote to the district attorney at once asking to have your appearance delayed until 2 P.M. on January 13. The district attorney replied as follows:

"January 4, 1954, C. Henry Nicholson, Attorney at Law, Warren, Pa., Dear Sir: In answer to your letter of January 4 you will remember that I have on previous occasions changed the time to accommodate you and Mr. Moon and he did not show up. I have written to you that he be here on January 13, 1954 at 10 A.M. and we must insist that he be present at that time. However, if he appears at 10 A.M. and asks that the case be continued until 2 P.M. so that you may be there I have no objection. We must stick to that time and if he is not here at 10 A.M. I will assume that he is not coming. Yours very truly, M.A. Kornreich, District Attorney."

Costs on an attachment against you would eventually have to be paid by you and therefore I recommend strongly that you be in court here on the day and at the time set forth above. Therefore please be in court at 10 A.M. and if you wish, ask the court to continue the hearing until 2 P.M. at which time I have no doubt that I will have returned from Jamestown and I will be able to be in court with you.

Yours very truly,
C. Henry Nicholson

On Monday January 11th, 1954, Norman went to The National Bank and Trust Company in Connellsville and bought a cashier's check made out to himself in the amount of $1,500. He also withdrew $500 in cash.

On January 12th he filled the tank in his mother's four-door Dodge sedan and drove to the Swap Shop which was located on the north side district of Pittsburgh. He had been in the store the past summer to buy a clip and shells for another gun.

"I was in the shop about 30 to 45 minutes," Norman later recalled. "I went in and asked to look at several different sizes and everything. I asked him to see a used .45 pistol and the purchase price was somewhere around $30. But I got to feeling fairly sick at the time so I said don't bother. I left and went across the street and went to the toilet, then came back and went in again.

"He asked me if I was feeling sick, and I said my bowels was bothering me some. So he went to a back room and got a bottle of medicine and gave me a teaspoonful. I got feeling better and decided to buy the .45 I had looked at.

"I was feeling despondent. I didn't know if they was ever going to get anything straightened out. I was just giving up on living."

Norman bought the gun and a box of shells and, after a brief detour into Ohio, drove to Warren. He got to the tourist house on Pennsylvania Avenue East at seven that night. He had no suitcase and no toiletries. After he checked into the tourist home, he went out and had a spaghetti dinner at a restaurant. Then he returned to the home and went to bed.

The next morning he woke at 8:30 and dressed in the same clothes he'd worn the day before: a dress shirt, gray flannel pants, a lightweight waist-length jacket, and over that a green plaid mackinaw, a woolen jacket, plus a fedora. He got in the Dodge and drove to the area around the Warren State Hospital.

"I loaded the pistol out there. I stopped a while and thought a while. I had many thoughts in my mind. I contemplated killing myself, different things. I had the urge to leave and go to another section of the country. I had the urge to kill myself and also had different urges. I didn't know whether, which way, or what to do. I had quite a desire to go to another part of the country more or less just see if I could stay away from her or something. Then I thought maybe it would come out pretty good, so I decided to come in court and see what the case actually was.

"I got to the courthouse about a quarter to ten. I was getting so wrought up to such a point I couldn't see it could be settled anyway. So I drove over to the post office and bought an envelope and addressed it to myself. I signed the cashier's check and the title to my trailer and put them in the envelope and mailed the letter to myself. Then I got in my car and drove back to the courthouse and parked there, right in front."

Norman stuck the .45 in the waistband of his pants, behind his belt, and buttoned his heavy woolen mackinaw so that the gun could not be seen. He walked up the courthouse steps into the foyer, then walked into the main courtroom and took a seat on the left-hand side of the aisle in the first position next to the aisle in the first pew.

There were three cases called before Norman's case that morning. The first involved a woman asking that her long-missing husband be declared legally dead so that she could be listed as the sole survivor in the settlement of an estate. The second case involved a group of businessmen who were setting up a corporation. The third involved Judge Wade, attorney Sam Bonavita, and court stenographer Bernice Seavy leaving the courtroom and going downstairs to the first floor of the courthouse so that they could take a statement from a woman who was disabled and was not able to walk up the stairs that led from the first to the second floor.

About 20 minutes later Judge Wade and Mrs. Seavy returned to the courtroom. The judge took his place behind the bench, and Mrs. Seavy took her place at the court stenographer's desk. As soon as they were settled,

District Attorney Kornreich announced to the court that defendant Moon was present and that the matter of the Commonwealth of Pennsylvania versus Norman W. Moon could proceed.

As Norman's attorney Henry Nicholson had stated in his most recent letter to Norman, he would not be in court that morning and he informed Norman that he would be able to be in court when the court re-opened after the lunch break at two that afternoon. Nicholson also advised Norman to relay this information to Judge Wade and ask that his case be set aside until two in the afternoon.

Norman did not take his attorney's advice.

♦

# ◆ JUDGE WADE

W as it the job? Was it the feeling of not only being the Law, but of being above the Law that led two of Warren County's most prominent judges to do the things they did? Or was it just a coincidence that two back-to-back president judges of Court had a hint of scandal during their tenure and that their scandals led to more than a little controversy and a division of opinion that continues today?

Delford Arird was born in 1851 in Sugar Grove. He graduated from the Collegiate Institution in Jamestown, New York, began his career as a schoolteacher in Warren County and later became principal of Union Schools in Youngsville. He then studied law and was admitted to the bar in 1892; in 1922 he was elected to the first of two 10-year terms as president judge of the 37th Judicial District, which is made up of Warren and Forest counties.

It was during Arird's watch, in 1936, that the murder trial of Russian immigrant Metro Seminuk, owner of the Airport Inn in Pittsfield, came before his bench. It seems that Metro's attractive younger wife Mary and her lover, John Polens, hired a hit-man, 19-year-old Joe Senauskas, to murder Metro so that they could be together, take over the thriving business, and live happily ever after.

The three were quickly apprehended and charged with Metro's murder. The first irregularity to occur in this sensational case was during the first few days of the proceedings. Joe Senauskas, the confessed triggerman was the first to stand before the court, and even though he had previously confessed to shooting Metro at the gas pumps of the Airport Inn a little after midnight on March 26th, 1936, when he came before Arird with his attorney Earle MacDonald, he pleaded not guilty.

His plea threw everyone concerned with the prosecution of the case a curveball. In fact, the Warren *Times-Mirror* ran the headline "JUDGE & DA MISTAKE DEFENDANT'S PLEA AS GUILTY INSTEAD OF NOT GUILTY."

The story continued, "From the actions of the DA and the officers of the court on June second, it appeared a guilty plea was expected and all seemed somewhat surprised when Senauskas changed his plea to not guilty and asked for a trial by jury."

The next day in court, after five jurors had been seated, Senauskas abruptly changed his plea from not guilty to guilty. Later that morning the second defendant John Polens was brought into the courtroom and he also pleaded guilty to murder. At 1:40 that same afternoon Mary Seminuk was brought before the court and she pleaded not guilty and asked for a trial by jury.

Courtroom watchers agreed that something didn't seem right here. Why the sudden switch in plea? And why did Senauskas and Polens ask for a bench trial, in which case, the judge is the sole arbitrator of not only who is guilty and who is innocent, but whether the charge is murder in the first degree or murder in the second degree and what the sentence will be? Was there some sort of deal in place? Was there some sort of behind-the-scenes hanky-panky going on?

Senauskas' attorney, Earle MacDonald, claimed that there was in fact a deal in place and that he had met with Judge Arird and that the judge had promised him that if his nineteen-year-old client pleaded guilty to murder he would take the death penalty off the table.

As a result of this alleged promise the second defendant, John Polens, pleaded guilty also. But when it came time for sentencing, Arird sentenced both men to the electric chair. The death sentences caused such a controversy—not because the men weren't guilty, they had admitted they were guilty, but because of the way the trial was handled—that the case went to the Pennsylvania Supreme Court twice and that Court sent a judge to Warren to conduct hearings to determine if Arird had made a deal, or had mishandled the case.

The visiting judge, Judge James Brownson, concluded that Arird had made mistakes in the case but since that court session was over, he could not legally reverse a decision that was reached in a former session. This, of course, was a technicality that further divided opinions on the case. Brownson added to this first controversial conclusion by saying that, yes, Arird had made a number of mistakes in the trial, but those mistakes did not affect the outcome of the trial. In other words, these were picayune mistakes that reasonable jurists would overlook.

Arird's decision stood and the death sentences were upheld. But this led to more controversy and legal haggling that lasted through nine appeals over the next three years. Finally the newly elected Attorney General, Joseph Margiotti, stepped in and informed the parole board and Governor George Howard Earle that, even though the men were guilty of murder, they had not received a fair trial in Arird's courtroom. No one, he said, was going to the electric chair on his watch unless they had had their day in court and had stood before a jury of their peers.

As a result of Margiotti's edict, Polens' and Senauskas' death sentences were commuted to life sentences and the men eventually got out of prison.

Judge Arird had another problem in this case. Mary Seminuk, Metro's wife was found guilty by a jury. And even though she had done essentially the same acts as Polens—that is, they were both accessories before the murder—she was convicted of second degree murder, whereas Polens had been convicted of first degree murder by Judge Arird.

Additionally, when the jury brought its verdict before Arird they recommended that Mary serve up to twenty years in prison. Yet for some mysterious reason known only to the judge, the 85-year-old bachelor gave the pretty young blond a sentence of 18 months in Muncy, a detention facility for women.

Judge Allison Wade followed—literally—in Arird's footsteps. In 1942, after Arird stepped down, Wade was elected for his first 10-year term. In 1951 his wife, Ruth Tillotson Wade died mysteriously at their home. Despite the controversy surrounding his wife's death, Wade was reelected to a second 10-year term in 1952. And like Arird, a scandal developed regarding the alleged preferential treatment Wade gave to another attractive young blond: Janet Schwab Moon.

Arird ran his courtroom the way he saw fit. Some have said he ran it like a fiefdom and was used to getting his way in county. One such self-proclaimed perk was that he had sheriff's deputies drive him home for lunch in a patrol car and wait while he ate then deliver him back to the courtroom. It was also thought by more than one Warren attorney that Arird was too old for the job and that near the end of his tenure his memory was failing him.

At any rate, the crimes and misdemeanors of President Judge Delford Arird pale compared to the crimes and misdemeanors of which President Judge Allison Wade was accused.

◆

Allison Douglas Wade was born on September 17th, 1902 in Warren to Alice J. and H. Douglas Wade. As his father before him, Douglas was in the oil business, and as he had with his father, Douglas had Allison working in the business during his school years.

Wade graduated from Warren High School in 1920. He received his bachelor's degree from the University of Virginia and his law degree from the University of Buffalo and was admitted to the bar in 1930. He worked as an associate in two Warren firms before he and Richard P. Lott formed a partnership in 1932. During that partnership, Wade became the County Solicitor, a position he held for nine years.

Those who knew Wade in the 1930s, when he was in his 30s, remember him as an idealistic young man, a staunch Republican who traveled the countryside organizing Young Republican clubs and speaking before civic groups about the evils of the Red Menace—communism.   Hinting that Wade was a less than scintillating a speaker, Mike Evan, police chief for many years, admitted, "Well, if he was going to give a talk, I don't think I'd go and hear it."

Wade spoke from one meeting to the next, and not surprisingly, one night he spoke before a group gathered at the Hunter Memorial School in Tidioute. It was here that the ambitious attorney first met Lou and Helena Schwab and began a friendship—most likely based on Schwab's financial contributions and support to Wade's career—that would last until Wade's death.

Nick Merenick remembered meeting Lou Schwab at the time he and Wade were out organizing the Young

Republicans. "Yeah, he was a supporter. It wasn't so much about money as getting people organized, getting people interested."

Chuck Sellin was another one of Wade's friends and traveling partners during this period. "Allie knew Schwab." Sellin recalled. "I knew this because the Schwabs was helping him out politically down in Tidioute. Allie was very active politically at that time and I imagine he had his eyes on the judgeship in future years."

Sellin also remembered Wade as a walking contradiction. Here was this ultra-ambitious politician delivering lecture after lecture about how we as Americans should stand up to communism and at the same time here was this naïve, ineffectual young bachelor in his 30s still living at home and still abiding by his parents' rules.

Nick Merenick recalled that, "One time we stopped at my parents' grocery store to pick up some snacks for lunch and he came upon cans of mustard sardines, and he said, 'Oh gosh, I like these but I can't have them at home; my folks don't go for them.'"

♦

Ruth Tillotson was born in Corry on October 19th, 1901. She graduated from Corry High School and received her bachelor's degree from the University of Pittsburgh and from there she did graduate work at New York University and studied in Europe. She then moved to Warren and lived at 305 Fourth Avenue. She began teaching in the Warren County School District, where she would eventually become the head of the commercial department.

In the summer of 1938, Ruth's mother, Florence Tillotson, introduced her to an up-and-coming 36-year-old attorney named Allison Wade. In December Ruth and Allison were married.

Like her husband, Ruth was active in civic affairs. She was vice president of the Woman's Club, a member of the Association of College Women, chairman of the program committee of the county Council of Republican Women, a member of the Philomel Club, the Shakespeare Club, the Blue Stocking Club, the Library Association, and she was on the Board of Trustees of Edinboro State Teachers College.

During the early years of their marriage, Wade finished his stint as county Solicitor, and in 1942 he was elected to his first 10-year term as county judge.

Life started getting busy for the Wades. Allison was also a member of the prestigious Shakespeare Club as well as a handful of other civic groups. In addition to all his professional and civic activities, he was a highly regarded painter, working mostly in oil. A number of his paintings won awards in local art fairs.

Ruth Wade could not have children, so in 1945 Wade suggested that they adopt a child. Ruth agreed. But Wade proved to be an unaffectionate father in the view of his Ruth Wade's second cousins, Lorraine Cole and Lynn Jordan (because Ruth Wade was so much older, Cole and Jordan usually referred to her as their aunt).

"You could see it when you were around them," Jordan remarked years later. "His daughter asked me and the other cousins one time how much their dad hugged them." Among other places, Jordan and Cole played with their adopted cousin on the Tillotson family farm in Sugar Grove.

Cole said that, even as a child, she recognized the strained relationship between her aunt and Allison Wade. "He wasn't what he projected. At home he was a tyrant. Ruth learned to go where he wanted, when he wanted. She was forbidden to call certain friends that he disapproved of. The only time we ever saw him smiling was at Ruth's funeral when he was teasing two kids."

It was well known in Ruth Tillotson's family that Judge Wade looked down on his wife's farm relatives. He complained about Uncle Harry's ramshackle farmhouse, and he didn't like the farm smells either. By contrast, Ruth loved visiting the farm; she thought it was charming.

Jordan and Cole remembered Aunt Ruth as an intelligent, worldly woman who had studied in Europe. She was kind to all the children in her family; she always brought them little gifts and made them feel special.

But somewhere along the line, Ruth Wade's life began to unravel. Lee Schaeffer, son of the Wade's housekeeper and nanny, Lena Schaeffer, used to tell him about the good times when Wade would complete an oil painting and Ruth would make the frame, then the couple would go together and display his paintings at local art fairs.

But she also recalled when things at the Wade household took an ominous twist. Ruth was ill. She would walk the house at night until finally the judge would call Dr. Valone to see what was wrong.

Patty Borger was a neighbor and friend of the Wades during those years. "He was a very kind, very pleasant man. He'd talk any time he was out. He liked to garden."

It appeared that Ruth Wade was slipping into an emotional abyss. "She was a very withdrawn type person," recalled Borger. "I don't think she was truly well. I believe that she went from doctor to doctor getting sleeping pills. And of course, I heard what everyone else heard—that she had tried to commit suicide more than once."

Judge Wade had friends just like everyone else. Some—perhaps most—were acquaintance type friends, friends from the courthouse, the neighborhood, the art league, the Shakespeare Club, the Republican organizations. But when his life starting spinning out of control, Wade went to his best friend and confidant Chuck Sellin.

"Allie's judgment then was beginning to be influenced by his domestic problem." Sellin recalled in later years. "He was very upset over Ruth's condition. She tried to commit suicide two or three times. They had to pump her stomach out. She'd really go off the button, I mean she carried on, was nude. Gail Reuhlsburger, her doctor, told me once, he said, 'Yeah, I slapped her backside real hard, picked her up and threw her down on the bed—to jar her to get her back to her senses.'

"He said just that she wasn't satisfied—sexually or something. Allie didn't understand that. As I say, he was a naïve individual with relationships."

When Wade and Ruth's physicians eventually decided she should be institutionalized, Wade called Chuck Sellin for a favor. "He called up and came over. He was going to drive Ruth to a private hospital down in Philadelphia. He wanted me to sit in the back seat of the car with her.

"I said, Allie, I'd like to help you, but I don't want to be responsible if anything happens in that backseat. She could jump out while you're driving.

"All he was trying to do was keep the expenses down. I said, you get an ambulance and go down; I'll go down in my car and bring you back.

"So Dr. Yerg came over and gave her the shots to subdue her. Allie, he was all emotionally broke up.

"She was in that hospital for a while and when she returned, he was to perform this routine set up by the psychiatrists—how to handle the situation—but she was still in this depression. There was two times I remember after that, rush deals to the hospital to pump her stomach out. I don't know why they issued the pills knowing that."

Monday, May 14th, 1951 started out like every other Monday in the Wade household. Wade went to work in the courthouse across the street from their home. But by early in the evening, Jordan and Cole believe, their aunt had worked herself into such an anxious state that she couldn't bear it any longer. She had demanded on a number of occasions that Allie move out and that they end the painful charade that their marriage had become. Quinn Smith, whose spinster Aunt Mabel Siggins lived by herself in a large house just a block from the Wades, remembers his Aunt telling him that Allison Wade approached her at one point about taking a room in the house. Mabel Siggins declined Wade's offer, and in any event, Wade remained in the Fourth Avenue house throughout the marriage. But on the evening of May 14th, according to Jordan and Cole, Ruth packed a suitcase, phoned her mother and told her that she was moving out that night.

That was the last anyone heard from Ruth Wade.

No one knows what happened later that night. But in the early morning hours of May 15th, 1951, Ruth Wade was found dead in her living room at the foot of the stairs that led to the second floor. "Physicians who were summoned," said a story in the *Times-Mirror* the next day, "informed Coroner Ed Lowrey that the demise probably occurred an hour or two before" her body was discovered by Allison Wade around 4:30 A.M.. Ruth Tillotson Wade was 49.

Speculation by friends, neighbors, police, relatives, and the man on the street ran the gamut. Ruth's nieces, Jordan and Cole, believe that over the previous months Wade was systematically overdosing his wife so that she would once again be committed to a psychiatric hospital. The nieces suspect that Ruth and Wade argued into the night of May 14th and in an effort to settle her down, Wade gave her the drugs that killed her.

Others, Wade's friends, acquaintances, and coworkers believe that Ruth Wade was mentally ill and that she took her life with an overdose of sleeping pills.

Still others in the community believe that Wade and Ruth argued and that Wade pushed Ruth down the flight of stairs and she broke her neck. Warren resident Donna Hartley, who had been a student of Ruth's, was in this camp. "It just seemed common knowledge in town," Hartley recalled later. "Everybody believed that."

During Norman's murder trial three years later, Norman's older brother Robert recalled being approached by Ruth Wade's sister outside the courtroom. "She told me that her sister and Wade were ready to go out one night to some social, and he threw her down the steps and broke her neck. She said she wished that could be brought out at the trial."

Years later even Norman Moon recalled hearing the rumor, while serving his 20-day stint in the Warren County jail, that Judge Wade had pushed his wife down the steps of their home and killed her. "It made me reflect," he later wrote of the incident, "on the character of Judge Wade."

The rumor spread like wildfire until people in other towns started repeating it as gospel. Chuck Sellin recalled stopping in a hardware store in Ridgeway and hearing the tale. "Fellow by the name of Eagen knew Doc Cashman here and he says to me, 'Boy you got some judge over there, he pushed his wife down the stairs and killed her.'

"I said, oh no. 'No?' he says, 'Doc Cashman told me.'

"You see, Doc Cashman was from St. Mary's and so was Eagen, a couple of Irish guys. But Cashman was not Ruth's doctor. And some people used to say they wouldn't believe Doc Cashman if he said he was all wet when he was standing in the middle of the Allegheny River. I think Doc Cashman liked to color the history."

But there was another twist. The state police began following Allison Wade around for a while after his wife's death. Exactly why they did so is not known. One theory is that they suspected him of foul play and were trying to see if he had another woman waiting in the wings. The other theory is that associates of Wade's were so worried about his mental state at the time, they enlisted police to keep an eye on him.

"One thing he said to me," Chuck Sellin recalled, "and I'm not surprised it bothered him. He said the state police followed him. This I know, he would drive around the country all alone and in the privacy of the car would have his emotional outlet—cry, whatever."

Mike Evan was Warren's chief of police at the time, and when confronted with the different scenarios surrounding Ruth's death, including the theory that Wade pushed her to her death, Wade overdosed her, or she overdosed herself, Chief Evan responded, "Well, she did have a fall. And it's possible she died from an overdose. We didn't investigate it. And if it was so, we should have investigated it."

Of course, throughout his career, Chief Evan had got to know Wade. "It was like this, Judge Wade was a witch hunter. He was always calling and saying, 'Hey, do you know what's going on down there? Gambling or something, you know. Yeah, we knew about them. In other words he was a witch hunter, you know, instead of taking care of his own business. In fact, I think he called Harrisburg one time to investigate something in town."

While there was nothing obvious or disrespectful in his behavior toward Judge Wade, it was clear that Warren's Top Cop was not a big fan of Wade's.

"I didn't warm up to him. I knew what he was before he got to be judge—he was considered to be a sissy and so on, down the line. But, he was a straitlaced guy, no problem there. But he was a gossiper. He was good, though, he was honest, I'll give him credit.

"We were on a business trip one time, I remember. Well, there were three of us, and you know how it is with a bunch of guys. But the judge would say, 'Wait, you know how it is, nature has a little call on me, I got to find a boys room. '

"Well, you know if it was me, I'd say, I gotta take a leak. But that's the kind of guy Wade was. He wasn't a homosexual, but he gave that impression, definitely so. And his talk, the same way. I just couldn't warm up to him."

Still others in the community in those days claim Wade was a regular Don Juan. As a child a woman who lives in Sugar Grove now lived with her parents on Prospect Street and ran around with two neighborhood girls who suspected their mother was spending time with Judge Wade when their trucker father was out of town. Together with one of the girlfriends, the Sugar Grove woman would sneak up to Wade's house on Beaty Street and watch them through a window.

"We would go up and watch her mother and the judge. He'd have a meal on the table. We'd look in the window of his house. This would have been around 1953, somewhere in there. Wade was quite a ladies' man."

Regardless of the rumors, there was one irrefutable fact in Judge Wade's life and career after May 15, 1951— his wife was dead and his actions or inactions kept the flame of scandal burning. Wade went on with his life and career, yet the questions remain to this day:

- ♦ Did Ruth Wade commit suicide by taking an over dose of sleeping pills?
- ♦ Did Ruth Wade accidentally overdose herself?
- ♦ Where did the pills come from?

♦ If Ruth Wade did accidentally or otherwise take sleeping pills, could she have accidentally fallen down the steps and broken her neck?

♦ Knowing that Ruth was suicidal, what physician would prescribe sleeping pills without first making sure that someone in Ruth's household would control them?

♦ Knowing her condition, why didn't Wade have these pills locked up?

♦ Did Wade push his wife down the stairs?

♦ Did Wade and Ruth argue and did she accidentally fall down the stairs?

♦ Why did Wade refuse the Tillotson family's request for an autopsy?

♦ Why wasn't Ruth Wade's death investigated by the police?

In 1951 everyone had their opinion of what had happened at 215 Fourth Avenue on the night of May 15th. But those opinions didn't mean a thing a year later when Wade's first term as president judge expired and the county needed to elect a new judge, or reelect Wade.

♦

In 1952 President Judge Allison D. Wade was reelected to his post for a second 10-year term. During the months since his wife Ruth had died Wade continued going about his affairs as usual. He attended meetings of the county Bar Association and Republican Party affairs, both of which were held at the Carver House Hotel, which sat on the corner of Pennsylvania Avenue and Hickory Street.

At that time the Carver House was the in-place for downtown businessmen, including private attorneys, DA's, and judges—even President Judge Allison Wade went there for a drink at the bar. After all, the 52-year-old jurist had been a widower now for a little over a year, and perhaps—like any other red-blooded man his age—he sought the company of female companionship. If he did, the Carver House was as good a place as any to meet a suitable female friend.

Sam Bonavita remembered the Carver House as an upscale place with a sports bar with a TV that showed the fights. "You'd see a local businessman and a single girl from New Process or Sylvania having a drink after work. It was a classy place. Even John Blair, owner of New Process, would stop in."

Former Carver House employee Donna Hartley later remembered how appealing it was. "Usually, you'd go in the corner of the building, which had a beautiful glass-brick entry into the lounge. There was a beautiful kidney-shaped mahogany bar, and then from the lounge you went up two steps to the dining area, tables or booths, and an organ. There were also booths in the lounge itself. It was a popular place with businessmen, a classy place."

Peggy Harp, another former Carver House waitress, even recalled Norman Moon coming into the hotel. "He was polite, soft-spoken. He wasn't handsome, but he was a nice looking fellow."

It is perhaps inevitable in small cities such as Warren that people's lives overlap. Here it was over 15 years since Judge Wade and his two pals Chuck Sellin and Nick Menerick had made the rounds of the county setting up Young Republican clubs one evening and warning the populace about communism the next. Here it was over 15 years since Wade had met Helena and Lou Schwab at just such a meeting in the Hunter Memorial School in Tidioute and struck a friendship that was as warm and friendly as ever.

And here it was 15 years later and here was the coincidence: the Schwabs' daughter Janet, now a pretty 25-year-old soon-to-be-divorcee, worked as a waitress in the hotel restaurant and lived in a room in an annex of the Carver House, the very same place where Wade and his friends held their meetings and where a few of them, perhaps those that didn't want to or need to go home, stayed after the meetings and repaired to the bar. Once again, in the enigmatic life of Judge Wade, things were being said regarding his visits to the Carver House, as well as other places, that were either true or false, reasonable or not reasonable. And once again, the opinions regarding Judge Wade and his amorous abilities and exploits were split down the middle.

In the late summer of 1952, Janet Moon separated from her husband Norman and returned to live with her parents in Tidioute. And, by all accounts, she continued in her predilection of seducing any man she chose. Mary Schwab, Janet's sister-in-law, recalled that period vividly.

"She continued her former life. Little incidents would happen and somebody would say they saw her on the street or with some hunter. And then she got a job at the Carver House. She wanted contacts, and I suppose it got dull around Tidioute."

Warren attorney Sam Bonavita corroborated that Wade was a frequent visitor to the Carver House when Janet Schwab worked there. But Bonavita did not see Wade as a Don Juan type. "Let me tell you something about Judge Wade. I didn't know the judge intimately. He was an artist, you know, he did some painting. When I first heard this rumor about the judge and Janet Moon, my remark—and I wasn't the only one who felt this way—was that if Marilyn Monroe was in Judge Wade's bedroom in the nude, he wouldn't climb in bed with her. He would have picked up his palette and his brush and he would have painted her. To me, Judge Wade just wasn't a womanizer."

Bonavita also remembered the rumors surrounding Janet Moon during that period. "As far as her running around—definitely. Frankly, it was common knowledge that she was running around."

Peggy Harp worked at the Carver House at that time. She worked with Janet and found her to be aloof, not very friendly. She couldn't remember anyone who had been Janet's friend at the hotel. Peggy, like most everyone else familiar with the Janet-and-the-Judge scandal, had heard the rumors, but she had also seen the two of them together.

"I wondered, you know, because I'd seen them sitting together in the lounge. Not real often, you know, but a few times—just sitting at the bar, talking, having a drink. It could have been innocent, I don't know. But Janet did have a reputation for hanging out in the bar and going with men."

In fact, Janet was ultimately fired from the Carver House for taking a man to her room and allowing him to stay all night. Donna Hartley worked at the Carver House at that time.

"The only incident I clearly remember is when the manager, Russ Lindberg, kicked Janet out of the hotel for taking someone up to her room all night. The next morning Russ tried to get someone to fire her, and no one would, so he did it himself. He just told her she had to leave. I took it that this was the kind of person she was. I wasn't there when it happened, but Russ talked about it, talked about how disgusted he was with her. He was furious. In those days that just wasn't something girls did."

Lynn Jordan, Ruth Wade's second cousin, had heard similar stories from her friend, Ed Peterson, who was a bellhop at the Carver House and lived in Sugar Grove. Peterson told Jordan that not only did Janet take men to her room but that he had once seen Judge Wade standing outside the door of Janet Moon's room in the hotel annex.

It would seem that if there were anything illegal going on in the city that Chief Evan would know about it. When questioned about the Janet-and-the-Judge Scandal, the Chief replied, "I never have heard that, never had heard that. And I would question that. It's ridiculous. Hell, I'd have known about it. This town is too small."

Martha Eaton was the vivacious, outspoken wife of a prominent Warren attorney, R. Pierson Eaton, who knew Allison Wade. She insisted years after the event that she had never heard the rumor of an illicit affair between Wade and Janet Moon. "That must have been something people dreamed up in later years," Eaton said, shocked by the idea. "I knew a great number of people around here, and Pete, my husband, would have told me. It just sounds like something made up out of whole cloth. No, that's the kind of stuff people in the sticks figure out.

"Oh, that's laughable," Eaton said—then added, pointedly, "I don't think Allison was that keen about women."

Years after Wade's death, Wade's close friend, Chuck Sellin, wasn't so sure anymore. Another mutual friend of both Sellin's and Wade's had told him that his wife had recently revealed something—that she knew for a fact Wade had had an affair with one of her girlfriends. "She was emphatic," Sellin recalled, "that Allie had extramarital affairs while married to Ruth."

At a minimum it's clear that Allison Wade and Lou Schwab were well acquainted. "Allie knew Schwab," Chuck Sellin maintained. "I knew this because the Schwabs was helping him politically down in Tidioute." Chief Evan conceded that some people in town suspected Wade had an ulterior motive for insisting that Janet's support case be heard in Warren. "I think possibly Judge Wade was mending political fences with the Schwabs—although Wade was pretty strict about abiding by the law."

◆

At two o'clock in the afternoon on September 26th, 1952, Janet Moon's legal suit asking for support in the amount of $30 per week went to court. Janet Moon, her mother, Helena Schwab, and their attorney, Harold Hampson, sat on one side of the main courtroom in the Warren County Courthouse. Norman Moon sat alone on the other side. President Judge Allison Wade was on the bench. Sixteen months later on January 13th, 1954, this case would come to an abrupt and violent end.

And again, just as when Wade's wife Ruth died, there were a number of questions regarding Wade's handling of this acrimonious support case.

◆ Given his relationship with the Schwab family, why didn't Judge Wade recuse himself from the case and find another, impartial judge—a visiting judge as he himself had been in Allegheny County—to handle the case?

◆ How did the prosecution arrive at the $30-a-week support payment? And why wasn't the $30-a-week payment adjusted after it was learned that Janet took a job at the Carver House?

◆ Why, on the morning of January 13, 1954, didn't Judge Wade postpone the Moon case until two in the afternoon when Moon's attorney, Henry Nicholson stated he would be there?

◆

# ♦ MURDER IN THE COURTROOM

A little bit before eleven o'clock on the morning of January 13th, 1954, 28-year-old Norman Moon was finally getting his day in court. It had been 16 months since his wife Janet had left him and had hired attorney Harold Hampson to represent her in her attempts to get Norman to pay her $30 a week in support.

Norman had come into the courtroom at 9:45 that morning and had taken a seat on the left side of the courtroom in the first bench in the closest position to the center aisle.

Judge Wade called the court to order and directed Mrs. Seavy to begin taking notes.

Hampson clearly felt he'd been on this case way too long. He had met and argued with Norman while Norman was being held in the county Jail. He had even made a 386-mile round trip to Norman's hometown of Connellsville to try to get Norman to give in to Janet's demands.

"Your honor," Hampson stood and addressed the court, "we have gone over backwards, going out of our way to be obliging to Mr. Moon. We have spent a great deal of time and we are coming to the point where we would like to have a settlement of this case and have some money."

Hampson sat down and District Attorney Meyer Kornreich spoke next.

"Mr. Moon, are you still unwilling to comply with the court order in this case?"

Norman stood and replied, "Absolutely. That is correct."

The courtroom went silent for a heartbeat as Kornreich shot a look at Judge Wade. Wade returned the look then cast his eyes downward at the paperwork on his desk. He arranged the sheaf of papers into a neat pile and squared it off by tapping the page bottoms against the flat surface of his desk. Satisfied that the pages were squared off, he carefully placed the papers on his desk and patted the pile with the side of each hand.

Satisfied that everything regarding this case was in order, Judge Wade stared down at Norman Moon a long moment.   Then he turned to the Prothonotary, Ralph Sires, chief clerk of the court, and directed him to make a note of the question that had just been put to Moon and of Moon's reply. Wade turned back to Moon. "Mr. Moon, come forward for sentencing."

Moon stood up and took a few steps toward the judge's bench. As he did, he pushed back one flap of his unzipped jacket and pulled the Colt .45 from his waistband.

◆

Reconstructing events, Kornreich may have shouted, "He's got a gun!" then run for a door behind and to the right of the judge's bench. Moon fired wildly around the courtroom, roughly in the direction of Kornreich, then Judge Wade, then attorney Hampson. By then court clerk Ralph Sires and stenographer Bernice Seavy had dropped to the floor and were hiding under Sires' desk. Harold Hampson had crawled into the witness box before slithering across the floor and, finally, through a door on the left side of the dais. Dr. John Thompson, in court on business of his own and a few rows back in the spectator gallery, was also on the floor hiding behind one of the wooden benches.

Moon walked through the opening in the railing that separated court officials from the spectator section, crossed to the left side of the judge's bench, mounted the dais and found Judge Wade hiding in the knee well of his bench. Seeing Moon approach, Wade crawled out slithered backwards, pleading, "I won't sentence you, I won't sentence you!" Moon, his mouth taut with anger, said, "*Fungu*, you bastard," using a common Italian vulgarism, pointed the gun in Wade's direction and pulled the trigger. *Click*. The gun jammed.

Meanwhile, Judge Wade had pushed himself backwards and right off the right side of the dais. There he grabbed a wooden chair and held it up to shield himself as Moon manually rocked back the muzzle of the .45, ejecting an unspent shell and automatically loading the chamber with a fresh bullet.

Moon paused. He stared at Wade lying on his back, shielding himself with the upended chair. Then he lowered the gun. Turned and walked toward the opening in the railing between the court officials' area and the spectator section. Abruptly Moon heard someone behind him, whirled and fired twice. Judge Wade, on his feet and moving toward Moon, was struck in the chest. "I'm shot, I'm shot!" he blurted out. Wade staggered a few feet before collapsing to the floor next to the witness chair.

Moon stared at him a moment. Then he rammed back the muzzle of the Colt, ejecting a shell. He walked deliberately to the spectator bench where he had been sitting, releasing the clip from the gun's handle as he did. He reached inside his coat jacket, took out a fresh clip and jammed it into the handle of the Colt. Then he gathered his fedora and wool coat and walked up the aisle.

Dr. Thompson, crouched on the floor behind a spectator bench half way back, saw Moon walk past, his heavy coat slung over one arm. Thompson cautiously raised his head and watched as Moon walked, unhurried, out the rear doors of the courtroom. Then Thompson got to his feet and looked to the front of the courtroom. Mrs. Seavy, standing now, cried out, "Help, help, the judge has been shot!"

Thompson hurried to Wade, who was lying on his side. The judge was breathing hard. It sounded to Thompson as if his lungs were filled with blood. Wade's color was ashen. His eyes were open but unreactive. Thompson checked the Judge's pulse. It was very weak.

Meanwhile, on the first floor of the courthouse, attorney Sam Bonavita stepped out of the County Recorder's office and into the large center hallway of the courthouse. He cocked his head, listening to the muffled shouting and commotion coming from the second floor courtroom. From the front of the building he heard a voice shout, "He just ran down the front steps!"

"And of course," Bonavita recalled years later, "having been in the service, sometimes you don't think of what a problem is. If anything happens, you immediately run to it. So I ran from the back of the courthouse all the way to the front."

Pushing open one of the heavy wooden doors, he found Peter Massa, the janitor, standing just outside. "He's down near his car," Massa said, pointing toward the street.

Bonavita looked down the wide stone stairs and saw Moon on the far side of his Dodge, parked at the curb about 30 yards away. Bonavita ran toward the car, shouting, "Hey, you're not going anyplace, bud!" Moon, his eyes fixed on Bonavita, came around the rear of the Dodge to meet the lawyer. Moon's coat was draped over one arm, and as Bonavita approached, Moon removed the coat with one hand. In the other was the Colt .45 pointing right at Bonavita. "If you are not looking for trouble, please leave me alone."

Bonavita stared in disbelief at the handgun. "I was in court that morning on another matter," Bonavita later recalled, "and so I saw Norman sitting there, and I said hello to him. He nodded and said hello, you know, just like that. He had a jacket on, sat there calm and collected, wasn't showing any emotion on his face. So personally I was shocked when I learned he had shot and killed the judge, because he sat there so quiet and collected and just listened."

Outside the courthouse, Bonavita looked up at Moon and said. "Hey, listen—you shouldn't get so excited over such a small matter." Moon stared at Bonavita blankly. "Look," the attorney added, "your wife will probably get married again and before you know it, it'll all be over." Abruptly Moon looked away, to his right, across the wide courthouse lawn. Bonavita followed his gaze.

A hundred yards away a man in civilian clothes and two uniformed state police officers hurried up a walkway leading to a side door of the courthouse. Moon walked past Bonavita, across the wide sidewalk and up to the chest-high wrought iron fence that surrounded the courthouse grounds. He raised the pistol and said, to no one in particular, "It's all over. I might as well finish it now." Moon aimed his pistol at the state troopers, but the trio disappeared into the side entrance.

Moon turned back to Bonavita. "Don't grab me or I'll shoot you," he warned the attorney as he circled past Bonavita to the driver-side door of his car. Bonavita watched Moon get into the Dodge and pull the door shut. The car started, backed up a couple of feet, then pulled out onto the street and slowly drove away. "You know," Bonavita later observed, "Norman could have turned around and fired again—there were one or two other people he passed on his way out. Or as I approached, he could have fired away easily. He heard me running after him. But he didn't shoot."

Bonavita ran back into the courthouse and found the three state troopers standing in the middle of the first floor corridor. At this point none of the men knew precisely what had happened in the courtroom, just that Moon had a gun and was escaping. "He just headed west on Fourth," Bonavita told them, after which four men burst out of the front doors of the courthouse.

Janitor Peter Massa was still standing there. "He went on down Fourth Avenue, that way," Massa said, pointing. Just at that moment a gray Ford state police cruiser rounded the corner of Fourth and Liberty one block west and headed up Fourth Avenue toward them. The troopers bounded down the courthouse steps, trailed by Bonavita, and one of them flagged down the cruiser. "Come on," one of the troopers called to Bonavita," You'll have to identify him for us," and they all piled into the patrol car.

Pvt. Paul Dell, driving, made a U-turn and floored the Ford, heading at high speed west on Fourth Avenue. At Pine Street where Fourth Avenue ended, Pvt. Dell swung left for one block, then right onto Pennsylvania Avenue. He floored the car again, roaring down the narrow two-lane avenue past grade school children walking home for lunch. At the edge of town the cruiser mounted a light rise, rumbled over two sets of railroad tracks and immediately ascended a short, steep grade before the highway flattened out again. Once more Pvt. Dell floored the accelerator.

As the state police car rounded a curve, a blue Dodge came into sight far ahead. "That looks like his car,"

Bonavita said. The patrol car roared right up behind the Dodge, the cruiser's dome light flashing. The driver of the Dodge kept on driving at a steady 45 or 50 mph. Through the rear window they could see the driver wearing a fedora. "It looks like him," Bonavita told the officers, "but I'm not sure because of the hat." The two-lane avenue had now turned into a three lane highway on the outskirts of town, an area known as Starbrick. Pvt. Dell eased the police car into the snow-covered center lane and pulled up beside the Dodge. Bonavita, sitting next to the passenger window, looked directly across at the driver, then turned back to the officers. "That's Moon, I'm positive."

Sgt. Charles Naddeo, sitting in the rear, rolled down the window and yelled at Moon, "Pull over!" Pvt. Dell pressed the foot control and sounded the siren. Moon glanced over his shoulder at the men in the police cruiser. "Moon wasn't going that fast," remembers Bonavita, "because he had a big lead, and by the time we caught up to him out on Route 6, Trooper Naddeo rolled the window down, you know, and pointed the gun right at him and told him to pull over. Norman looked a little bit ashen when he looked back. But he just kept going. He wouldn't stop."

The police car started to fishtail in the snow, and Pvt. Dell dropped behind the Dodge, sounding his siren again. Still the Dodge plodded on at a steady 45 mph. Sgt. Naddeo turned to Pvt. Dell. "All right, crowd him off the road!" Bonavita turned to look at Sgt. Naddeo over the back seat. "I don't think that would be such a good idea. He's got a gun. He threatened me with it." Naddeo hesitated. "Okay, pull up beside him again," he instructed Pvt. Dell. Dell eased the Ford back into the center lane and pulled up beside the Dodge. Two of the troopers thrust their guns through the open window. The barrels of the service revolvers bobbed about a foot away from Moon's driver-side window, and one of the troopers hollered out the window again, "Pull over! Right now, pull over!" Moon glanced at the officer, then stared straight ahead again without changing speed.

Sgt. Naddeo ordered Pvt. Dell to drop back 10 feet. Then the Sergeant leaned out the rear passenger-side window—and began firing at the left rear tire of the Dodge. Abruptly the three-lane road narrowed to two lanes again, and Pvt. Dell had to ease the Ford behind Moon's Dodge once again. For a mile or so the two cars wound along the curving U.S. Route 6 at a steady 45 mph. Then, on a straightaway, the Ford swung into the left lane and Sgt. Naddeo, joined by Pvt. Joseph Mastrian, leaned out their windows and began firing at the left rear tire of the Dodge. Finally, just as the car started up a railway overpass, the tire blew. Moon's Dodge careened from lane to lane across the bridge and down the other side, sliding across the left lane and coming to a halt on the left shoulder of the highway. Pvt. Dell pulled the police cruiser off on the left side as well, about 30 yards behind Moon's car.

Moon got out of his car and turned to look at the troopers. All four had leaped out of the car along with Bonavita and taken up defensive positions behind their vehicle with guns drawn. Moon raised his right arm, and the officers could see the Colt .45 automatic. "I wouldn't do that!" Sgt. Naddeo shouted at Moon. Moon's arm continued up in a smooth motion, however, until the muzzle of the gun rested just below his right ear. A shot exploded from the Colt, spinning Moon around and knocking him to the ground. He lay stretched out on his back in the snow, blood gushing from his neck and mouth.

◆

The following is Norman Moon's testimony from his subsequent murder trial about the shooting of Judge

Wade. He is under direct examination by his attorney Samuel D. Braemer. [Authors' note: Because Norman had chestnut colored hair, friends sometimes called him "Red."]

Q: I asked you what you did.

A: I stood up and got rather excited. I pulled the revolver out from my belt—I had it under my belt—and I don't know, I knocked the safety off and shuffled the sliding mechanism of the gun—that part on the top—and a shell came out. I had anticipated killing myself but pretty much in the excitement I just started shooting. I got awfully mad. I was pretty much mad, extremely, and when the case hadn't even been called into court and I was sitting there and was just called before the bench for sentence. I started shooting and I have a faint idea of what I did but exactly what I done—I have ideas on that, on what I did since. But as far as exact actions I can't explain every one of them because I have a much different vision of what happened in the court that day than what I have heard so far.

Q: Go ahead.

A: The way I can remember it is that Kornreich got up. He was standing over there and he said, "Look out, he has a gun!" I remember he was running. He started going toward the door very fast, running toward the door. He was almost through the door when I believe I shot over in that corner. As I shot he hunched down pretty much and went out the door.

Q: Were you shooting at him?

A: Not exactly. I was shooting very high. I have no exact notion of where I shot and what I shot. That is something I can't recall exactly, I can only give you a general idea of what happened. I can't tell you just exactly what happened, every step I did and such, I can only relate it as best as I can remember. If I remember right that was the first shot. If I remember rightly I continued walking and came through where Mr. Secor is sitting and walked around the bench and came over here. Mr. Hampson was lying pretty much back here where those two men are, lying there. I never shot in his direction, he was just lying there. Mrs. Seavy was standing behind the desk, merely standing there in a daze. I walked past her over here and shot down here.

Q: Where did you shoot next, what were you shooting at there?

A: I was just shooting.

Q: Into the floor?

OBJECTION BY MR. KOHN: Just let him testify, Mr. Braemer. I think this is very important and the witness shouldn't be asked leading questions.

BY THE COURT: "Down here" from where he is sitting couldn't be anything except down in front on the floor.

BY MR. KOHN: I agree that is the presumption. That possibly follows. I think he is—

BY MR. BRAEMER: We will refrain from interfering with the witness.

(Resuming before the jury) BY MR. WAGGONER:

Q: Tell us what else happened?

A: From there on out?

Q: Yes, sure.

A: Well, I mean actually I couldn't have walked in here and showed you where I shot or anything. I found out from sitting here beside you where those holes have actually been found but as far as my being able to walk in and lay my finger on any places where I shot I couldn't—I doubt if anybody could do that if they knew what they were doing, to find the places where they had shot. The next thing I remember, I believe I walked up here and I shot in this place up here. I believe Judge Wade was lying on the dais in back of the bench on the floor. He started crawling and crawled away and he got pretty far to the other end almost to the corner and I shot on the floor there. He fell off the other side or crawled off the bench on the other side, seemed to crawl backwards more or less shuffling backwards on his back. How he did it I don't know. As far as I can recall that is what he did. He ended up in front of the bench on the other side as best as I can remember and was laying there with a chair over him. He was on top of the dais if I can remember rightly is when he said, "Don't shoot, don't shoot, I won't sentence you" and he more or less shuffled off the dais and fell on the floor with the chair over him. As I can remember I walked around the end of the dais and was walking out going by—

Q: Did you walk past him?

A: Yes. The best I can remember, I was about to kill myself then and there. The last I can remember and what I have a slight memory of is was that way—it has come back to me kind of slow that he got up and started coming toward me and then two more shots were fired. As far as I can remember, I can't remember how a loaded shell—they say they found a loaded shell at that end of the bench—but I can't remember because the gun was empty when I was over there. I went to kill myself and the gun clicked and nothing happened, the gun was empty. I picked up my hat and coat from where Mr. Hoskins is sitting and if I remember rightly my jacket was over my left arm and my hat was in my left hand— no, my jacket was over my left arm and my coat was in my left hand and I went outside and was going to get some ammunition and kill myself out there and I thought, or I was thinking, the clip for the gun was in the car, but I didn't see it there and I felt in my pocket and it was there and I put it in the car. About that time, I didn't know his name at the time but I know it now—Mr. Bonavita—came up to the other side of the car and more or less rapped on the other side of the car or was trying to open the door or something. This is all as best as I can recall. I can't guarantee it is going to be a hundred percent, but I recollect he said, "You are not going anywhere, Bud" or "Where do you think you're going, Bud" or something like that if I remember rightly. I got out of the car and turned around and I said, If you are not looking for trouble, please leave me alone."

Q: Directing your attention back to the courtroom for a moment, one question I want to ask, Red. Will you tell us why you did it?

A: What?

Q: Why did you do it, Red?

A: Which part do you mean?

Q: The shooting.

A: You mean the Judge?

Q: Yes, coming in here and the events that you told us about. Tell us why you did it if you know.

A: Well, at the time I can't say, I really don't know why I did it. I can tell you what my thoughts have been since that has graduated out of me. I didn't actually have a reason at the time. I can't really give you an out and out reason. He started coming at me and he was shot twice. The only thing I can remember as happening is he said, "Oh" and turned and started walking this way. He said it in a little bit different tone than that. As far as where he ended up or anything like that I can't tell you except what facts and statements have been made in here. Why I shot him I can't tell you that, at the time, but I can tell you what is more or less come into my mind since or what angle I had at the time. Seems like there wasn't anything that you could call a trial or anything.

BY MR. KOHN: What?

A: Wasn't anything in the way of a trial, it just seemed like I was here to go through the back door to the jail is all I was here for. That's why I started to kill myself. I had pretty much become reluctant—not reluctant, but I foresaw what I was going to, or coming to and I got tired of trying to get it out in court and get it settled and in Fayette County. It seemed I had spent quite a bit of money, had a five hundred dollar cash bond up here. And I think I skipped this part—when I was sitting back there Mr. Kornreich came to me and asked if I wanted to wait until two that afternoon and I said I might as well get it over with now and see what is going to happen.

BY MR. KOHN: What's that? (last half of answer read to Mr. Kohn by the reporter)

(Resuming before the jury) BY MR. WAGGONER:

Q: Go ahead.

A: When he spoke to me about that I asked him where or how my five hundred dollar cash bond was at that time and he said it had been forfeited. It looked like there was nothing to stand on and was just ready to go. I mean pretty much, and it seemed like I had no way of carrying on. The money that I owed was pretty well tied up and I got reluctant to even pay them so that morning I sent it back home. I just got so I didn't care any more you might say, and I had spent quite a bit of money on attorneys and hotels and expenses each time coming up here. It seemed like it was piling up too much. I couldn't see anything in the future, it seemed. I hadn't enough money to take it to the Superior Court to see what the heck was going on—it just seemed like there was no foundation to stand on. I got extremely mad or furious or whatever you want to call it when I was called before the bench without any chance to testify or to find out what was going on or what had happened. I went pretty much what I call berserk or whatever you want to call it but I didn't exactly especially try to hit anyone. It seemed like it wasn't really the court, those things come on you all of a sudden. You can try to think them out but it hits you all of a sudden, it seemed like there was no justice in it, that there wasn't any chance to say anything or do anything, seemed like one road and not too far to the end.

Q: Red, have you finished?

A: Well, I suppose there are some more thoughts came in my mind but I can't gather them all. Things come to you slow, you don't just remember everything in your past at one time.

Q: Tell us if you have anything else?

A: Just seemed like I was being pressed down and had no chance to get up and walk more or less. This firing everywhere—I was ready to commit suicide. I don't know whatever made me start firing everywhere to begin with. Just exactly what the motives were for it or the why of it or just what, I can't say. That's what the jury is here for I guess.

BY MR. KOHN: What's that? (last part of answer read by reporter)

(Resuming before the jury) BY MR. WAGGONER:

Q: Red, after you walked out of the court and got in your car, you testified that Mr. Bonavita rapped on the side of the car, is that correct?

A: Yes.

Q: You told us what he said—what did you do from then?

A: What did I do then? I can't remember if I was in the car or just standing there beside it but I know I came back around the back and as best as I can remember I told him if he wasn't looking for any trouble to leave me alone. Any other action besides getting back in the car and driving away I can't tell you exactly for sure if I did or I didn't.

Q: Do you remember seeing the State Police?

A: I can remember seeing the state police behind me on the highway and along side of me such as that to a certain extent.

Q: Can you tell us if you knew what the state police were doing?

A: As I remember it, as they said, they blew the siren and came along back of me and came along side of me. One time they pulled over in front of me and I went around them and went on down the highway and then they started shooting at the car if I can remember, I remember hearing shots. I can slightly remember they had pistols pointed at the car. Then I can slightly remember going across the overpass or bridge or whatever it is on the other side of Warren and pulling off the road. The last thing I can remember is shooting myself. I have other things vaguely come in my mind. Those things that happened quickly have come back gradually and now is the time they are really developing in my mind but I didn't know it at the time. All that I can remember after I shot myself, I sort of come to slightly. I was on the ground and I sort of moaned and rolled up if I remember rightly, or somebody rolled me up I couldn't say for sure, but I can slightly remember the motion. I can slightly remember the officer throwing my green jacket pretty much over me and covered my entire head or I seemed to black out. I can't tell whether my vision went out or whether I had the vision but I sort of remember at the time of a jacket being put over my head. Then I was put in a rubber blanket more or less and put in the ambulance. I think I made a moan or so on the way to the hospital. I believe I saw an officer sitting beside me in the ambulance at one time on the way to the hospital. The last thing I can remember for quite a while is the stretcher coming out of the ambulance and being shifted into the hospital. To a certain extent I remember a few people around me. The last I can remember until I was in the hospital, I kind of remember the first persons I noticed in the hospital but whether it was some relatives or something I don't know—it's vague—I can't remember. I can't tell you the rotation they came in or anything but I can slightly remember one time waking up and more or less and a cellophane cage was around me. Naturally, for a long period of time I didn't feel very good. The thing I can remember very vividly is getting my jaw wired together. I can remember officers being in the room before that, some.

Q: Do you remember when that was, Red, when you got your jaw wired?

A: If things date back right I think it was the last part of a week I was in there, Thursday or Friday or something such as that.

Q: Do you know when it was that this took place?

A: You mean the jaw getting wired?

Q: Yes.

A: I remember being up and around pretty much but I don't have any recollection of that time or what day it was. I hadn't started to realize where I was but if I remember rightly I was moving around, was up and about to a certain extent. Actually for any of this description to a certain extent things have just developed in my mind. I believe when you talked to me I said, "Where is that in the courtroom"—I didn't even remember there was two entrances, one here and one there (indicating). They are just vague things in my mind and I can't actually state everything that happened. I can remember that jaw getting wired together and seeing some officers in the hospital—I have recognized some of them since—saw them and spoke to them but actually for knowing everything that I did in there I have no recollection of most of it. For any ideas of the time I was in there it was maybe about a week before I came out that I started to remember things fairly well."

# ♦ RUMOR & INNUENDO

I n 1954 Warren County had a population of 42, 698. The city of Warren, which was then still a borough, had a population of 14,849. In a community the size of Warren there were three ways that people learned what was going on: the local radio station WNAE, which was located at 310 Second Avenue, the Warren *Times-Mirror*, located at 203-295 Pennsylvania Avenue West, and the local rumor mill.

By dinnertime on January 13th, 1954 probably every adult in Warren County and a lot of others around the country as well as in a number of foreign nations knew Norman Moon had shot and killed Judge Allison Wade in the courtroom that morning.

Just the day before, on Tuesday, January 12th, Norman's brother Melvin had had an ominous feeling that Norman should stay in Connellsville. "The weather was bad that day, but he stopped in the office for a few minutes and he said he wouldn't be around that day. And I said something about, You got something real important? Where you going? And he said I'm going out of town. Well, I assumed he was going to Warren, but I really had no idea. I tried to talk him out of it and said, Well, do you really have to go? You know, the roads were bad. And he said something to the effect, Well, I'm gonna go. Warren was the only place he'd take off to from time to time."

The general media view was that Norman Moon was some kind of maniac and that he was as guilty as sin and that he would surely fry in the electric chair. But the local rumor mill saw it in a different light. Waitresses, barkeeps, construction workers and folks who knew Norman and Janet Moon and perhaps had moved in that same social circle saw things a little differently.

Mary Schwab, Janet's sister-in-law, remembers hearing about the murder on the radio. "Norman seemed like such a nice quiet fellow. My sympathy was always with him because it ruined his life totally. You can be driven to insanity and do things you'd never do otherwise. That was my feeling the day we heard about the shooting. Everybody in town was buzzing."

Mary was a home economics teacher at the Hunter Memorial School in Tidioute. "I went to school and a schoolgirl came to me and said, 'Is that your daughter that's married to that guy? He shot the judge up there!'"

The only purported record of Janet Moon's response to the shooting was carried in a monthly newspaper published in nearby Erie called *Jack Ducy's Town-Crier*. Ducy, who was unapologetic in viewing Norman Moon as a victim of political corruption, wrote in a *Town-Crier* column published shortly after Norman's murder trial that Janet Moon was asleep in room 108 of the Carver House Hotel at the moment the shooting took place. "Told what had happened by a maid," Ducy wrote, without indicating the source of his information, "she rushed to a telephone in her pajamas and said to her mother at the other end of the line in Tidioute: 'Norman just shot Judge Wade. If you and dad wouldn't have been so crazy about money, it would never have happened.' She hung up the receiver," Ducy added, "and burst into sobs."

Janet's girlhood friend Marcella Flasher Stover first heard about the shooting over the radio. "I remember Leroy Schneck talking on the radio. And he was running at the mouth. He was really condemning Moon, and Janet was fine and dandy and all this and that. And that was far from the truth, because I knew he didn't know what he was talking about. God, he really—I mean Jeezuz, I'd be listening to him on the radio and he'd be telling the darn stuff, and I'd think, God, you don't even know what you're talking about, and you're telling everybody this. And of course, a lot of people didn't know not to believe what he said.

"Norman was wrong to shoot like he did," Stover added. "But she was wrong, too, to do what she had done all her life."

Robert Moon had gone to work that day, and, as he normally did, he came home for lunch. He was sitting at the table eating when it came on the radio that Norman had shot and killed Judge Wade. Robert went immediately to his parents' home and picked up his mother and father, Dolly and Fred Moon, and started for Warren.

In its afternoon edition on January 13th, 1954 the *Times-Mirror* came out with this headline in half-inch bold type: JUDGE WADE VICTIM OF ASSASSIN.

A head-shot photo of Judge Wade ran under the headline. The headshot, which was three columns wide by six inches high, showed the judge in a suit, a white shirt, and a diagonally striped tie. Wade's hair is clipped short and his hairline is receding, his eyes appear deep-set and his expression is serious.

Another photo showed the Judge's chair where he sat behind the bench. The caption states—erroneously—that this was the chair where Wade was sitting when Moon started firing bullets into his body.

The story goes on to give an account of what had happened that morning in the courtroom, followed by a write-up of Judge Wade's life and career and his involvement in the Republican Party, as well as his talent as a painter. The article continued, naming Wade's next of kin: his nine-year-old adopted daughter; a sister, Mrs. Lucille Wade Williams of Harrisburg; a sister-in-law, Mrs. Harriet Wade, of the Overlook Sanitarium in New Wilmington, and ended with the announcement that Wade's body had been removed to the Lutz-VerMilyea Funeral Home.

There were photos on page six which showed the 1950, four-door Dodge sedan Moon was driving still parked along Route 6 west of Warren.

By nightfall that day Robert Moon and his parents, Fred and Dolly, had made it to Warren General Hospital, but they were refused permission to see Norman, who was unconscious. The doctors met the family in the hall and told them that they didn't expect Norman to live.

The next day, Thursday, January 14th, the *Times-Mirror* ran a smaller page one story with an accompanying headshot of Norman Moon in a suit and tie and his hair cut neat. In the photo, which looks as though it might have been taken by a professional in happier times, Norman looks directly at the camera. Above the photo the caption reads: "Clinging to life."

The headline of the article reads: SLAYER HAD SECURED NAMES OF ALL SEVEN HIGH COURT JUDGES

The article, which was attributed to an anonymous Pittsburgh source, went on to report that 10 days earlier, on January 4th, Moon had driven from his home in Connellsville to the office of the prothonotary of the Superior Court located in the City Council Building in downtown Pittsburgh and requested a copy of the appeals court decision upholding Judge Wade's jurisdiction in his support case.

According to the story, Norman sat down and read the report, then asked the deputy prothonotary who had waited on him which judge had written it. She informed him that Judge J. Colvin Wright had actually written the decision but that all seven judges had made the decision. At that point Norman asked her for the names and addresses of the judges but she denied his request and was quoted by the anonymous Pittsburgh source as saying she refused to divulge the judges' names on the grounds that she "didn't like the look in his eyes."

But, as far as the rumor mill was concerned, questions still remained as to how such a relatively minor court case had ended up with Moon shooting Judge Wade. Even legal minds like local attorney Sam Bonavita—who was involved up close and personal in the case—had concerns over certain aspects of Norman's support case.

"Now, back at that time, thirty dollars was a higher order of support than we had seen for a wife in her situation," Bonavita recollected. "If somebody would have been getting twenty dollars a week, a single woman, we would have considered it a fairly generous order. I was working on a lot of these cases at that time, and girls working at the New Process—heavens, thirty dollars a week, I don't think they had take home pays of thirty dollars a week. I know they didn't. I don't know of any explanation of why it was so high. I was flabbergasted when I heard the amount. I felt that it was out of line, no question, way out of line. No one could figure it out."

In the same edition of *Jack Ducy's Town Crier* mentioned earlier, Ducy claimed to have investigated 11 of Judge Wade's most recent support orders and found the $30 per week he awarded Janet Moon was the highest. "He was ordered to pay his errant, incorrigible wife $30 a week," wrote Ducy, "while the next highest, $25, was ordered in the case of a woman having six minor children." Ducy listed all 11 of the most recent support orders, which included a $10 per week order for a wife with two children and a $17.50 order for a wife with four children.

Bonavita also knew that Norman had a temper. "I had seen him in court a couple of times, and he had exhibited a bit of temper. He deeply resented the fact he had to pay support to his wife and the amount of the support. It was the way he answered questions. I think he had suspicions his wife was running around."

A gifted attorney, Bonavita lays out both sides of the case. "To me the shooting of Judge Wade had to be willful and premeditated, because he carried the gun with him. He felt he had been wronged by the local court—that's the only thing I can surmise. Then as he sat there something set him off.

"You know," Bonavita added, "a lot of guys who were in the war, it changed them. When you live with the fact that every day might be your last, you can get to the point where—maybe you're fatalistic. Maybe Norman just got to the point where he felt there was no use in going on—after what he'd been through in the war and then with his wife and then with the courts. And if he thought he was going to face prison, I can see how he might have thought there was just no use going on. In which case, a plea of voluntary manslaughter might have been more appropriate. I think something might have just snapped when Judge Wade called him forward to sentence him."

Ironically, in October of 1953, just three months before he was killed, Wade served as a visiting judge in the manslaughter trial of James Benford in the Allegheny Criminal Court in Pittsburgh. Wade found Benford guilty and sentenced him to two to four years in Western Penitentiary.

Meanwhile, the atmosphere surrounding the courthouse and downtown Warren was crackling with excitement. Telephones were ringing day and night all over the county as distant cousins and long-lost uncles who hadn't called home in years were suddenly trying to get a hold of any relative who would talk to them to find out if there were any sordid details that the media had left out—the way the media always did in big-time cases. Warren's four hotels and the local tourist homes were filling up fast as newsmen from all over flocked in to cover this tragic yet bizarre murder story.

The Wade Murder was big news, not just locally but all over the United States and in a number of countries around the world. As far as anyone could remember, Judge Allison Wade was the first judge in the 20th Century to be shot and killed in his own courtroom in the middle of a trial. Within days of the shooting, the *Times-Mirror* reported that its phone lines were jammed with calls from most of the major news services, including the Associated Press and the International News Service; it even received a call from NBC News.

Don Allen, Jr., later to become Sheriff, got the news of the shooting while he was stationed with the 82nd Airborne in North Carolina. "A buddy of mine called over, 'Hey. Al, aren't you from Warren, Pennsylvania? Good God, what kind of country is that up there? They just shot the judge right off the bench!'

"I said, hell, Norman Moon?! I couldn't believe it. Cause to see him, he is the mildest man you'd ever want to see. First time I saw him, he was sweeping the floor in the jail—that first time he was in the county lock-up. My dad was the warden, and I remember him saying that Norman had the money to get out but that he thought it was a matter of principle. But he was only hurting himself. My dad commented about him being so bullheaded."

Police Chief Mike Evan saw Moon in an entirely different light than Sheriff Allen. "To begin with he was a spoiled brat, by his father," the Chief said years later. "And I think any trouble he had down in that county where he lived, I think perhaps a lot of fixes were made on his behalf. I think, in my own mind, he had the feeling that nothing would happen to him as a consequence of shooting Judge Wade. He just decided that, 'I'm not going to let them crap on me,' in other words.

"It was not only premeditated but well thought-out. When he bought this gun down there in Pittsburgh, he got two clips with it, filled both clips. Then he took the gun out and tried it out someplace in a gravel pit. [Authors' note: This often repeated accusation was never made in court and certainly no proof was offered to support the accusation.] He was dead set in his mind no one was going to get the best of him. And I think he took the idea, 'I'll get out of this.' He growed up with that."

On January 14th the *Times-Mirror* ran an editorial piece titled Mirrored in Our "Times", which ended: "Among a long and impressive list of civic activities and a remarkable record during his time on the bench, the Hon. Allison D. Wade leaves a host of friends and admirers, not only in this community, but throughout those areas which he most ably served. His quiet sense of humor, sense of fairness, as well as many other personal attributes made him one of Warren's outstanding citizens. His interest in problems of juvenile delinquency as well as ardent anti-communistic attitudes made him a much sought after speaker for many organizations and occasions. One may well feel that it will be impossible to replace him with anyone of equal caliber.

"Each summer, the judge, and daughter Noel, enjoyed the quiet beauty and woodsy surroundings of Cook Forest Park, spending several weeks at the old Cook homestead there. In addition to being a fine jurist, he was an equally fine father, preferring the company of his daughter whenever his busy schedule permitted, and oft times when it didn't. There is little one can say by way of consolation to a nine year old child, but it may be stated that the entire community is well aware of the effect such tragedy may have."

In a page one story which it ran on January 14th, the *Times-Mirror* reported another misstep in this case. It appeared that everyone in this case—from Judge Wade on down—considered Norman Moon a relatively harmless defendant, a typical, angry, soon-to-be ex-husband faced with support payments. But there was one participant in this soap opera who saw Norman in a much different light.

At 9:30 on the morning of the murder, DA Kornreich went to the Sheriff's Office to request that a deputy be stationed in the court as he was concerned that Norman Moon, whom Kornreich considered to have a violent temper, might cause some trouble. But when he got to the office, he learned that Sheriff Larry Linder was in an Erie hospital recovering from back surgery and that deputy Sandy Secor was out serving papers in Russell.

Deputy Secor was quoted later as saying that if the Sheriff's office had been equipped with a two way radio, he could have been summoned and would have returned to the Courthouse at once. He added that anytime he or the sheriff were in the courtroom, they would be armed.

◆

After his arrest Norman Moon was brought by ambulance to Warren General Hospital where he was admitted in serious condition. The .45 caliber bullet he had fired through his neck had shattered his trachea, and he was choking on the blood and breathing through the bullet hole. His attending physician, Dr. William Cashman, immediately performed a tracheotomy which allowed Norman to breathe normally.

By the next day, Thursday, January 14th, Norman's condition was upgraded and he was expected to recover.

That same day, the Judge's sister, Mrs. Lucille Wade Williams, arrived from her home in Pottstown and set about to make the funeral arrangements for her brother. The body would lie in state in the Trinity Memorial Episcopal Church from 11 a.m. until 2 p.m. the following Saturday. At 2 p.m. the Reverend Beecher M. Rutledge would conduct the service, which would be followed by internment in Oakland Cemetery.

In its January 14th issue the *Times-Mirror* carried the following headline over a page one story, which appeared first in the Titusville Herald. KILLER VIOLENTLY JEALOUS OF HIS BLONDE BRIDE, MOTHER-IN-LAW IS SAID TO HAVE DECLARED.

According to Helena Schwab, when Janet's father Lou kissed Janet right after the wedding, Norman flew into a tantrum. Another time, Helena said, Norman came barging into her home with a shotgun. "He flew right through the house, looking for Janet. When he stormed upstairs, I ran out of the house as fast as I could. I was so frightened. It's a wonder we didn't all get shot."

On the other hand, Helena said that both she and her husband thought a lot of Norman. "He normally was quiet, as nice as could be, and we liked him an awful lot." She said Norman often described Janet as "the most beautiful girl in the world."

Apparently Helena didn't think there was anything inappropriate with Judge Wade handling her daughter's support case. She told the reporter that she "was also grieving for Judge Wade, a personal friend of the family."

Regarding her daughter's marriage, Helena said, "She wanted to go back to him. She still loved him. And we thought that perhaps they could come back together eventually and everything would be all right."

The following day, however, a follow-up story in the *Times-Mirror* about the shooting of Judge Wade reported that, "Resentment was expressed today over quotes contained in a story copied from The Titusville *Herald* and which included an interview with Moon's mother-in-law, Mrs. L. H. Schwab of Tidioute." The *Times-Mirror* report did not explain who voiced resentment or precisely what the complaint was. But if Norman had, in fact, ever barged into the Schwab house threatening to shoot people, it's hard to believe Lou Schwab wouldn't have made sure the authorities knew about it and did something about it.

Also, years afterward a number of Tidioute residents, many of whom had known Norman Moon at least a little, said they did not share Helena Schwab's views. "I think public sentiment was pretty much for Norman here in Tidioute and throughout the county," Bill Johnson maintained, adding, "with the exception, of course, of your lawyers and attorneys in Warren. All they could see was, well, you shot our beloved judge. I've always felt it depends on who you shot. If you're going to murder someone, it depends a lot on who that person is as to what the consequences will be. At least in our courts.

"Well, the public sentiment was people felt he was dealt unfairly with in the courts. It seemed like the judge was expecting too much in support payments for a person without a child. There was other cases where the wives did have children, and they didn't get nearly as much in support. There were those who said it possibly had to do with the friendship between the judge and the Schwabs."

Bill Johnson, like many others, felt that something in Norman just snapped. "My impression of Norman was, Here's a person who had served his country in wartime. And had never really done a wrong thing in his life. I don't know what his record would show, but I have an idea he'd never had a brush with the law and was just a good citizen. I just felt sorry for him. The nervous tension must have built up in him to the extent that he was kind of insane at the time of the shooting. Not responsible for his actions. And I was disgusted with our attorneys in Warren, because their attitude was, well, he shot our judge—he's the worst criminal ever. But I didn't look at it that way. But the little I'd seen him, I just felt this was a quiet, reserved type person who had never done anything wrong. And then he got involved with these marital problems and—something snapped."

◆

On the morning of January 15th, Norman Moon woke up to discover that the oxygen tent, in which he had been placed since his tracheotomy, had been removed sometime during the night. For the first time since shooting himself, Norman was given water and orange juice to drink.

That same afternoon tributes and memorials honoring and remembering Judge Wade began appearing in neighboring counties. From Forest County, the editor of The *Forest Press* praised Wade for his distinguished career. He wrote also of Wade's stance on communism. "He was many years ahead of his time in grasping the ominous threat of communism to America. He waged relentless war against communism, and he contributed much in ridding this region of the hidden dangers from within."

The editor of the Titusville *Herald* admitted that while Wade had no official dealings with the courts in Crawford County, he was nevertheless highly regarded as a top notch jurist. He went on to offer, "It is apparent that no person in official position failed in his duty in this matter. Certainly, nothing villainous was expected from a man who had only to answer why he had not obeyed a court order growing out of a rather unimportant case."

Also on January 15th, reports were received in Warren that the owner of the Pittsburgh gun shop where Moon had illegally purchased the murder weapon, had been arrested and remained in jail. All the way from Harrisburg, Governor John S. Fine commended the police officers who were responsible for their "fast apprehension" of Norman Moon. And finally, Allegheny County Sheriff William H. Davis announced his new policy that his deputies would search for weapons on all defendants who had been free on bond, before their appearance in court.

There was also a telegram received in Warren that day from United States Supreme Court Justice Robert H. Jackson, himself a former Warren attorney and friend of Wade's, expressing regrets that he could not attend the funeral service.

♦

The funeral ceremony for Judge Allison Douglas Wade was a simple affair. A steady stream of mourners began filing past the body at eleven in the morning and continued without letup until two that afternoon when Reverend Beecher M. Rutledge, pastor of the Trinity Memorial Episcopal Church, read the hymn "Crossing the Bar."

As the procession formed in front of the church on Pennsylvania Avenue at 2:30, the courthouse clock began to toll—its deep resonating tone reverberating through the streets of Warren every fifteen seconds until 2:45, when the procession arrived at Oakland Cemetery.

Hundreds of the Judge's friends and fellow members from the various fraternal, civic, political, and legal organizations to which he belonged, stood on the frozen ground of Oakland Cemetery, their long woolen topcoats flapping in the brisk January wind.

Meanwhile, just a mile or so from Oakland Cemetery, Norman Wilfrid Moon spent the weekend tossing and turning in his private room in Warren General Hospital. He was visited by his parents, Fred and Dolly Moon, and his brothers, Melvin and Edward, who had driven from their home in Connellsville. Out of the family's presence and even though Norman was medicated and unable to talk, he was questioned by Chief Evan and State Police Sergeants John Mehallick and Charles Naddeo.

DA Meyer Kornreich stated that he has been in communication with Pennsylvania Attorney General Robert E. Woodside regarding the issues of trying to get the Moon case before the next Grand Jury, in February, and the assignment of a judge to preside.

In nearby Crawford County it was reported that Sheriff J. Floyd Van Winckle and Judge Herbert A. Mook met to set up a policy in that court which would serve to protect persons in the courtroom. Van Winckle told reporters that he is always armed when he is in court and that he is considering adopting a policy of searching all defendants who have been out on bond.

A *Times-Mirror* article published that same day praised State Police officers Sgt. Charles Naddeo and Privates Paul Dell, Joseph Mastrian, and George Kaliena for their roles in the speedy capture of Moon. The unnamed writer stated that it was a good thing the officers were able to stop Moon before he reached the intersection on Route 6 and Route 62 because, had they not, they wouldn't have known which route Moon had taken. The writer went on to say, "It is thought the probable reason Moon attempted suicide was that he was confronted with a display of firepower so much superior to his own, that he might have tried conclusions with one or two officers, but not with four."

On Monday, January 18th, Chief Evan served Norman with a warrant for his arrest for the murder of Judge Wade. Donnell F. Allen, warden of the Warren County Jail, accompanied Chief Evan on the three o'clock visit. Immediately after the warrant was served, The Chief posted two police guards at the door to Moon's room, where they would stand watch 24 hours a day, seven days a week until Moon was well enough to be transferred to the county jail. Prior to the serving of the warrant there had been only one police guard at the door.

Years later Chief Evan explained how he was able to question Moon, even though Moon could not talk at the time. "So this was three days after the shooting. What we did—he couldn't speak, as I recall. And so we would—we asked leading questions is what happened, because a good investigator doesn't let any grass grow under his feet."

Although there was much to do in the way of preparing the case against Moon, including assigning a judge to cover the trial, prothonotary Ralph Sires sent notices to 23 county residents stating that they were in line to serve on the February grand jury. The notices didn't state it, of course, but no one knew at the time whether or not the Moon case would make it to the grand jury by February and that some of these jury members would decide the first step in the Moon trial.

On Tuesday, January 19th, the St. Mary's Press, in Elk County, ran an editorial that praised Judge Wade and called him "one of the most able young jurists in the state," but then the editorial slipped away from reporting and slid down to merely printing rumors when it stated, "His wife was killed about two years ago when she fell down the stairs at their home and broke her neck."

The rumors and innuendos continued. And the one that just wouldn't go away, the one that had more tongues wagging than any other was the one that alleged that Norman's wife Janet and Wade were having an affair at the time of her support trial. Even Norman's older brother Robert believed it was true, and he was willing to put his money on the line to prove it. Robert hired an attorney, and the attorney turned up the name of a man in the Navy who the attorney believed could testify that Wade and Janet had had at least one rendezvous in a nearby hunting cabin.

"An uncle of mine and I, we drove into New York state to a naval station," Robert Moon recalled later, "I don't think it was Buffalo, but I traveled all day to get there and back. I knew what ship to find him on. And on the deck they said, 'Oh, he's in his room, just go down. I went down in the bottom of the ship to find this seaman. It was night. He knew that Wade had a cabin in the woods someplace and she was a guest.

"But that was not allowed to be brought out at the trial," Robert added. "I don't know the guy's name or anything. But I interviewed him personally. His home was in Warren and he'd had contact with Janet in his younger days. He wouldn't sign anything—we had an affidavit with us—because it was embarrassing for him. But he said Judge Wade had a cabin in the woods and that Janet said she'd meet him there."

Of course Robert had heard the other rumor—the one going around that said that Janet and his father, Fred Moon, had had an affair. At first, he recalled years later, he seriously doubted the rumor but he did not entirely rule it out. "I know he did buy her a dog. But his animosity toward her was too great, so I'd say it was unlikely. But then—a man's a man."

Candis Snyder, a Connellsville resident who knew Norman's father, maintained in later years that, "Fred, he had roving eyes." Snyder grew up with the Moon family. She even went on picnics with them. Candis was at work at her job as the town telephone switchboard operator the day of the shooting. That was when she heard the news of the shooting. "But Dolly, she stayed with Fred," Snyder remarked. "She went to our church. In fact, when they laid Dolly out, Fred had his girlfriend there. Fred was one of the best people in construction in this town. He was very good at his job—though his morals weren't too good."

Another rumor stayed in Robert Moon's mind. He believed that Janet was using her room in the Carver House to make money, just as he believed she had at the Frontier Café in Colorado, where they had rooms upstairs. Robert summed up his feelings about Janet in one sentence. "She was just too loose, she was sex crazy."

On Wednesday, January 20th the Franklin *News Herald* ran an editorial with the headline: MURDER IN COLD BLOOD.

The writer praised Judge Wade for his exemplary and important career. The reporter went on to say, "We hope that the psychiatrists will not be permitted to have a field day with this murderer. Undoubtedly some interesting experiments can be conducted and the evidence will show in all likelihood that the killer wasn't exactly satisfied with some aspects of his childhood."

The Harrisburg *Evening News* carried an editorial that day as well. After its opening paragraph outlining the shooting, its writer stated, "Scarcely a day goes by without a report from some part of the nation of wanton killing and, while it may not be properly described as an epidemic, it undoubtedly is reaching new and unprecedented heights.

"How much of this frightfulness stems from contempt for the law and how much from the failure in many areas to take prompt and definite action against those responsible for the awful record may be a matter for argument, but the undeniable fact remains that we live in a state of lawlessness not even exceeded in the wild period of prohibition gangsterism."

On Thursday, January 21st, doctors at Warren General wired Norman's fractured jaw together.

The case against Norman Moon was moving forward. Also on January 21st Chief Evan along with State Police Sergeants John Mehallick and Charles Naddeo returned to the site on Route 6 about five miles west of Warren where Norman had shot himself. Initially, due to the deep snow, they had suspended their search for the shell casing from the bullet that Norman had fired into his neck. But the rain from the day before had melted the snow to a point where they were able to resume the search and to find the casing. Chief Evan stated after the successful search that he now had all the casings from all the bullets that Norman had fired.

That same day DA Meyer A. Kornreich reported that Deputy Attorneys General David Kohn of Dauphin county and Harrington Adams of Northumberland county had been assigned by the state's Attorney General to prosecute the Moon trial. "They just come in here," recalled Chief Evan, "and took it over on their own."

At 2:30 in the afternoon on Friday, January 22nd Warren attorney Alexander C. Flick was sworn in as President Judge of the 37th Judicial District. Prothonotary Ralph E. Sires administered the oath in the main courtroom before the county Bar Association and assorted friends and dignitaries from other counties. This ceremony was followed at 3:30 by a tribute to Judge Wade conducted by the bar association. State Senator

Rowland B. Mahanay, of Forest County presented the tribute.

"His judicial qualities were recognized and appreciated by this bar and he won its confidence and respect early in his judicial career. His humor and patient approach to litigation over which he presided won the personal regards of all persons familiar with court procedure."

On Tuesday, January 29th, Norman's physicians at Warren General decided that he was well enough to be discharged. A little before two that afternoon, Chief Evan entered Norman's room and handcuffed his own right wrist to Norman's left wrist. The Chief then led Norman to a waiting police car and took him to the Warren Municipal Building at 318 West Third Avenue, where he was arraigned for murder before Justice Tracy M. Greenlund. Norman pleaded not guilty, and a hearing date was set for February 10th. After the arraignment Norman was taken to a cell in the county jail.

By this time Norman's parents, Fred and Dolly Moon, had moved into the Carver House Hotel. Former Carver House waitress Donna Hartley remembers waiting on the Moons and how she felt. "I really didn't know Janet, but I didn't like the things I heard about her. And, I felt sorry for Norman. His parents seemed to be lovely people. I really think he was driven out of his mind, by being driven from one court system to another. I think he didn't know what end he was on.

"His parents stayed at the hotel during the trial, and I waited on them. They seemed to be very nice middle-class people." Robert Moon, Norman's older brother, later recalled that he and his mother would go to church on Sunday while in Warren, "And the whole congregation just seemed to come to us and offer anything they could do to help us."

"Like I say," Donna Hartley added, "I didn't know Janet, but I knew all this stuff was going on, because I kept hearing all these things in the Carver House—about her and men and how she dragged Norman from one court to another and made a nervous wreck out of him."

◆

In the annals of Warren County history, January, 1954, will surely be remembered as the month that lasted a year. But, on Sunday January 31st, it did end, and, the new month began just as it should, on Monday, February 1st. On that day at 10 in the morning, the February grand jury was sworn in by Prothonotary Ralph Sires in the main courtroom. Newly appointed Judge A.C. Flick, Jr. convened with the jury and informed them that at the end of that day's session they would be recessed and that they would be subject to the call of the court any time before May 1st. He included the proviso that they may be called in to address the Norman Moon case, and the jury was dismissed at 12:30 that afternoon.

Meanwhile, the Moon case was being tried in the court of public opinion. Zo-Ann Nicholson remembers that her father worked with Norman and that her father felt that Norman was getting a raw deal. "My dad worked with Norman, and Dad always felt the poor guy got railroaded. I never knew Norman, I just know what my father said, and he thought Norman was a wonderful boy. Dad just thought the fellow was being shoved to the hilt, you know, that I guess his wife was after him for nonsupport and she was just out to make a bundle off him, I think. I mean, it's too bad it happened the way it did. But you know, under the same conditions, you don't know—maybe anybody, if they were pushed that hard, you don't know what you would do."

Also on that Monday DA Kornreich, Chief Evan, and Sgt. Naddeo spent the day in Harrisburg where they met with the two deputy attorneys general—Harrington

Adams and David Kohn—who would be prosecuting the Moon case. The two prosecutors would be in Warren for the next step in the case, Moon's preliminary hearing on February 10th. Chief Evan and Sgt. Naddeo spent the day going over ballistics evidence with state experts.

On Friday, February 5th, the Sheriff's office informed the 52 residents, who were selected for criminal jury duty that was scheduled to start on Monday, February 7th, that their services would not be needed. The Moon case would not be ready by the court's end and there were no other criminal cases to be heard during that quarter session.

While he awaited his hearing, Norman Moon was confined to his cell and was allowed to walk around the adjacent cell block corridor. He was under 24-hour armed guard and locked in his cell each night at 10.

On Wednesday, February 10th, the hearing for the Commonwealth vs. Norman Moon began at two in the afternoon before Justice of the peace Stacy Greenlund. Moon had two of his attorneys, Samuel Braemer of Connellsville and Warren attorney E. H. Beshlin with him. Deputy attorneys general Adams and Kohn called just two witnesses to provide probable cause to bring the matter to trial. Stenographer Bernice Seavy testified that she saw Moon shoot Judge Wade. She said Moon mounted the dais and followed the judge with the pistol as the judge pleaded, "Don't shoot. Don't shoot. I'm not going to sentence you."

Dr. J. R. Thompson testified as to what he saw in the courtroom that day from his seat just three or four rows back from Moon and on the opposite side of the courtroom. Thompson stated that after Moon left the courtroom, he ran to the judge and that Wade was breathing shallowly and had little or no pulse and that Wade died three or four minutes after he reached him.

At 10 on the morning of March 3rd, the 23-member February grand jury reconvened in the main courtroom, and, after an hour of deliberation, indicted Norman Moon for the murder of Judge Wade. The jurors were then dismissed and the trial date was set by Judge Flick for Monday, May 10th.

While attorneys on both sides prepared their cases for trial, Norman remained in jail without bail. On March 31st, Norman had the wires in his jaw removed by a Warren dentist. His attending physician reported that Norman had a case of yellow jaundice associated with this jaw wound, but he added that Norman was responding well to its treatment and that overall his condition was good.

◆

The wheels of justice turn slowly—but inexorably— toward the meting out of justice. As the winter of 1954 turned to spring, the wheels kept turning until, like the seasons, they changed the manner of things. There would be no delays; there would be no turning back: spring was here and it would soon be time for Norman Moon to stand in front of those wheels.

On April 30th, Judge Flick announced to the media that there would be no photos taken in the courtroom during the trial. Flick also informed members of the media that on the first day of the trial, which would be taken up with jury selection, the 104 prospective jurors in the pool would enter the courtroom and sit in the first three rows while roll was called. When each person's name was called, he or she would leave the courtroom and be called back in, one person at a time. After all three rows were vacated, those seats would be available for the media.

Saturday, May 1st, was a busy day for Judge Flick and his courtroom staff. In the morning they finalized the court personnel changes that would be necessary for the trial because some of the court staff would be called as witnesses during the trial. Prothonotary Ralph Sires was listed as a witness and would perform his duties until he was called. To act as his substitute and as an overall assistant, the court appointed Don Shuler of North Warren. Shuler had previously worked as a Recorder for eight years and was then a state tax appraiser.

James Maines, the court crier from Judge Laub's courtroom in Erie, would assume those same duties in Warren during the trial. Maines, along with Lena Schaeffer, Judge Wade's former housekeeper and a retired probation officer, would be in charge of the jury. Their job would be to escort the jurors to and from the Carver House Hotel and to make sure that they were contacted by no one and did not read the newspapers or magazines. Four members of the State Police would report to Sheriff L.E. Linder. These men would provide security where the sheriff felt it was needed.

Warren's two main hotels, the Carver House and the Exchange, were booked solid as out-of-town attorneys for the defense and the prosecution and media representatives checked in over the May 7th weekend. The Associated Press News Service would set up its headquarters at the *Times-Mirror* and would install a special news service wire and modern equipment for wire transmission of photographs, used for the first time in Warren. The media would use the weekend to get familiar with Warren, and the attorneys would get themselves ready for the jury selection process, which would begin Monday morning.

The rumor mill was still in business, but as the start date of the trial drew nearer, there was a last-minute hush as if everyone in Warren was holding his breath, waiting for the trial to begin.

At 9:30 in the morning on Monday, May 10th, Sheriff L.E. Linder and his deputy Sandy Secor prepared

Norman to leave his cell and walk the 200 feet to the front of the courthouse. As they made their way from the side of the courthouse to the front, they met up with Norman's parents, Fred and Dolly Moon, who were walking up the front sidewalk. Norman waved at his parents and his father raised his right hand and tried to smile. Dolly, perhaps too deflated to even look at her son, kept her eyes downcast. As the pair made their way from the jail to the courthouse steps, news photographers took advantage of the situation to get photos that would accompany their stories.

Norman Moon entered the courtroom a few minutes before ten, just as he had entered the courtroom 117 days earlier, only this time he was escorted by Sheriff Linder.

At ten the jury selection process began as the prosecution asked the same questions over and over:

◆ Have you ever been employed by the Commonwealth?
◆ Are you an acquaintance of the defendant, his family, or the family or person of Janet Schwab Moon?
◆ Have you ever been given legal advice by attorney Beshlin, Hampson or Kornreich?
◆ Did you know Judge Wade?
◆ Would Judge Wade's high position in this county or the fact that the act took place in this very courtroom influence your decision in any way?
◆ Have you talked the case over, heard it discussed, or read about it in the newspapers?
◆ Is there any reason at all why you should not serve as juror in this case?
◆ Are you in the military and, if so, what branch?
◆ Do you have any children and, if so, what is the age of the eldest?
◆ What are your feelings on capital punishment?

The defense asked one and only one question of every prospective juror:

♦ Would you abide by the instructions of the Court if the insanity issue was to be considered?

By the noon recess only one juror had been chosen: 33-year-old Richard Curtin from Barnes. By 5 o'clock the attorneys had questioned 15 more prospective jurors and were successful in accepting only one more juror: 34-year-old William W. Rhoades of Clarendon. By Tuesday at noon three more jurors were seated: Mrs. Lucille McKelvy of Warren; Harold Joy of Kinzua; and Allen Porter of Bear Lake. At the end of the afternoon session, one more juror was selected: Mrs. Hazel Witz of Warren. The seventh juror was selected Wednesday morning: Howard Clark of Warren.

At this point in the jury selection process, the pool of 104 candidates had been depleted. To procure more candidates Judge Flick selected two Warren residents— H.B. Pettit and E.R. Sanford, Jr. to go out into the borough and county and serve papers on whomever they ran into, quite literally. Pettit and Sanford were sworn in as special deputies by Clerk Don Schuler and instructed "to go forth into the borough and county to round up 60 talesmen to report to the court at 10 o'clock Thursday."

Donald Rice of Barnes, 25 at the time, was one of those corralled as a prospective juror and remembered that many residents literally were afraid to go out on the street for fear of being snagged into the jury pool. Nonetheless, at the beginning of court on Thursday morning, the prosecution and the defense had 59 new prospective jurors to choose from. Four jurors were selected Thursday but the number of total jurors rose only by three because juror number three, Mrs. Lucille McKelvy, was dismissed when she became ill. Harry W. Johnson of Warren took her place. J.W. Mock was selected as juror number eight and Robert Honhart of Youngsville became number nine. Court opened Friday morning with nine jurors having been selected. At 2:15 Friday afternoon William Reiff of Clarendon became juror number 10 and Don Rice was seated as number 11 at a special Saturday session.

During the Saturday session, Deputy Attorney General Kohn made it known that he had received a message from the *Times-Mirror* that was from a local couple who wanted to make sure that juror Robert Honhart be identified correctly so that he would not be confused with another Robert Honhart who lived in Youngsville. This prompted an investigation by Kohn that resulted in Honhart being released as juror number nine. But before the extended Saturday session was over, at 10:30 that night, two more jurors were seated: Elizabeth Hunter of Fifth Avenue Extension, who would be the new number 11; and Harold Nelson of Warren, number 12.

The Monday, May 17th issue of the *Times-News* carried the following editorial headlined, ACT TWO.

"It is now one week since there came into our midst four attorneys from distant points in the State, two from Harrisburg to represent the Commonwealth in its case against a young man accused of fatally shooting our County Judge in the Courtroom where he was presiding, and two others from Connellsville and Uniontown to represent this young man in his efforts to escape the death penalty.

"During this week these four attorneys, each one just short of middle life, have impressed the people of this community with their evident possession of every trait which goes toward making a fine gentleman. Their treatment of each other and of the defendant has not lacked the rudiments of efficiency, but has been tempered with understanding, unstudied poise, gentlemanly conduct in and out of Court, and at all times it has been quite evident that each one of these lawyers has great respect for the other three as well as for the dean of Warren lawyers who also represents the defense. In an entirely new capacity for him, our Warren county sheriff has sat at the left of the prosecution all week and the same tributes paid the other five apply to him.

"Warren and Warren county, known for quiet living and good living, are fortunate in having this sort of talent in the Court Room, and the entire countryside is pardonably proud of its President Judge, The Hon. Alexander C. Flick, Jr., whose splendid conduct in Court has withstood a number of delicate and could-be embarrassing situations during the first week of the trial. It is difficult for one to believe that Judge Flick is presiding over his first major case. It has been necessary in at least one incident for Judge Flick to clearly search his mind and bring forth a measure of wisdom closely akin to that of Solomon.

"Not even in the Warren County Courtroom did the full import of this trial descend upon participants and spectators until two prominent Warren men were summoned to appear before Judge Flick to be named as elisors for bringing into Court additional jurors, the original panel being exhausted. A new hush fell upon the big room, and within a matter of minutes this new aspect of the case began to evidence itself throughout the town. The quiet efficiency with which everything had been handled to facilitate the Court procedure had taken many off their guard, and their false composure was suddenly penetrated.

"As has been pointed out from the bench, 'We have gone through a hard week,' but that was as far as Judge Flick could go. He realizes, as do most of us, that difficult situations may arise as the trial goes on. It is reassuring to know that matters at the Courthouse are ruled by such a fine Judge and that the out-of-town lawyers who have come into our midst, together with Hon. E.H. Beshlin and Sheriff E.E. Linder, are of the same caliber.

"The attorneys for both sides have evidenced to the judge their impenetrable intention that the defendant shall receive a fair trial. The people of this town and this county have no fear on that score. Warren has again come into the national spotlight, this time because of an incident few county seats escape during the passage of years. Let us maintain a tranquility, retain our good sense, and view all developments from an unbiased standpoint. We are not the Jurors, it is not our privilege to decide this case in advance in our homes, taverns, business places, or on the streets. Excitement over the issues that may develop will do no one a whit of good. Fairness to the extreme is the procedure of our Court; we should sit back and be calm and undisturbed, let come what may. Events to come most certainly do cast their shadows before."

# ♦ THE COMMONWEALTH VS. NORMAN MOON

A t 10:36 on the morning of May 17, 1954, the Honorable Alexander C. Flick Jr., the newly appointed President Judge of the 37th Judicial District, banged his gavel and the murder trial of the Commonwealth of Pennsylvania vs. Norman W. Moon began.

Norman and his attorneys, Samuel D. Braemer, Thomas A. Waggoner, Jr., and E.H. Beshlin, sat at the defense table. First Deputy Attorney General Harrington Adams and Deputy Attorney General David S. Kohn, who were assigned as special prosecutors for the trial, sat at the prosecution table.

The jury was ushered into the courtroom and directed to the jury box. Judge Flick opened the proceedings by addressing the jury: "I am sure you have been impressed with the care exercised in choosing you. Now it will be very different. You are now to listen to the evidence upon which you will decide this case."

Court Clerk Don Shuler then had the jury stand as he administered the oath: "You and each one of you do swear by Almighty God, the Searcher of all hearts, that you will well and truly try, and true deliverance make, between the Commonwealth of Pennsylvania and the prisoner at the bar, whom you shall have in charge, and a true verdict give, according to the evidence, and that as you shall answer to God at the Last Great Day."

The jury, which was comprised of 10 men and two women, was as follows: (1) Richard E. Curtin, Barnes (2) William W. Rhodes, Clarendon (3) Harold Joy, Kinzua (4) Allen Porter, Bear Lake (5) Hazel Witz, Warren (6) Howard L. Clark, Warren (7) Harry W. Johnson, Warren (8) J.M. Mock, Warren (9) Warren Reiff, Clarendon (10) Donald E. Rice, Barnes (11) Elizabeth Hunter, Warren R.D. 1 (12) Harold Nelson, Warren.

The two alternates are Paul R. Smith, Warren R.D. 1, and Robert Geiger, Conewango Avenue.

Prosecutor Adams was the first to speak and he addressed his opening remarks to the jury. "The Grand Jury has indicted Norman W. Moon on a charge of murder. It will be your duty to decide his guilt or innocence. It will be our duty to prove his guilt. As the District Attorney of this county is to be called as a witness, we are to prosecute the case in his stead.

"Now on behalf of the Commonwealth, I state that on January 12 Norman W. Moon purchased an automatic Colt pistol in Pittsburgh, then proceeded from Pittsburgh to Warren, spent the night in a tourist home, and on January 13 appeared in this Court Room and occupied a seat for about an hour. At 11 o'clock the matter involving Norman W. Moon was brought to the Court's attention and Moon's attention. Moon rose from his seat and started to discharge a pistol and started toward the bench and fired shots at close range at Judge Wade. By that pistol and the shots therefrom, Judge Wade was killed.

"We now will show you that Moon went downstairs, entered a car and proceeded to flee.

"We will ask that you bring in a verdict of first degree murder and the death penalty because this was cold-blooded, deliberate murder."

◆

The jury sat stunned. It was as if all the hours they had spent waiting then answering all those questions and then trying to prepare themselves for this moment had meant nothing. There was no way to prepare yourself for the electric surge of emotion that ran through each fiber of your body as you realized, once and for all, that you held a man's life—his very breath—in your hands.

Adams returned to the prosecution table and sat in his chair. His opening remarks had filled the great room with a tension that you could almost taste. From the front of the courtroom there came a sharp intake of breath followed by the half-audible sobs of Dolly Moon, as she sat beside her husband, alternately twisting a white handkerchief around her fingers then dabbing her eyes. Her son Norman sat just twenty feet away, but he might as well have been on the other side of the moon.

Prosecutor Kohn rose and called his first witness, Court Prothonotary Ralph Sires. Sires raised his right hand and was sworn in by Court Clerk Shuler. Sires' testimony set the stage, which was, of course, the very same courtroom where the trial was now taking place. It was established that the following 10 people were in the courtroom at one time or another on the morning of January 13th: Judge Wade, Norman Moon, District Attorney Meyer Kornreich, attorney Harold Hampson, court stenographer Bernice Seavy, court crier George Todd, attorney Sidney Blackman, James Scalise, prothonotary of the court, Ralph Sires, and Dr. John Thompson.

Q: Just tell us what happened.

A: The district attorney indicated to the court that Moon was present and that this case should have some attention that morning. There was some conversation back and forth and the Court directed me to make a note of the district attorney's questions to Moon's answers. The DA asked Moon if he still refused to abide by the Court's order and Moon replied, "Absolutely. That is correct." As I made notes, Mrs. Seavy spoke to me over my right shoulder. I continued to make a note of the questions and answers as directed by the Court. It was while I was so engaged that I heard a shot, looked up and stood up. I saw Moon standing inside the rail at a point between the west post and the lawyers' table.

At this point Sires was directed to leave the stand and go to where Moon stood when he fired the first shot. Sires showed that Moon was about 18 inches inside the rail, in front of the left gatepost. Then he resumed the stand.

Q: What, if anything, did you see Moon have?

A: As I observed Mr. Moon at that point he was bringing a gun in an arc from above his line of vision down to a firing position in the act of firing the gun. He was looking in the direction of the judge where he was seated at this end of the bench and the gun was pointed in that position as he fired the shot. I dropped to the floor behind my desk just before the shot was fired but I saw the gun descend to the firing position in the act of firing the gun. Kohn then established that Sires had his head down at the time of the first shot and it was as Moon was preparing to fire the second shot that Sires dove under his desk. Sires was still under his desk when he heard the third shot, which he said came from a position on the end of the platform on which the bench is located, the end toward the jury box.

Q: Then what happened?

A: It was at that time just before the shot or just after, I don't recall which, that I heard a noise immediately back of the bench which indicated that the judge was scrambling along—

At this point there was an objection by Braemer that Sires could not testify as to what he saw because, as he was hiding under is desk, he didn't see anything. The Court directed Sires to just say what he heard. Kohn then directed Sires to leave the stand again and assume the position he had been in when he heard the shots. He did and it was while he was in this position that he heard, in rapid succession, the final two shots that had hit Judge Wade.

Q: Then what happened next?

A: I then observed the judge fall from the east side of the platform.

Kohn then enlisted the help of State Police Sergeant John Mehallick to assume the role of the judge. Sires positioned Sgt. Mehallick where the judge lay after he was shot.

Q: What if anything did the judge have?

A: The chair which normally sits to the left of the prothonotary or clerk's chair for the convenience of the attorneys or others who may wish to converse with the clerk during actions of court was in his hands. He had grasped it by the arms with the feet extended upwards and his legs were drawn up. That is about it, and the feet were pointed at a position toward the bench.

Q: What conversation took place at that particular point?

A: The judge had let go of the chair and had turned about and toward this general direction. And then I heard Moon say, "You will back down now, you bastard, you will back down now." And that was followed by the two additional shots.

Q: Then what happened?

A: I then saw the judge as he stood up and he called, "I am shot. I am shot," and he then started and ran or limped very badly in a running gait past the front of my desk, and around toward the chambers.

Q: Then what happened?

A: I did not see Moon. The next thing I heard was a clicking noise immediately in front of my desk. That is from a position immediately in front of the center of my desk. I identified this noise as being made by the gun, a noise such as changing the clip in the gun. That is what it sounded like to me. Then I heard footsteps on the linoleum heading toward the back of the courtroom.

Q: What did you do after that?

A: I waited until the footsteps had receded to the back of the room and I heard the lock of the door as it opened and it was at this point that I heard screams at the entry door to the east of the bench as spectators entered the room.

Kohn ended his direct examination and Braemer began his cross examination by going over the details of Sires' testimony. Braemer, it seems, went over each statement Sires had made looking for him to slip up or add something new. When nothing came of this, Braemer asked him questions regarding how the case came to be called that day and whether or not minutes were made of the trial up until the time Moon started firing. Braemer continued to question Sires about the proceedings that morning.

Q: Then am I correct in understanding that the Court had stated that there was no record being kept in this case at that particular time?

A: There had been no witnesses sworn, and the proceeding was very informal.

"Yes, it was," Braemer responded in a sarcastic tone.

At this, Kohn jumped up and asked that the remark be stricken from the record. He added, "I think it is very improper." Judge Flick agreed with Kohn and said it was an unnecessary remark. Kohn continued saying that "It is the tone of voice in which he repeated it." In the end Braemer apologized.

Kohn then stood up and started his re-direct questioning.

Q: You testified that Moon used the word bastard toward Judge Wade while he was lying on his back. Now I ask you whether or not you recall any other obscene words that were used by Moon at that time.

A: There were some additional words.

Q: Repeat them.

A: There was only one word that I recall.

Q: Tell us what it is.

A: The word was fucking.

Sires' testimony ended at noon and the court adjourned for the lunch hour until 1:30 in the afternoon.

♦

At 1:30 the prosecution called its next witness, William Kress, the operator of a sporting goods store in Pittsburgh where Moon had purchased the .45 automatic on January 12th, the day before he shot Judge Wade.

Q: Was there any conversation between you and Moon in regard to the purpose for which he was purchasing the gun?

A: Moon said he wanted to shoot target, that he had been in the army and was familiar with a gun like that and would like to possess one of his own.

Kress stated that besides the pistol Moon bought 50 rounds of government surplus ammunition.

Q: Do you have a record showing the serial number of that gun?

A: The number I have on my application, which is signed, is for a revolver, a Colt automatic, caliber 45, length of barrel five inches, serial number 2251839.

Kohn then entered the Colt .45 as Commonwealth Exhibition #1, the box of shells as #2, and the clips for the automatic as #3.

Braemer's cross-examination started off with him asking the witness the very same questions that Kohn had asked. Braemer then questioned Kress about the 48-hour waiting period that is used when a handgun is purchased so that the authorities can investigate the purchaser to see if he qualifies to own one.

Kohn stepped up for a re-direct and had Kress tell how Moon had talked him into letting him take the handgun with him. He brought out the fact that Kress had said that Moon was sick and had to go across the street to use the men's room.

A: His argument was that he was so far from home and being in his condition it would be way out of his way to come back for his gun. Kohn then brought to light the fact that Kress was in trouble for selling the gun.

Q: You are under prosecution for that in Allegheny County now aren't you?

A: Yes sir.

Prosecutor Kohn called his next witness, William E. Lutz, Warren County Deputy Coroner. Lutz testified that, as deputy coroner, he was called to the courtroom shortly after 11 o'clock on the morning of January 13th.

Q: Did you do an autopsy of the body after you removed it?

A: We took the body out after Dr. Thompson confirmed the death. Yes I did. Not me, Dr. Sugerman did.

Q: Did you see the cause of death at the time of the autopsy?

A: Yes sir. Two wounds on the left side between, about at the elbow made by bullets.

After an objection by the defense was denied by Judge Flick, a photograph of the judge after he had died was admitted as Commonwealth's Exhibit #4. The photo was then passed around the jury. Kohn produced a copy of the photo and directed Lutz to stand up and indicate where the bullet marks were on the judge's body.

A: They entered there on the left side, almost at the armpit. About four inches apart.

It was then established that one bullet passed through the body and the other one did not. The bullet that passed through, did so at a 45 degree angle and exited just below the floating rib on the right. The one that remained in the body had reached the skin on the right side and it had also taken a 45 degree trajectory.

Q: Did you remove the body?

A: That's right. The clothes were removed and turned over to the Warren Department of Police, to Chief Michael Evan.

Q: Besides yourself, Dr. Sugerman was present and performed the autopsy?

A: Dr. Sugerman, Dr. Thompson, Dr. O'Connor, and one of our employees, Mr. Ver Milyea.

After some discussion at the prosecution table, Kohn recalled William Kress, and Kress was able to produce the application for purchase of a firearm that Moon had signed. This application was offered as Commonwealth Exhibit #5. Kress' in-house receipt from his business, the Swap Shop, which was for the Moon transaction, was entered as Commonwealth Exhibit #6.

The Commonwealth then called DA Kornreich as a witness. Kohn established that Kornreich had lived in Warren County for 45 years and has been the district attorney for the past nine years. Kohn brought out that Kornreich was present in court the day of the shooting and that he knew Moon and had worked on the Moon case.

Q: At the time you came in did you have any conversation with him?

A: I came in the back way to the courtroom. At that time there was a hearing in progress here and Mr. Moon was setting in that seat and I went up to him and I believe I first extended my arm to shake hands with him but he turned away. I told him that I had been advised by his attorney, who at that time was Henry Nicholson, that Mr. Nicholson could not be here in the morning but that he could be here in the afternoon and I told Norman Moon that we would defer his case until that afternoon but Norman Moon answered, "No, I want to get it over with now" or words to that effect. I believe those were the words he used.

Kohn responded to Norman that as soon as an opportunity arose, he would get Norman's case before the court.

Q: Was it your request that Moon was in court?

A: It was at the request that I made to his attorney, Henry Nicholson, that he be present that day.

Q: And subsequently did you see Nicholson and try to find out whether Moon would be here or not?

A: I met Attorney Nicholson in the elevator at the Warren National Bank Building where both our offices are located, and I asked him whether Norman Moon would appear on January 13th and he told me that he had sent him a notice and he held up a postal receipt, return receipt, one of those little red cards, and showed me that it was signed by Norman W. Moon or by somebody on his behalf that he had received the notice but he didn't know whether Moon was coming or not.

Kornreich continued saying that Judge Wade had gone downstairs on another court matter and that when Wade came back to the courtroom, he followed him in. As soon as Wade was seated behind the bench, Kornreich told him that Moon was in the courtroom and briefly reviewed the history of the case. Among other things, he mentioned that Moon had lost his appeal in the Superior Court, that the case had been going on for more than a year and that it was time to take action. Kohn continued to question Kornreich.

Q: Just tell us what happened. Tell us everything.

A: Attorney Hampson made a statement to the court and when he had finished Judge Wade also asked Norman Moon whether he did not want to wait until that afternoon when his attorney could be in court. Moon stated that he wanted to proceed then. Judge Wade then directed Mr. Sires to take minutes of the proceedings. The next thing that I recall Judge Wade looked at Moon and said, "Will you come forward please?" or something like that, I don't recall the exact words. It was at that moment that Moon stood up where he was sitting behind the railing and he had a jacket that apparently zipped down the middle. He stood up, deliberately opened the right flap of his jacket, and from where I was sitting I could see the outline of his gun stuck in his belt.

Q: What did you do and what did he do?

A: I immediately jumped up from the chair and ran toward the door which is immediately to the left of this dais and ran downstairs to the sheriff's office and called the state police.

Q: Now, while you were proceeding towards the exit from the courtroom, which is to the right of the courtroom facing the bench—did you hear or see anything further?

A: When I got approximately to the corner of Mr. Sires' desk I heard one shot. I ducked momentarily but not feeling anything I kept on going.

Q: Fast?

A: Very fast.

At this point Braemer stepped before the bench and began his cross-examination.

Q: Mr. Kornreich, I believe you stated that Mr. Hampson was a private prosecutor in this case?

A: Well, he was attorney for Mrs. Moon, yes.

Q: Will you tell us when you got into the case in your official capacity?

A: Mr. Hampson represented Mrs. Moon when this information was filed before Justice of the Peace Greenlund. Under our practice in this county all transcripts from the Justice of the Peace come through my office. When I received this transcript I filed it in court and I arranged the schedule for hearings. I then arranged with Mr. Hampson first as to when this hearing will come up and I was present at that hearing.

Q: So you came into this case in your official capacity at the time the transcript came over into your office?

A: Yes, except there were two or three continued hearings at which I wasn't present. Mr. Hampson carried on at those hearings.

Q: When did you get into the picture again?

A: When Moon filed the petition through Attorney Nicholson, questioning the authority of the court to make the order. On the technical legal questions—I worked with Mr. Hampson on the law and I also appeared before the Superior Court and argued the case for the reason that Mr. Hampson was tied up in civil court that week.

Q: Can you tell me, Mr. Kornreich, when was the first time you knew that Nicholson was representing Moon?

A: The first time I knew that Nicholson had any interest in the case was when he stopped me on the street one day last summer and said that he had received a call from the jail from a man named Moon and he asked what the case was all about.

Braemer continued hammering away at Kornreich, asking him if he could recall certain hearing dates. Kornreich conceded he couldn't remember, at which time Kohn jumped in and objected to that line of questioning, stating, first, that all those dates are on the record and, second, that those questions were to be asked during the presentation of the defense case and not as a part of cross-examination. Braemer withdrew his last question and stated that he would ask the following question, which was all he wanted to know anyway.

Q: When you first knew that Nicholson was representing Moon until January thirteenth the date that you were in court and that Moon was in court at your request made to Nicholson—during that entire period you knew that Nicholson was the attorney for Moon?

A: Why, yes.

Apparently getting the answer he wanted Braemer moved on.

Q: Directing your attention to the morning of January thirteenth will you tell us why you went to Moon and offered your hand?

A: The last time I saw Mr. Moon was in September. This was January. We had just received word about his appeal from the Court. I wasn't mad at him. I went up to say "Hello."

Q: Did Moon ever advise you that he was mad at you?

A: No, that is not the reason I offered to shake hands with him.

Q: You wanted to show him that you weren't mad at him, is that the purpose?

A: I wanted to show him that there was no hard feelings over this appeal which he had taken and the fact that the Superior Court has upheld Judge Wade.

Q: So you went over and offered to shake Norman's hand and he refused, is that correct?

A: He lifted his head—

Q: But he didn't say anything to you at all?

A: Not at that point.

Q: Will you tell me again when you were advised by Nicholson that he could not be here on the thirteenth of January?

A: About a week or ten days before that Nicholson advised me that he couldn't be here in the morning of the thirteenth but that he could be here in the afternoon.

Q: At the time Nicholson advised you did you notify the court?

A: Not at that time.

Q: Did you notify the court at any time between the time Nicholson advised you that he couldn't be there until two o'clock in the afternoon of the thirteenth?

A: Not until this morning.

A: Did Nicholson ask you to change the date of the hearing?

A: I don't believe he did, not that I recall.

Q: And are you testifying that you did not advise Judge Wade that Nicholson had informed you that he couldn't be here at ten on the morning of the thirteenth?

A: I advised Judge Wade that morning.

Q: Not until that morning?

A: That's right.

Braemer switched gears and began asking questions about who was sitting where and where was Moon sitting and did he leave the courtroom at any time. Kornreich answered as had every other witness as to where Moon was sitting. Then Braemer abruptly switched back to his previous line of questioning.

Q: At approximately eleven then you addressed the court and advised him that Moon was in court?

Q: You say that was the first the court knew that Moon was there that day?

A: That was the first I had mentioned it to the court.

Q: Mr. Kornreich, did you at any time prior to January thirteenth advise the court that you had notified Nicholson, Moon's attorney, to be present in court on January thirteenth?

A: No I did not. Do you wish to know the reason?

Q: Not particularly. Did the court, Mr. Kornreich, when you arrived at ten after ten that morning indicate to you or ask you why Moon was in court that day?

A: At ten after ten the court was busy with other matters. I had no opportunity to talk to the court until 11 o'clock until the previous business had been finished and the court was ready to hear what was coming next. That was the first I advised Judge Wade that Moon was in court.

Q: You did testify to that earlier. My question was: Did Judge Wade, when he saw you in the courtroom at ten after ten ask you as district attorney, what Moon was doing in the courtroom that morning?

A: No, he did not.

Q: When did you speak to Moon next? The first time I think was when you offered your hand to him. When was the next time if there was any?

A: When I rose to make the preliminary statement and advised the court that Moon had informed me that he wanted to proceed then. I believe I did ask Moon whether he came prepared to do anything about the order. I believe I asked him that while I was on my feet addressing the court.

Q: And what was his answer?

A: I don't recall the words but he said he was not prepared to do anything on the order.

Q: Mr. Kornreich, at that time did you have any other words with Moon?

A: I don't recall.

Q: Didn't you advise him that you knew that Nicholson, his attorney, could not be there?

A: I had already told him that at 10 after 10. Are you speaking now of eleven o'clock?

Q: No, I'm trying to get the sequence of events as you recall them. I said earlier that you had your first conversation with Moon when you walked up and offered your hand to him. I then asked you when next did you speak to him?

A: The next time was approximately eleven o'clock when I arose to make the statement to the court and I believe I addressed a question or two to Moon while I was standing talking to the judge about the history of this case.

Q: We may still be confused. When did you tell Mr. Moon that you knew that Nicholson could not be there that morning?

A: When I first came in at ten after ten.

Q: At ten after ten you advised him that you knew that Nicholson could not be there?

A: That's right.

Q: What did Moon say to you then?

A: Well, I went further than that. I said, "Your attorney told me that he could not be here this morning but could be here this afternoon. We are willing to defer your case until this afternoon," and Moon said, "I want to get it over with now," or words to that effect. In other words he led me to believe that he did not want to wait for his attorney, Nicholson, for that afternoon.

Q: Mr. Kornreich, did you make an effort, as district attorney of Warren County, to have the hearing continued until two o'clock that afternoon?

A: I made no effort to continue the case because I had told Moon that in view of his wishes I would take it up with the court as soon as court was available and see what the court wanted to do. I felt that was a matter for the court.

Q: In other words, you felt the court should decide?

A: That's right.

Q: Whether this man should be heard that morning without his counsel or whether he should not?

A: That's right. In view of his own statement that he wanted to go ahead without his counsel.

Q: Without his counsel being there?

A: That's right.

Q: When you advised Judge Wade of your decision in the matter, that you wanted the judge to determine whether the matter should be heard then, what did Judge Wade do?

A: I did not tell Judge Wade of my decision in the matter. I merely stated to the court when the time came that I had talked to Moon and that he had expressed a desire to proceed; that his counsel could not be there until that afternoon. Judge Wade then repeated the question to Moon.

Q: What question, Mr. Kornreich?

A: Whether Moon did not wish to wait until the afternoon when his counsel could be there and Moon again answered he wanted to go ahead then.

Q: On direct examination, Mr. Kornreich, you said you believed that Judge Wade asked that question—are you now positive that the judge asked that question?

A: As near as I can recall he asked him again in open court.

Q: You are now speaking from a positive recollection?

A: As near as I can recall and I think it is fairly positive.

Q: Mr. Moon said he wanted to proceed?

A: I don't recall the exact words but he intimated he wanted to go ahead at that time.

Q: Mr. Kornreich, do you recall whether anything was said to Moon about having other counsel present?

A: I don't recall that that was mentioned.

Q: Was it mentioned?

A: By whom do you mean, by him, or by one of us?

Q: I meant by the court, Mr. Kornreich.

A: I don't recall that myself. He may have asked him that.

Q: After this question and answer then am I right in this, that Mr. Hampson then made a statement to the court?

A: It was a very brief statement, maybe a minute or two, I don't remember.

Q: Tell me, Mr. Kornreich, was Janet Schwab Moon in the courtroom on this particular day?

A: She was not here.

Q: She wasn't here but Mr. Hampson as her counsel was here, is that correct?

A: That's right.

Q: After Mr. Hampson's statement to the court, was it then, Mr. Kornreich, that the court indicated that a record should be made?

A: Well, I don't believe he used the word "record." He used the word "minute," that a "minute" be made of the proceedings.

Q: That a "minute" be made of the proceedings?

A: Yes.

Q: You have been district attorney of this county now for nine years or better, is that correct?

A: Not quite nine, this is my ninth year.

Q: During that time, has the expression "a minute be made" been used in this courtroom?

A: Oh yes, several times.

Q: What was meant by a "minute being made"?

A: When there is no formal court and a matter is brought up or presented. At times it was the custom of Judge Wade to ask the stenographer or the clerk to keep a record of that proceeding in his Minute Book, under the court records of his Minute Book.

Q: You say in his Minute Book?

A: No, I mean the Clerk's Minute Book.

Braemer kept on about notes being taken, whether Wade had told Mrs. Seavy or Sires to make a minute, where each had been sitting, where Kornreich had been sitting, and if anyone else was sitting near him.

Q: Now when the judge called Moon, when he said "Would you step forward?" did you retain your seat at that point?

A: I continued sitting there.

Q: Referring to the proceedings at the time the court called the case, as district attorney in charge of the case was it your place to be present before the bench when the court called the case?

A: As I understand it the court never called the case. We did not know that Moon was going to be in court that morning.

Q: Isn't it a fact that you had asked him to come into court?

A: Yes, I did, but his attorney told me he did not know whether he was coming or not.

Q: But he was here at ten that morning, here in court?

A: That's right.

Q: The time I am now talking about is something that happened at approximately eleven.

A: You must remember that we still didn't know whether this case would be considered at that time or whether Judge Wade intended to defer it until the afternoon. I did not—

Q: You were in charge here when—

A: Let me answer that please. I did not consider that this case was being called. This was more of a discussion that was going on.

Q: When you advised Nicholson to have Moon in court, did you advise Nicholson that the purpose of bringing Moon into court was for the purpose of discussing the case?

A: I didn't advise Nicholson of any purpose. I assumed he knew the purpose.

Q: You did say earlier that you had sent him a communication?

A: I believe I sent him a letter.

Q: You state now that Moon was not in court for any particular purpose except for the purpose of discussing the Moon case?

A: I don't know what purpose he was here for.

Q: Mr. Kornreich, you sent for him.

Kornreich went over his previous statements about times and dates in a long discourse. The DA eventually admitted Judge Wade had not requested Moon's appearance but that Kornreich had taken it upon himself to send Moon's attorney, Henry Nicholson, the letter which demanded that Moon appear in court on January 13th. Braemer then continued with his cross-examination.

Q: Can you now, Mr. Kornreich, tell me the purpose of having Moon in court that morning?

A: The purpose? There was an order of support on record in Warren County against Moon for one whole year. He had had several hearings. He had taken an appeal to the Superior Court. We had just received the decision of the superior court. Up until that time he had not paid anything. Now this order—I felt it was my duty to make some disposition of the case because it is the duty of the district attorney to enforce court orders.

Q: With that history—with that record of proceedings which had gone on in Warren county and the appeal to the Superior Court, do you still say when you sent this notice out, you wanted Moon brought into court for the purpose of discussing the case?

Kornreich again went over the time line of events that he had previously stated, ending with his decision to turn the matter over to the court.

Q: Your first thought was that you should continue it until the afternoon?

A: That's right.

Q: Then your next thought was to repost the matter to the court and let the court determine what the court wanted to do?

A: That's right.

Q: When Moon stood up was his jacket open or closed?

A: It wasn't zipped, if that's what you mean.

Q: It was hanging loose?

A: It was hanging loose but was fairly close together.

Q: At any rate, as he came through the opening, you say you noticed an outline of a gun?

A: I did not see him come through the opening. I saw him stand or rise from his seat, throw open his jacket. It was then that I could see his gun. I saw him start to reach—

Q: Which side was it on?

A: It was on his right hip under the belt.

Q: You say you saw him reach for it with his right hand, is that correct?

A: That's correct. As soon as I saw him reach I left the courtroom.

Q: Did you make an outcry, Mr. Kornreich?

A: No, I did not.

Q: Did you make any effort to try to talk to Moon?

A: When he had the gun?

Q: Yes.

A: No, I didn't.

Q: When you first saw the gun did you make any effort to dissuade him?

A: When I first saw him reach for the gun, I sort of felt that we were going to have trouble and I started for the door. I didn't stop to argue.

Q: You didn't stop to argue?

A: I didn't stop.

Q: You didn't stop—you went right on?

A: That's right.

◆

Prosecutor Kohn called his next witness, attorney Harold Hampson, and once again set the stage as he learned that Hampson had been an attorney for 25 years and that he had arrived in the courtroom that morning at 10:40.

A: My best recollection is that I was addressing the court, on that occasion I noticed out of the corner of my eye that Norman had got up from his bench. As he got up he reached into his clothing and pulled something out and I saw him point it and before I knew what was happening a shot had been fired.

Q: Do you know where Norman was at that time?

A: He was approaching the railing. He had gotten up and taken a step or two from the front bench where he had been sitting. As soon as I heard that shot I fell to the floor and I crawled.

Q: Where did you fall?

A: Right down here about where the feet of these two alternate jurors are.

Q: About four feet in front of the rail?

A: Right. I crawled on my stomach expecting another shot any minute until I got in immediately behind this witness stand where I am now sitting. I paused there for just a moment to see whether there would be any more shooting. When I heard nothing I crawled on my stomach into the door that goes into the judge's chambers over to my right. I went in there and called the local police. The line was busy and I had to report to the operator that—

Q: You can't tell that. Do you recall any conversation between the judge and the defendant, Moon?

A: I don't recall it specifically. As a matter of fact, I don't recall whether the judge asked Moon to come forward but that may well have happened, but I have no recollection of it.

Q: Do you have any recollection in regard to any conversation about his attorney or whether he wanted to proceed.

A: No. I wasn't in on that. That was a matter, as I recall it, between Mr. Kornreich and Mr. Moon.

Q: And you were in the judge's chamber. While there did you hear any more shots fired?

A: Yes. As a matter of fact, before I got into the judge's chamber I heard a second shot. I didn't see from where the shot came or what it may have hit but I heard it. Then after I got into the judge's chamber I heard other shots.

At this point Braemer stepped up to the bench and began his cross-examination. He asked Hampson about the original support case and established that all the proceedings in that case had been conducted in the Warren County Court before Judge Wade. Braemer then asked Hampson where he was standing that morning and established that Hampson had never left the courtroom from the time he came in until the shooting began.

Q: I believe you stated to Mr. Kohn on direct examination that you did not hear any discussion between Mr. Kornreich and the court with respect to the absence of Mr. Nicholson, Mr. Moon's attorney?

A: Well, I wouldn't say that I didn't hear the district attorney tell the judge that fact but I didn't hear him discuss it with Moon. He may have said that.

Q: Do I correctly understand you to say that while you heard Mr. Kornreich report the matter to the court that you did not hear Mr. Kornreich discuss the matter with Mr. Moon?

A: That is not a correct statement of what I said.

Q: Will you tell us what you said?

A: I said that I didn't hear any discussion between Mr. Kornreich and Moon about the matter, that Mr.

Kornreich may have told the judge but that I had no specific recollection of it, but that if he did say it I undoubtedly must have heard it because I was here all of the time.

Q: Am I right in assuming that now you can't recall it?

A: I can't recall it.

Q: Am I also right in assuming that during this entire period you were within 10 or twelve feet of the bench?

A: Oh, Yes, that is right.

Q: I believe you stated that it was while you were making your statement to the court that out of the corner of your eye you noticed Norman Moon stand?

A: Yes.

Q: Are you positive of that?

A: That is my recollection and I think it is pretty good.

Q: That is all.

♦

The prosecution called its next witness: Chief of Police Michael Evan.

[Authors' Note: No one in the courtroom that morning knew exactly how many shots Moon fired. That is not surprising. Amidst the roar of the .45 and the scrambling of the survivors, it would not be expected that any one of them could say with any certainty how many shots Moon fired. The only witness to even offer a number was Ralph Sires, who testified that there were six shots. That, we are about to find out was not correct. By the time Chief Evan got to the scene, the danger was over; he and his team of investigators had the advantage of cool detachment as they searched the courtroom for bullet holes and shell casings.

It is often said that eyewitnesses make the worst witnesses. This is because they have only their perception of what happened and no other proof. What Chief Evan did when he found the bullet holes and spent and unspent shells, was to provide proof: the bullet holes and the shells are the proof of how many shots Moon fired that morning.]

Q: What is your name?

A: Michael Evan.

Q: You are chief of police in Warren Borough?

A: Yes.

Q: How long have you been chief of police?

A: About four or five years.

Q: You may state whether or not after this occurrence you made an investigation of this occurrence.

A: I did, sir.

Q: Were you present and did you yourself engage in the extracting of certain bullets from the courtroom?

A: Yes.

Q: When was that done?

A: January thirteen, 1954 and January twenty-fifth, 1954.

Q: Will you point out to the jury where these bullets had lodged?

A: One bullet (1) was removed from this dais here. It entered right here.

Q: That is about three inches from the lower step of the witness stand. Is that correct?

A: Yes.

Q: Did you remove the bullet from there?

A: Yes.

Q: Would you mark that with a pencil?

A: Yes.

(Witness did so.)

Q: Did you mark the bullet that was taken out of there?

A: Yes, I did.

Q: Will you take it out of that particular box you have it in?

A: I will have to refer to my notes.

Q: I think it is on the front of the box.

A: That is the one.

Q: That is the one that you recovered from the floor here that you just testified to?

A: Yes.

Q: Put it back in the box.

A: I was accompanied by Deputy Secor when I recovered this bullet.

Q: Where else did you recover a bullet?

A: At the rear of the witness chair in this panel right here. (2)

Q: Stick a pencil in it.

(Witness did so.)

A: That was recovered on January 25th.

Q: That was about eight feet above the lower step on the left hand side of the platform that the judge sits on.

A: That is right, sir.

Q: By left hand side I mean the left hand side facing the judge's bench. Do you have that bullet?

A: That is it.

(The jurors left the jury box and examined the bullet holes.)

Q: Where did you find another bullet?

(Witness marked the location with a pencil.)

Q: The location of the third bullet (3) is at the east end of the judge's platform and approximately three inches behind the top of the judge's desk. Now the fourth bullet hole is found where?

A: In the northeast corner. (4)

Q: Northeast corner at about a height of eight feet from the platform of the northeast corner of the courtroom, approximately four feet from the door that goes into the attorney's room. Is that correct?

A: Yes.

Q: Is there any other?

A: Yes, a spent bullet (5) was found about three feet—

Q: By a spent bullet may I ask you whether you mean a bullet that has been fired or a bullet that has not been fired?

A: Has not been fired.

Q: You found the lead part of that bullet at this particular location you are about to describe? Is that correct?

A: About two and one-half feet from the east end of the bench and I would say about three feet east of the prothonotary's desk.

Q: That was found on the floor there?

A: Yes.

Q: Were there any marks found close thereby on any of the paneling of the bench?

A: Yes, about two feet from the top of the bench and down, about three feet east of it, is a mark of a bullet that we called it key holed, hit sideways.

Q: Hit sideways?

A: Yes.

Q: In addition to that do you have any other bullets taken from Judge Wade's body and turned over to you by the coroner and Dr. Sugerman?

A: Yes. (6)

Q: Were there any other bullets found by you on January thirteenth that had any relation to this gun, as far as you know?

A: We found some empty cases or housings, as we call them, and two loaded shells that were not discharged.

Q: Do you recall where you found the empty hulls?

A: May I point?

Q: Yes.

A: The two hulls were found right here. (indicating)

Q: By hulls you mean discharged bullet shells?

A: Yes, cartridge cases.

Q: They were found where?

A: One was found about here.

Q: To the right of the post of the aisle bisecting the courtroom and immediately right prior to the entrance to the part separating the courtroom from the spectators and the bench?

A: Yes.

Q: Where was the other found?

A: The other was found the opposite side of same.

Q: Where did you find anything else?

A: Found a loaded bullet about a foot ahead of the first pew and toward the easterly end of that pew.

Q: That is about the place that was described previously as the where Norman Moon was sitting?

A: Yes.

Q: That was a completely loaded bullet that had not been discharged?

A: That is right.

Q: Anything else?

A: And there were three empty ones and one loaded one found about right in this area which is halfway between the judge's bench and the railing.

Q: So that completes eight shells altogether, two loaded and six empty ones?

A: That is right.

Q: Do you have those all there?

A: Yes.

The box of shells was admitted in evidence as Commonwealth's #7.

Braemer went over everything that Kohn had brought out. He had Chief Evan go back over inserting the pencil into the bullet holes and then he asked the Chief where the shooter might have been standing in order for the bullet to take on the angle that it had. The Chief held the pencil in his hand and with the other he directed Braemer to move to a certain spot where he felt the shooter had stood. They did this for a few bullet holes and then Kohn objected to that line of questioning because it called for a conclusion from the witness, who was not there at the time. Judge Flick intervened and asked that the jurors get up from their seats and take another look at the bullet holes.

At this point Kohn stood up and began re-direct questioning.

Q: Did you receive that gun which was admitted into evidence from the state police?

A: Yes.

Q: Did you receive the clips that were in the gun?

A: Yes.

Q: At that time you received the gun I ask whether or not there was a clip in the gun?

A: Yes.

Q: How many shells were in that clip?

A: As I recall them, there were six.

Q: I show you these and ask you whether or not these are not the shells that were in the clip after it had been taken from Norman Moon?

A: Yes.

The clips and the shells were admitted as Commonwealth Exhibit # 8

Kohn then established that the coroner's office had given Chief Evan the clothes Judge Wade was wearing when he was shot. The Chief had marked the clothing and brought the items to court in a paper bag. He then held up the judge's bloody handkerchief that had been in the judge's left hand lapel. Then Kohn held up the sweater the judge wore that day.

Q: This sleeveless green sweater. Are there any holes in that?

A: Two holes in that.

Q: Where are the holes? Hold it up please.

(Witness did so.)

Q: Indicating sleeveless green sweater with two bullet holes at the left armpit, front of the left armpit, and one bullet hole on the right hand side of the same jacket at the lower right pocket. Show that to the jury.

(Witness did so.)

Q: They are about how many inches apart?

A: About four inches apart.

Q: Where is the other hole?

A: About four inches from the bottom on the right side.

Q: Would that be the approximate position described by Coroner Lutz as to the entry of the bullets into the body?

A: Just about.

Q: Here is the white shirt. Show that to the jury.

(Witness did so.)

Q: Indicating bullet hole at the left armpit and one about four inches below that.

A: And one on the right side.

Q: About the same place as was indicated on the sweater?

A: Yes.

Q: Would be on the body? Is that correct?

A: Yes.

The white shirt, the handkerchief, and the sweater were entered as Commonwealth Exhibit # 9.

Q: I show you this brown suit coat. Does it have any holes in it?

A: Yes. One just at the top of the lapel pocket, and one about four inches below that. A third one about four inches below that also. There were three holes in this one coat.

The brown suit coat became Commonwealth Exhibit #10. Before moving on to the next witness, Judge Flick spoke to the jury:

BY THE COURT: These are offered for the purpose of showing where the bullets entered and where the holes are. You understand that in a murder case they have to

# WARREN TIMES-MIRROR

The Only Paper in Many Homes • The Only Paper in Most Homes

VOLUME FIFTY-FOUR. — NEA and AP Features — WARREN, PA., WEDNESDAY, JANUARY 13, 1954. — The Associated Press — PRICE FIVE CENTS

# JUDGE WADE VICTIM OF ASSASSIN

## ALPINE AVALANCHE DEATH TOLL SOARS TO OVER 200

### 135 PERSONS REPORTED TO BE MISSING

## REDS AGREE TO RESUME PEACE TALKS

## MAN IN COURT CHARGED WITH NON-SUPPORT GOES BERSERK AND FATALLY SHOOTS JURIST

### High Tribute Paid Jurist By Allegheny Co. Officials

### 55 Pennsylvania Citizens of Note Recipients of Honorary Keystone Farmer Awards

### Accepts Chairmanship Of '54 Cancer Crusade

### Martyr to Cause of Justice

JUDGE ALLISON D. WADE

### Number of Attorneys and Officials Have Close Call

### California Is Shaken By Earthquake and A Shower of Rain

### Firemen Form a Human Chain To Rescue Child

### Annual Meeting of Warren C. of C. Thursday at Four

### Barnes Resident Is 97 Years Old Today

### Six Dead in Crash Of Plane Into Home At Long Beach, Cal.

### Stockholders of Warren Banks Hold Annual Elections

### Radio Announcer Is Father of Twin Girls

### Committees Are Set Up For The Mothers on the March

### Cold Front Plunges Mercury To Zero In Some Districts

---

Afternoon edition of the Warren *Times-Mirror*, Jan. 13th, 1954.
(ALL PHOTOS COURTESY THE WARREN COUNTY HISTORICAL SOCIETY, EXCEPT FOR NORMAN MOON MUG SHOT, COURTESY ROGER THELIN, AND RUTH WADE WEDDING PHOTO, COURTESY LYNN JORDAN.)

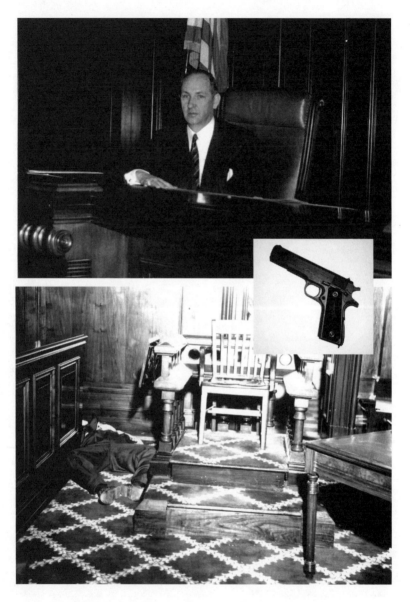

TOP: Judge Allison Wade on the bench circa 1954; BELOW: Wade as he was found dead by police sprawled next to the witness chair, feet toward the camera; INSET: the Colt .45 automatic, currently in the archives of the Warren County Historical Society.

Warren Police Chief Mike Evan and State Police Sgt. D.L.Holmes escort Norman Moon from Warren General Hospital to his arraignment and mug shot.

Janet Schwab's 1945 high school graduation photo.

CLOCKWISE FROM TOP:
Carver House Hotel;
Fred and Dolly Moon
during Norman's
trial; Allison and
Ruth Wade wedding
photo; Janet Moon
classmates Marcella
Flasher Stover and
Phyllis Grettenberger
Hunter in 1945.

CLOCKWISE FROM TOP LEFT: stenographer
Bernice Seavy, Prothonotary Ralph
Sires, DA Meyer Kornreich, Norman
Moon's attorney Henry Nicholson,
Janet Moon's attorney Harold
Hampson; eyewitness Samuel Bonavita.

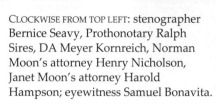

The Warren County Courthouse circa 1936; INSET: the view from the judge's bench.

CLOCKWISE FROM RIGHT; Deputy
Attorneys General Kohn (left)
and Adams; defense attorneys
Beshlin (left), Braemer,
Waggoner; the jury being
escorted to court; Norman Moon
led to court by Sheriff L.E. Linder.

prove that someone was killed, and how they were killed, and this shows how the bullets entered the body and you are to observe them for that purpose only and you are not to allow the unpleasant site to stir your emotions in any way.

◆

Kohn called his next witness: Edward H. Crowthers, small arms and ballistics expert with the Pennsylvania State Police, where he had worked for the past 18 years. Crowthers reviewed his background, saying he had started with small arms in 1932 in the National Guard of Pennsylvania and continued his training after he enlisted in the U.S. Army Ordnance Department during World War II and again when he was called up to the Korean War. Kohn established that Crowthers had testified as an expert in a number of murder trials in the state. The prosecutor then focused on the .45 automatic that had been taken from Moon and the shell casings and bullets that were gathered from the courtroom and Judge Wade's body.

Q: Will you give us your opinion?

A: My opinion is that the bullet removed from the body of one, Allison D. Wade, was originally discharged in Commonwealth's Exhibit No. 1, the Colt automatic, serial No. 2251839.

Crowthers then went over his testing procedures and how he came to his conclusions. He said that when he examined the shell casings under a microscope he was able to determine that each shell carried the same markings, created when the hammer came down on the shell, as the test bullets he had fired. Kohn questioned him about various technical aspects of the gun and how the clip is loaded in and how the spent casings are ejected.

Q: How powerful is a gun like that?

A: That gun has terrific shocking power. That is one of the reasons it was designed and adopted in the U.S. Army. The muzzle velocity is comparatively low to other types of weapons. The muzzle velocity of this is around 870 feet per second compared to a .357 Magnum which is up around 1700 or 1800 feet per second. But the density, size of the bullet, the bullet in this gun and the kind that is in evidence here weighed 230 grains compared to 154 to 160 grains of the average .38 special.

Q: That (the .38) is what is used by police is it not?

A: True.

Crowthers then explained how much pressure it takes to pull back the loading mechanism—12 to 15 pounds—and that, as the shells are ejected from an automatic pistol by the ejection mechanism, this action leaves distinctive markings on the shell casings, whether they were fired or not. He added that with the live shells he couldn't determine with 100 percent certainty that these two shells came from Moon's .45 automatic.

Q: In other words, they had been in an automatic weapon and had been extracted by the marks on the rims?

A: By the extracting marks left on the rims of the shells.

Q: So that they had been in a .45 but you can't tell whether it was this one or not?

A: Correct.

There was no cross-examination.

Kohn then called Dr. Joseph Richard Sugerman as his next witness. Kohn established that Sugerman had graduated from The University of Pittsburgh School of Medicine in 1934, was a physician, specializing in pathology, and that he had conducted a number of autopsies, including the one on Judge Wade.

Q: Will you please exhibit to the jury the perforations or wounds you found on the body of Allison D. Wade?

A: I would like to use my notes, with your permission. There was a tear in the left sleeve at the level of the armpit. There was also a tear where the sleeve was attached to the coat, and another tear just to the left of the upper part of the breast pocket.

Q: Are you talking about his coat now?

A: Yes, all on his coat. There was a tear through the sleeve at the level of the armpit. There was also a tear where the sleeve was attached to the coat, so there was here, right in front of that. There was a further tear in a similar line just to the left of the upper part of the breast pocket. The sweater beneath the coat was blood-soaked along with the shirt and undershirt and there was a hole there and there was a second tear in the coat. I mean second in the sense that it was below this line of tears here, about five inches below the breast pocket in the midline of the coat on the left side.

Q: Is that three tears?

A: No, there was a tear here, a little tear here, another tear here and a fourth tear here.

Q: Two tears you indicated under the left armpit, were they—

A: They were part of the same line, actually, but they were separated.

Q: Was there another tear on the coat besides those two?

A: Yes, one in the back on the right side.

Q: And I imagine that the bullet holes that you found in the body were located approximately the same place that you have indicated the tears in the coat?

A: Yes. There was a wound in the chest wall at the level of the fifth rib and in the anterior axillary line. The anterior axillary line is an imaginary line that goes from the front of the armpit straight down, and at the level of the fifth rib there was a wound.

A: Approximately how many inches was that apart?

Q: That was at the level of the fifth rib. There was a wound nine centimeters below the first, also on the anterior axillary line, and two and one-half centimeters is about one inch, and I guess that would be about four inches below, three and one-half to four inches below where the second would be. There was a single wound on the right side of the chest posteriorly, approximately two centimeters in diameter—that is a little less than one inch—at the level of the tenth rib in the posterior axillary line, and the posterior axillary line is a similar imaginary line on the posterior part of the armpit going straight, so there was a wound at the level of the tenth rib in the right posterior. That was about two centimeters in diameter. This wound was filled with protruding particles of fat and bone.

Q: Did you extract the one bullet from Judge Wade's body that was found there?

A: I did. I eventually turned it over to Chief Evan.

Q: There was an indication from your description that the one bullet had gone through?

A: Yes. This wound posteriorly was a typical wound of exit. Wounds of exit carry along with them bone, fat, whatever tissue has been encountered and pushed out ahead of it. It comes out with explosive force.

Q: Will you state the cause of death of Judge Wade?

A: Cause of death: death resulted from cardiac tamponade due to a bullet wound to the right ventricle, and the anatomical finding was that he had a laceration of the right ventricle with hemopericardium, homothrax left, laceration of the base of the left lung with collapse of the left lung; puncture wounds of the liver, and multiple fractures of the ribs and laceration of the chest wall due to bullet wounds.

Q: Speaking a little more plainly, there is no question that the two bullets that struck him were the cause of death. Is that correct?

A: Correct.

Q: And from your medical experience did he die immediately after being shot?

A: I would say so. I don't see how death could be long delayed.

There was no cross-examination.

♦

Kohn called his next witness for the prosecution: Samuel P. Bonavita, and established that Bonavita was an attorney in Warren County for the past 11 years and that he had served four years in the U.S. Army.

Q: On the morning of January thirteenth, 1954, were you anywhere in the courthouse about eleven A.M.?

A: Yes. At approximately eleven A.M. I was in the Recorder's Office which is on the first floor of the rear of the courthouse.

Q: Did you see Norman Moon any time that day?

A: Yes, I saw Norman at approximately ten A.M. on the morning of January thirteenth sitting near the aisle at the end of the first row. That was in the courtroom.

Q: And how long did you stay in the courtroom?

A: I was in the courtroom until approximately twenty minutes of eleven.

Q: Was Moon there all that time?

A: Mr. Moon was sitting in the same position during that entire time.

Q: Then what did you do?

A: At approximately twenty minutes of eleven, together with Judge Wade and Mrs. Bernice Seavy, court reporter, and attorney S.D. Blackman, we went downstairs to the Recorder's Office where we took testimony of a witness.

Q: Then what happened?

A: At exactly ten minutes of eleven we completed our testimony downstairs.

Q: Can you tell us the reason you had to go downstairs?

A: The reason we had to go downstairs with the Court is because the woman who was to testify was unable to climb the stairs and we had asked the Court if the Court would permit us to take her testimony downstairs and that is the reason why the judge and the court reporter were down in the Recorder's Office.

Q: You say at ten-fifty this testimony was completed. Then what did you do?

A: The judge and Mrs. Seavy went upstairs. I noticed the time particularly because I happened to look at the clock and I stayed in the Recorder's Office.

Q: In what part of the building is that?

A: That is in the rear of the first floor. That is the north end of the Courthouse.

Q: Then what happened?

A: After being down there for a few minutes I walked down the corridor and I heard quite a bit of confusion and commotion and I heard quite a few statements and people hollering but I didn't hear what they said, and as I started down the corridor to the front door and I opened the front door and the janitor, Mr. Massa, said, "He is down near his car." I looked down in front of the Courthouse on the street directly in front of the sidewalk that led from the front door of the courthouse to the street and I observed Norman W. Moon on the left side of his car.

Q: At that time what was the condition of the sidewalks and the streets?

A: The sidewalk was clean leading from the Courthouse to the street, but there was snow shoveled and piled approximately perhaps two feet high on both sides of the sidewalk in front of the Courthouse.

Q: Was the walkway clear down to Moon's car where he had his car parked?

A: That is right. The walk was clear down to moon's car and his car was parked, rear end of his car was approximately even with the north curb of Fourth Avenue, and the edge of his car was at about the edge of the sidewalk that leads from the courthouse to the street.

Q: You say you saw him standing there. What was he doing when you first saw him?

A: When I first saw him I couldn't see what he was doing, but he had the driver's door open. The door on the driver's side was open.

Q: What did you do?

A: Well, at that point I yelled down to him and I said, "You are not going any place, bud," and I raced down to his car and I stopped at the right rear. His car was parked headed west up against the north curb.

Q: At that time did you know what had happened?

A: No. At that time I did not know what had happened and I had not heard any shots.

Q: Did he get into his car then?

A: No, he didn't. At that point he circled toward the back of his car and I was standing at the right rear when he got around to the left rear of his car, he had a jacket in his left arm and it was covering his right arm. Then when he got about three feet from me he removed the jacket and he had a .45 colt automatic in his right hand and he pointed that at me directly and he said, "Don't try to stop me or I will shoot you."

Q: As I understand it, he had the door open and had either been in the car or was getting out of the car when you first yelled at him?

A: I couldn't tell what he was doing except I saw his head and shoulders and I observed that the door was open.

Q: Then he closed the door and came back from his car towards the rear of his car and towards you?

A: Correct. Then when he said that I started talking to him. I don't recall my exact words except that I told him that he should not get so excited over such a small matter and I said other things to him. As I recall, he did not say anything further to me at that time.

Q: When he came to you with his left arm covering his right hand and pointed the gun at you did he say anything to you?

A: That is when he told me, "Don't try to stop me or I will shoot you."

Q: Then what happened?

A: It was just a very few seconds I observed out of the corner of my eye that there was a man in civilian clothes, whom I later recognized to Sergeant Naddeo, and two state police officers crossing Market Street going into the side entrance of the Courthouse. The other two police officers I recognized as Privates Kaleina and Mastrian.

Q: The State Police barracks are located on Market Street?

A: Market Street.

Q: There is a direct alleyway from the substation to the back entrance of the courthouse? Is that correct?

A: Yes.

Q: What happened then?

A: And at that particular time Moon, when he observed the police officers, started across that front walk and he went up to the fence directly in front of the courthouse—that is on the right side as you face the courthouse—and I moved along with him. I was about three feet away from him at all times. He walked over to the fence. He stopped and he said as he raised his .45and pointed it in the direction of the officers, "It is all over. I may as well finish it now."

Q: Did he shoot?

A: No, he did not.

Q: Was he pointing the gun in the direction that the police were proceeding?

A: That is right. As he walked over and he got to the fence he got down in a crouched, sort of half crouched position, pointed his gun straight ahead. Then, as the police officers continued on into the side entrance of the courthouse, Moon then turned and he pointed his gun again at me and he started to walk back towards his car and I moved back with him and I was approximately three feet away from him, then, as we approached his car, Moon had his gun in his right hand. As he moved toward the left side of his car he moved his body to the right so that his back was not turned to me at any time and, in so doing, he kept his gun on me at all times, and as he passed me going to his car I stopped when I got to the curb. At that point to pass me he was within about eighteen inches of me and as he went past me at that point he said, "Don't grab me or I'll shoot you."

Q: Are you familiar with .45 firearms?

A: Yes, because I carried the same type when I was in the service.

Q: Then what did Moon do?

A: He then got in his car and he backed up a few feet and he pulled away. His motor was not running before he got in the car. Then he drove forward and went west on Fourth Avenue.

Q: Were you with the state police that went after him?

A: Yes. When Moon pulled away I immediately ran into the courthouse through the front door and in the middle of the corridor of the first floor I saw Private Mastrian and Private Kaleina and Sergeant Naddeo. I told them that he just pulled west on fourth Avenue and then the officers ran out front and I followed them, and the janitor indicated that Moon had continued west on fourth, so at that time Private Dell came around the corner from Liberty Street onto fourth. He was stopped by Sergeant Naddeo and the officers got into the car and they told me to go along with them so that I could identify Moon. We then drove west on Fourth down to Pine Street. We turned south on Pine to Pennsylvania Avenue, then we turned west on Pennsylvania Avenue and headed toward the edge of the Borough, as we were rounding that corner, I observed this blue Dodge with a man driving and he had a hat on, and the officers asked me if that was him and I said, "It looks like him but I'm not sure because he has his hat on." Then as we rounded the curve and just at the start of the three-lane the officers pulled the car alongside of Moon's car and I said, "That is Moon. I am positive of it."

Q: Do you know whether or not Moon observed you at that time you pulled alongside him?

A: When we pulled alongside of him at the start of the three-lane, yes. He looked over and observed us.

Q: Did the officers give him any motion to pull over?

A: Immediately after that, after I identified him, they did. They sounded the siren and they rolled down the windows and they told him to pull over.

A: I would say he was traveling approximately forty-five miles an hour, which with the conditions of the road, was rather speedy.

Q: What were the conditions that day?

A: The highway had snow in more than the center lane of the three-lane and there was snow on the edges of the road.

Q: When the officers sounded their siren and hollered at him to stop what did he do?

A: He just kept looking over his shoulders and he kept driving and he didn't slow and he didn't pull up.

Q: How much farther did they pursue him?

A: Then the officers dropped him at that particular point and they sounded the siren again and Sergeant Naddeo ordered  Private Dell to crowd him off the road, and at that point I told the officers that it would not be advisable because Moon was armed and that he had threatened me, so then the officers pulled alongside of the car again and they rolled down the windows and they pointed their service pistols at him—that is, Sergeant Naddeo and Private Mastrian pointed their service pistols at him, and they hollered and told Moon to pull over and he continued on. That is, he was going west.

Q: Then what happened?

A: Then when he refused to pull over and refused to heed the siren Sergeant Naddeo told private Mastrian to start shooting the rear left tire. I don't know how many shots they took, and by that time we were at the end of the three-lane. We were down by the lily pond.

Q: How far is that from the point where you first saw him?

A: It would be approximately five miles.

Q: Then what happened?

A: At that point they had not hit his tire and when we reached that crossing at the lily pond they decided to wait until we got around the curve at the straight-away before the first overhead and that is where they shot and hit the tire.

Q: That is on the other side of that concrete bridge?

A: No, that is on this side. I don't imagine it is more than three-hundred yards prior to the first overhead. He started to pull over to the right and stop his car and as the police car approached behind him he took off again and he was sliding all over the road. By that time he was at the approach of the overhead and he went up the overhead and over the other side and he was sliding.

Q: That is a very dangerous bridge there, is it not?

A: Right. It has a sharp curve at the top of it, and he was sliding down and as he went down he pulled over to the left-hand side of the road approximately one-hundred to one-hundred-and-fifty yards beyond the overhead, and he stopped his car and the police officers stopped their cars perhaps seventy-five to one-hundred feet behind Moon's car.

Q: Did Moon get out of his car?

A: Yes.

Q: His car was parked on the wrong side of the road to the direction he was traveling?

A: Right, right on the left-hand side. He had pulled clear off of the left-hand side of the highway and got out the driver's side.

Q: Then what did he do?

A: As he got out of the driver's side the police got out of both sides of the police car and they stayed alongside of their car. As Moon got out he had his .45 in his right hand and he was facing the officers, he was turned halfway and he raised his gun level with his—even with his body alongside at his chest.

Q: Are you certain of that?

A: Positive. As he started to raise his gun alongside his body, Officer Naddeo yelled out at him, "Don't do that" or "I wouldn't do that," and as the officer was saying that to him the shot rang out and Moon spun around completely and he dropped and he stiffened out and after he dropped I went over and looked at him and the blood was gushing from his neck and his mouth.

Q: When he raised his gun were you able to tell whether he was going to shoot at the officers or shoot himself? Was there any way of telling?

A: There was no way of telling from where I was watching.

Q: At the time the officers got out there did they have their pistols in their hands.

A: That is right, they did.

Q: Had you known Moon previously?

A: Yes. I knew who he was because I had seen him on two occasions in court prior to January thirteenth.

Q: Did you observe at the time you saw him by his car with the left door open, how he acted? Were his actions deliberate, hurried or how?

A: His actions were slow and deliberate.

Q: How did he act when he pointed the gun at you and said, "Don't grab me or I will shoot you"?

A: At that particular time his movements were precise and deliberate because he was moving his body as he was walking in a well, it was a clockwise manner, because he was turning from left to right in order to keep his gun covering me at all times, and that is what he did, and he kept me completely in front of him at that particular time that I was with him. I can't tell you how he appeared or how his looks were but he kept me before him at all times.

Q: Can you describe his actions in regard to proceeding from the curb to the iron railing and leveling that gun at the police who were coming in back of the courthouse?

A: Yes. When he observed the police and in walking over there it was slow, well, it was a normal gait, it was about the same rate that we would use in walking in the army, about 120 cadence per minute.

Q: Did you call his attention to the police that were coming out of the state police barracks or did he notice that himself?

A: No. He noticed the police at the same time I did. We didn't notice them until they were across Market Street.

Q: Then it was his own actions that carried him from the curb to the fence there?

A: That is right.

Q: You say you had some conversation with him down there at the back of his car saying, "Don't do that" or something to that effect. How did he answer you?

A: He did not reply at that time.

Q: Did you have any other conversation?

A: No. That was the extent of my recollection.

Q: At the time you were pursuing Moon what type of car was being driven by the state police? Was it a marked car, gray, black or what?

A: It was, as I recall, a gray Ford with Pennsylvania State Police printed on the side (Author's note: in fact, photographs indicate it was a Chevrolet).

Q: How many officers were in that car?

A: There were four altogether, three in uniform and Sergeant Naddeo was not in uniform.

At the end of Bonavita's testimony, it was almost five in the afternoon of the first day of the trial. A brief recess was called and as court reconvened, Braemer asked that court be adjourned until the next morning. Kohn agreed but was given permission to recall ballistics expert Crowthers on a technical question regarding the shells recovered. Crowthers answered the question and Braemer stated that there would be no cross-examination of Crowthers.

◆

Day two of the trial began on Tuesday at 9:30 A.M.. Braemer began his cross-examination of Bonavita and essentially asked him the same questions that Kohn had asked him the day before on direct examination. There was one new point that Braemer put forth: by questioning Bonavita he was able to establish that the police officers who had walked across Market Street and went into the courthouse by a side entrance were about 150 feet from where Bonavita and Moon were standing on the sidewalk in front of the courthouse.

Q: During your army service, Mr. Bonavita, did you have some training in the use of a firearm?

A: Yes.

Q: It was while these officers were coming in that Norman said something about, "It is all over. I may as well finish it now"?

A: Correct.

Q: From your knowledge of side-arms, at that time would you say he was outside of effective shooting range with that kind of a weapon from the officers?

A: I will say this: for accurate firing, yes. For accurate firing I would say yes at that distance. However, he could have still fired perhaps effectively when there were three moving targets.

Q: That possibly is true, but to hit anyone at that distance a man would have to be pretty good with a weapon, wouldn't he?

A: That is right.

At this point Kohn objected, saying that this line of questioning was not brought out on direct examination. He told the court that if Braemer wanted to pursue the matter with Bonavita, he could call him as his own witness. When the court asked Braemer if he wanted to pursue it, Braemer declined.

♦

Bonavita was dismissed and Kohn called his next witness, Warren photographer, Philip W. Coyle, who was called in by the Commonwealth to take photos of the scene in the courtroom that morning, including photos of Judge Wade's body. On cross-examination Braemer brought out the fact that Coyle could not have known where the body was before he got to the courtroom.

Q: Of course, you do not know whether that was the original position in which the judge fell or not?

A: No. I do not.

Q: That picture shows the position as it was when you arrived?

A: Yes.

Q: That is all.

Kohn called James C. Scalise as his next witness. After establishing that Scalise was in court that morning on another matter, Kohn had the witness describe what he saw and heard that morning—his testimony corroborating what the other prosecution witnesses had testified to. Kohn's next witness was Warren attorney Sidney W. Blackman, who testified that he was in the attorney's room behind the courtroom when he heard five or six shots being fired. He peered into the courtroom and saw Norman Moon at the rear of the courtroom just leaving. Blackman said Moon didn't appear to be in a hurry as he left. Braemer's cross-examination went over the same material and added nothing new to the story.

There was a recess of 15 minutes and court resumed at 10:45, at which point Kohn called his next witness, Dr. John E. Thompson. Kohn established that Thompson was a physician and had been in practice in Warren since 1934. Kohn then led Thompson through the same questions that he had asked his other witnesses about where Thompson was sitting that morning and about his seeing and hearing Norman Moon firing the shots that killed Judge Wade.

Q: Did you hear anything after the first shot to that side of the courtroom, did you hear any sound of the bullet entering anywhere?

A: The first three shots came so close that you didn't have time to adjust yourself.

Q: Then could you tell in which direction he fired the second shot?

A: The flash of the gun was toward the witness stand.

Q: Do you know in which direction the third shot was fired?

A: The third shot was fired toward the bench.

Q: Before you went down under your bench, did you have an opportunity to observe what Judge Wade did?

A: No. I didn't pay any attention to Judge Wade. I was watching what was happening down front here.

Q: Did you hear any other shots?

A: I heard three other shots.

Q: Was there an interval between shots that you heard before you went down under the bench and the other shots that you heard later?

A: Yes. There was a short interval. There was a single shot and then two other shots.

Q: Dr. Thompson, did you hear Judge Wade say anything while you were under your bench?

A: I heard him say, "I'm not going to sentence you. I am not going to sentence you."

Q: That was before or after the last two shots were fired?

A: That was before the last two shots were fired.

Q: Was this after that statement made by the judge that "I am not going to sentence you. I am not going to sentence you"?

A: Yes.

Q: What did you hear after the two shots, if anything?

A: The judge said, "I am shot" and then I heard a few footsteps and then a thud.

Q: Now, did you hear anything while you were still crouched down?

A: After the thud, I heard footsteps and then the ejection of two more shells from the gun and then it sounded as if it was being reloaded.

Q: Then what happened?

A: Then a few seconds later I heard footsteps up the aisle. I looked up to see Moon leaving the courtroom and then the doors swinging shut and then Mrs. Seavy crying, "Help, help, the judge has been shot. After that I came over to where the judge was lying.

Q: Now, when Moon passed you walking up the aisle, how was he walking?

A: Casually, normally. He wasn't hurrying. He walked up the aisle just like a man who has done a job, wasn't in any hurry to get out. He just walked up the aisle. Nobody was moving in the courtroom. He just walked up the aisle and out the door.

Q: Judge Wade was lying to the rear of the witness stand?

A: Yes, lying on his left side.

Q: Was he breathing?

A: He was breathing as though his lungs were full of moisture or blood and his color was ashen gray. His eyes were open but there was no reaction to light and his pulse was almost imperceptible.

Q: At the time he was lying there you may state whether you moved him and in what way, if you did?

A: I didn't move him until after he ceased to breathe. The reason I did was because I thought if he had anything in the chest, if we moved him to the left side until we could get to an ambulance, possibly by keeping him on his left side we could keep him from bleeding any more into the pericardium and relieve the tamponade, relieve the pressure.

Q: Did he die in your arms?

A: He did, right there as I had my hand on his wrist. He died right there.

That was the end of Thompson's direct testimony. Braemer then began his cross examination repeating virtually each question that Kohn had asked. After a few minutes of this repetition, Braemer ended his cross-examination.

◆

Kohn called his next witness, Pennsylvania State Police Sgt. Charles C. Naddeo, who told the courtroom that he had been with the State Police for 25 years. Kohn went over that part of his testimony that corroborated the Bonavita testimony as to how he had come to the courthouse that morning and how he and Privates Kaleina and Mastrian had met up with Bonavita and how they had commandeered a patrol car driven by Pvt. Dell to give chase after Moon.

Q: Will you give us the license number make and year model and ownership of the car Moon was driving?

A: It was a 1950 Dodge sedan bearing 1953 registration 318VK. It was owned by Dolly Moon, 339 Arch Street, Connellsville, Pennsylvania.

Q: What happened, just tell us what happened.

A: When we first sighted the car Bonavita recognized the car and said, "It looks like the car." I then ordered Private Dell to pull alongside the car.

Q: Do you know whether or not Moon saw you when you pulled alongside of the car?

A: Yes.

Q: What notice, if any, did you give Moon that you were pulling alongside?

A: We sounded the siren on our car and motioned Moon to pull over to the right. He looked over his left shoulder and shook his head in a negative manner.

Q: Go ahead.

A: After positive identification had been made by Bonavita that that was Moon, we then let Moon's car go ahead a little bit and attempted to stop it again by sounding the siren and pulling alongside of it. Moon kept going. This was for about a mile and then I ordered my men to shoot at the car.

Q: At what part of the car did they shoot?

A: The left tire.

Q: Was it hit?

A: Yes.

Q: After it was hit how far did Moon proceed?

A: We followed his car for approximately four miles and when it came to an overhead pass on the highway, just before coming to that, the tire went completely flat and the driver didn't have control of the car and it swerved from one side of the road to the other but it did manage to negotiate this overpass and approximately a hundred to two-hundred feet beyond the overpass the car went onto the berm and stopped.

Q: How far after you hit the tire did he go?

A: The tire was hit about eight times and it didn't go flat until he came to this overhead. I don't know where we were when we hit the first shot.

Q: Moon was out before you got out?

A: Yes, and I had my gun leveled at him with my hammer back ready to shoot him if he was going to shoot in my direction.

Q: Did you know what he had done?

A: We didn't know what he did except that he had a gun in his possession.

Q: Did you go forward toward Moon?

A: Yes, I did.

Q: Now, up to this time, had Moon done anything at all regarding either shooting you or himself up to the time you hollered "drop that gun" or "don't do it?"

A: When I ordered him to drop the gun, almost simultaneously he pulled the gun to his neck and fired. He whirled around and fell on his back.

Q: At that point did you or one of your officers take possession of the gun which he had?

A: The gun dropped from Moon's hand and fell approximately three feet from him.

Q: Was the gun admitted as Commonwealth's Exhibit #1 the gun that you are now describing that fell from Moon's hand?

A: That's correct.

Q: Now, from Moon's automobile you may state whether or not there was any articles of evidence taken and tell us what they were.

A: We removed thirty-five cartridges in a box. We removed a target and the application for the purchase of the .45.

Q: Do you recall the amount of money that Moon had on him?

A: About a hundred and thirty dollars, close to that.

Sgt. Naddeo then explained that Moon was taken to Warren General and that at three the next afternoon, January 14th, he and Chief Evan and Sgt. Mehallick went to Moon's room to interview him. Sgt. Naddeo added that Chief Evan had received permission to visit from Moon's physician and that Mrs. Marian Freeborough was Moon's nurse.

Q: Officer, you may state whether or not Moon was able to talk?

A: At that time he was not.

Q: Officer, you may state whether you checked as to when he had last received any narcotics of any kind previous to two twenty-five, did you make a check?

A: Yes.

Q: Who made that check?

A: The nurse in charge, Marian Freeborough.

Q: How did she make that check?

A: She referred to the chart.

Q: Mrs. Freeborough will be called as a witness will she not?

A: Yes sir.

Q: She was present during the time the questioning took place?

A: She was.

Q: What method was used in the questioning of Norman Moon?

A: He, being unable to talk, Sergeant Mehallick proceeded to ask him questions. The first thing he said to him, he introduced himself—

Q: Who did?

A: Sergeant Mehallick.

Q: To whom?

A: To Norman Moon.

Q: And you may state whether or not he introduced you and Chief Evan?

A: He introduced Chief Evan and he introduced me.

Q: Now, was there any conversation between Mehallick and Moon at that time as to how he would answer questions and in what manner he was to answer them?

A: Yes, there was.

Q: What was said in regard to that?

A: Sergeant Mehallick—

OBJECTION BY MR. WAGGONER: This is objected to until the commonwealth has established that this man, on the day this occurred, was conscious and had realization of what was going on. It was only, as I understand it, the following day.

BY THE COURT: The testimony so far is that Moon was unable to talk on this particular day. You have asked if there was any conversation about the method of questioning. Perhaps if you ask that, you might find out if Moon could understand or appreciate what was told to him.

(Resuming before the jury) BY MR. KOHN:

Q: Prior to this you may state whether or not you had consulted with Dr. Cashman regarding Moon's condition as to whether or not he could be interviewed and was sufficiently aware and able to understand questions which might be put to him.

BY MR. WAGGONER: This would be hearsay.

BY MR. KOHN: We will have Dr. Cashman here.

BY MR. WAGGONER: If the Commonwealth plans this with competent testimony by Dr. Cashman—

BY MR. KOHN: I will follow the testimony of Sergeant Naddeo with testimony of Dr. Cashman that the facts now elicited are true and correct facts.

BY THE COURT: Then there is no objection.

BY MR. WAGGONER: No objection if it is properly followed.

Q: What efforts did you make to ascertain from Nurse Freeborough (whom I also intend to call as to his condition) as to whether or not he was able to understand questions and answers in the manner in which you have indicated. Was there any effort made at that time?

A: Yes.

Q: What did Mrs. Freeborough state in regard to his condition as to understanding the questions and signifying the answers?

A: Moon at the time was sitting up and we had checked the chart that he was not under any sedatives and having had permission from Dr. Cashman that we could talk to Moon, that he would be unable to talk but could understand—

Q: Who said that?

A: Dr. Cashman.

Q: What about Nurse Freeborough?

A: Mrs. Freeborough said the same thing.

Q: And the chart indicated that he had had no sedatives or narcotic from what time?

A: Six thirty that morning.

Q: Is it normal procedure of all police officers to interview the defendant as soon as possible?

A: That's right.

BY Mr. WAGGONER: That is objected to. It is not what the normal procedure would be.

BY THE COURT: Let's stick to this proceeding.

BY MR. KOHN: I am sorry. I have no objection to its being stricken out.

(Resuming before the jury) BY MR. KOHN:

Q: Did you then continue to question, or did Sergeant Mehallick then continue to question Moon?

A: Yes.

Q: Approximately how long did this questioning take place on January fourteenth, approximately what time elapsed between the time you started and the time you finished?

A: It may have been, oh, probably half an hour.

Q: During the time of this questioning did it appear to you that Moon understood the questions that were asked of him and did he appear to intelligently reply to them?

A: Absolutely.

Q: You may state whether or not he intelligently replied to the best of his ability by the method you described?

A: Yes.

Q: The method used for his replies—how were they made?

A: By the nod of the head for yes and a nod of the head for no.

Q: And previous to the questioning was there any explanation or understanding between Mehallick and Moon as to what each nod should signify?

A: Yes.

Q: Who made that explanation to Moon?

A: Sergeant Mehallick.

Q: Mehallick is in the court is he not?

A: Yes.

Q: Subpoenaed here as a witness?

A: That is right.

Q: Can you give us the gist of the questions and answers at that time?

A: Yes, I can.

Q: Did you make notes of the questions and answers at that time?

A: I did.

Q: Are these your original notes made at the time?

A: These are my original notes.

Q: Will you give us the entire gist of that questioning, tell us who asked the questions, and the answers?

BY MR. WAGGONER: As to the gist of the questioning, we will object to that. If certain specific questions were asked and the answer that would be—

BY MR. KOHN: We will withdraw the question about he gist of the questioning.

(Resuming before the jury) BY MR. KOHN:

Q: you may state whether or not he was asked the question, "Do you realize what you did in the court room?" —was that specific question asked?

A: Yes, we asked that question.

Q: What was his answer?

A: He nodded in the affirmative.

Q: You may state whether or not you asked him this specific question: "How many people did you intend to kill?"

A: We asked him that question.

Q: How did he indicate his answer?

A: He held up two fingers.

BY MR. WAGGONER: If the Court please, the only method that has been described here is one by which only yes or no could be recognized. Then if some question was asked which was incapable of a "yes" or a "no" answer, it could not be answered by that method.

BY THE COURT: That's not the same type of answer but if there was a code by which he was being asked questions and he was answering—anyone could ask a question about numbers by indicating with the fingers, and probably that's the way he indicated. It seems to me that is perfectly proper.

BY MR. WAGGONER: There was no testimony that anything like that was explained to him.

BY THE COURT: I don't believe it would have to be explained. (To Sergeant Naddeo:) You may answer.

A: He held up two fingers.

Q: You may state specifically whether or not this question was asked him? "I will name these people and you shake your head "yes" or "no" with regard to the people you intended to kill."

A: It was.

Q: Was the next question: "Was it the District Attorney?"

A: That was answered.

Q: How did he indicate his answer?

A: Negative answer.

Q: I ask you whether or not the next question was: "Was it the judge?"

A: That was answered in the affirmative.

Q: Was the next question: "Was it Hampson?"

A: That was asked.

Q: What was his answer?

A: He answered in the affirmative.

Q: Was the next question asked him: "How many days in advance did you plan this? I will hold up the number with my fingers," and than Mehallick held up one finger and what did Moon do?

A: Moon held up one finger and nodded in the affirmative.

Q: You may state whether or not the next question was: "Did you intend to kill any other judges in Pittsburgh?"

A: We asked that question.

Q: What answer did you receive?

A: He shook his head in the negative answer and held up two fingers.

Q: Now at that time did you ask the questions, Sergeant Naddeo?

A: Yes, I did.

Q: Did you ask him: "Did you plan this the same day you bought the gun?"

A: I asked him that question and he answered in the affirmative by nodding his head.

Q: I ask you whether or not you followed with this question: "Did you buy the gun for that purpose?"

A: I asked him that question and he nodded in the affirmative.

Q: Was that the extent of your questioning that day?

A: That day, yes sir.

The court then asked Kohn to ascertain exactly who was present at the time these questions were asked and the answers given in this fashion.  Sgt. Naddeo responded:

A: Sgt. Mehallick, Chief Evan, Nurse Freeborough, and that State Police Private George Kaleina was standing guard at the door and was in and out of the room.

The court recessed at noon and reconvened with Sgt. Naddeo still on the stand. Kohn continued with his direct examination.

Q: Officer Naddeo, I think we finished with your statement of the conversation that was had with Moon on the fourteenth, is that right?

A: Yes sir.

Q: When did you see Moon again?

A: On January sixteenth at the Warren General Hospital.

Q: And in whose company were you?

A: In company with Sergeant Mehallick, Chief Evan, Mrs. Mong.

Q: What about Dr. Cashman?

A: We met him at the hospital.

Q: Did you inquire of Dr. Cashman as to the condition of the defendant in regard to whether or not he could talk and be interviewed at that time?

A: Yes, we did.

Q: You may state whether or not you had Dr. Cashman's permission to interview the defendant at that time?

A: We had his permission at that time.

Q: You may state whether or not Dr. Cashman was the physician attending Norman Moon at this particular time and on January fourteenth?

A: Yes.

Q: During the interview, was Dr. Cashman present?

A: Yes.

Q: And you may state whether or not, at that time, you questioned the defendant as to who, if anybody, he intended to kill?

A: We asked him whether or not he intended to kill Judge Wade and Mr. Hampson and he replied "Yes."

Q: You may state whether or not you asked him when he formed the intention to do that?

A: He said he didn't know but we did ask him whether it was one, two or three days and he replied, "Yes."

Q: Was this statement that you took from him taken down by Mrs. Mong in shorthand and later transcribed?

A: Yes, it was.

Q: Upon the transcription of these questions and answers, you may state whether or not Moon read the typewritten statement?

A: Yes, he did.

Q: Will you tell us approximately how long it took him to read this statement?

A: To the best of my judgment I would say about half an hour.

Q: You may say whether or not Norman W. Moon signed that statement after he read it?

A: He did.

At this point Waggoner began his cross-examination. He went over Sgt. Naddeo's explanation of how he, Bonavita and the other state troopers ended up chasing Moon's car out of town. Waggoner then asked about the questioning of Norman which took place the next day in Moon's hospital room.

Q: Was there any question asked at that time as to whether he wanted counsel?

A: I do not recall, sir.

Q: You don't know if any such question was asked?

A: No sir.

Q: Was there any instructions given him at that time that he was not required to make any statements that might be incriminative?

A: I didn't hear any.

Q: Of course if it had been, you would have heard it?

A: Yes.

Q: Was he advised that he had a constitutional right to refuse to answer any questions?

A: Not that day.

Q: Did you know whether he was still in shock at that time?

A: Well, I am not a professional man. The only thing I knew was the information we got from the doctor. Apparently he was all right or we wouldn't have been able to talk to him.

Q: Was his doctor present at any time during that interview?

A: I don't recall seeing Dr. Cashman.

Q: Only the nurse?

A: The nurse.

Q: Then I believe the second question you asked him—
or that Mehallick asked him—was, "How many people
did you intend to kill?"

A: That was asked, yes.

Q: Don't you consider that a somewhat leading
question?

BY MR. KOHN: I object to this. I don't see that that
means—whether he considers the questions that were
asked leading or not, doesn't matter.

BY THE COURT: The defendant's intent is an
extremely important item. I think if you ask this witness
what questions were asked and the answers he got—I
think all the facts concerning that should go to the jury.

(Resuming before the jury) BY MR. BRAEMER:

Q: There was no question asked him first as to whether
he intended to kill anyone was there?

A: I don't recall, sir.

Waggoner went over the way that the investigators
had Moon nod in reply to the questions, reiterating what
Sgt. Naddeo had said on direct examination. Then he
moved on, asking about how Naddeo had obtained
permission from Dr. Cashman to interview Moon. Sgt.
Naddeo said that permission was given to Chief Evan
via a telephone conversation with Dr. Cashman and that
neither he nor the Chief knew if Cashman had consulted
Moon before giving permission. From there Waggoner
asked about the questioning on January 16th and
established that Cashman was present at that time.

Q: Was Norman still bandaged around the head then?

A: Yes, he had bandages on.

Q: Was he then, on the sixteenth, able to talk, to
articulate words?

A: Yes.

Q: Easily, or with difficulty?

A: Well, to the extent that we could understand what
he was talking about.

Q: Were some of the words garbled in pronunciation?

A: Somewhat, yes.

Q: Were there some sounds that he, with the condition of his throat, had difficulty in making?

A: Well, until he cleared his throat, then he was able to pronounce them audibly.

Waggoner had Sgt. Naddeo give a timeline of the events on the 16th. The sergeant testified that the oral part of the Moon interview started at 10:45 in the morning and took about an hour; and it took another three or four hours to have the interview transcribed and typed and returned to Moon's room.

Q: Was the doctor also present when you brought the typewritten statement back to him?

A: No, the doctor had left.

Q: Who was present then?

A: Sergeant Mehallick, Mike Evan, Mrs. Mong, and myself.

Q: No nurse?

A: No, not that day.

Q: Do you remember how many copies were presented to him for his signature?

A: Two copies.

Q: Do you know how many were prepared?

BY MR. KOHN: I object to this cross examination, it has nothing to do with the direct examination. If they have anything it is a matter of defense.

BY MR. WAGGONER: I think any proceedings to the taking and the signing of this typewritten statement is a matter of great importance.

BY MR. KOHN: I objected to the question of how many were prepared.

BY MR. WAGGONER: We intend to follow it by asking if there weren't more than two presented to him.

BY THE COURT: Ask him that question.

(Resuming before the jury) BY MR. WAGGONER:

Q: Were there more than two presented to him for signature?

A: Two copies.

Q: At first. Were there more later?

A: Yes, there were.

Q: A moment ago I asked you how many copies were presented to him for signature and you said—

A: Two.

Q: Now I ask you if there not more than two copies presented for signature and you say, "Yes."

A: Yes, but I wasn't there when he was to sign the others. I don't know anything about that. There were four additional copies prepared to be signed by Moon later. I was not there when they were signed.

Waggoner went over Sgt. Naddeo's testimony as to how many persons were in the room when the document was signed. He then asked if on the 16th any of Moon's family members were in the room when Moon was asked to sign the statements. The sergeant couldn't remember anybody from Moon's family being in the room. Kohn then opened a re-direct examination. His first concern was that Waggoner had called Moon's Dodge "blue" while Sgt. Naddeo called it "bluish green," to which Waggoner said he had no objections to this reference. Then Kohn moved on to the question of informed consent.

Q: At the time the second statement on January sixteenth was taken, you may state whether or not previous to taking any facts in relation to what happened at the court rooms, the defendant was instructed that anything he might say might be used against him?

BY MR. WAGGONER: I object to the leading form of the question, if the Court please.

BY MR. KOHN: You would like to know the answer, wouldn't you?

BY MR. WAGGONER: I would rather the answer come from the witness.

(Resuming before the court) BY MR. KOHN:

Q: What instructions, if any, were given to the defendant prior to the time any questions were given to him about the facts as to actually what happened?

A: I can't repeat it word for word. He was asked this: "Moon, we are going to take a statement from you but you must bear in mind that whatever you say can be used against you in the event this case goes to trial before court. Are you willing to make a statement under these conditions?" or words to that effect.

Q: What was his reply?

A: He said yes.

Q: Was that reply audible or was the reply made by a shake of the head?

A: That was an audible reply.

Q: Did you make a list of the items taken from the car at the scene.

A: Yes.

Q: Will you tell us the contents?

A: Number One: Superior Court ruling; one range target; one box containing thirty-five .45 caliber automatic loaded shells. Personal effects: clothes and stuff like that.

Q: That doesn't mention a second clip, do you know where the second clip came from?

A: The second clip was taken from the person by Officer Dell.

Q: Now, this target that you are talking about, how big was that—was it one single target; sheet of paper target, wasn't it?

A: Yes.

Q: Was that new or old?

A: Was pretty much soiled, it wasn't new.

Kohn brought out that the officers found the empty shell casing from the bullet that Moon had shot himself with and that the Commonwealth's expert, Edward Crowthers, had testified that this shell came from Moon's gun. Sgt. Naddeo then stated that Pvt. Mastrian stayed with Moon's car until it was towed to Warren County Motors. Waggoner's cross-examination consisted of several questions about Moon's personal effects that were found in his car that seemed to lead nowhere.

♦

Kohn called his next witness for the Commonwealth, Dr. William Cashman who stated he has been a physician for the past 23 years and that he was an attending surgeon at Warren General Hospital. Kohn went directly to the questioning of Moon that took place on January 14th, and Cashman, seemingly upset with Chief Evan's behavior, threw Kohn a curve.

Q: You may state whether or not you gave the chief and the officers permission to interview Moon on January fourteenth?

A: No, I didn't give them permission.

Q: Do you recall him calling you?

A: Oh, yes.

Q: Will you tell us just exactly what the conversation was?

A: He asked me when it would be the first possible moment for him and his friends to examine Moon and I told him as soon as he was able I would let him know.

Q: You are sure that you didn't tell him that they could—

BY MR. WAGGONER: I object to counsel cross examining his own witness and ask that the question be stricken out.

BY THE COURT: Strike it out.

Kohn kept pressing the doctor about the Moon interviews, about whether Moon was in any condition to understand and answer questions that were asked of him on January 14th and 16th. Cashman stated that he had been in the room and that he thought Moon was able to understand.

(Resuming before the jury) BY MR. KOHN:

Q: You may state whether or not Moon was asked if he intended to kill Judge Wade.

A: He was asked that question.

Q: Do you recall his reply, sir?

A: He said, "Yes."

Kohn then asked if the doctor had heard Sgt. Mehallick use the words "anything you say will be recorded." Cashman stated he had, indeed, heard the trooper express the warning and that Moon appeared to understand and answered yes. Kohn concluded by asking Cashman when sedatives were given to Moon on the 14th. Cashman replied at 6:30 in the morning and that this would not have affected Moon later in the day, at the time of the first interview.

Waggoner began his cross-examination by going over the questions that Kohn had asked then switched to the medical aspects of Moon's case.

Q: What did you find his condition to be when you first examined him?

A: He was in shock. He was bleeding from two wounds in his neck. He was suffering from loss of about two quarts of blood. He was in severe pain. He was severely anemic.

Q: Will you describe the two wounds in the neck that you referred to?

A: He had an opening in the right side of his neck about one inch below his jaw and he had an opening on the left side of his head about an inch behind his left ear.

Q: Could you tell which was the point of entrance and that of exit?

A: Yes. The point of entrance was the larger opening and it had powder burns around it and the edges of the skin were irregular. The point of exit was smaller, about a third as large.

Q: Doctor, referring to the chart, can you tell us what Norman's temperature was on the fourteenth in the afternoon?

A: At four o'clock his temperature was 101.2. His pulse rate was 140; normal is 72.

Q: What does that mean, tracheotomy tube?

A: Well, in the course the bullet took, it went through his throat and he had severe bleeding, and all that blood would, by gravity, drop into his lungs and gastro-intestinal tract. When it would drop into the lungs, of course he would become embarrassed in his breathing so in order for him to live it was necessary to put a small metallic tube in his trachea (that is the tube that goes from the throat into the lungs).

Q: If I could see your papers once more, if I may. I will ask you doctor whether or not on your record of his condition on the fifteenth you found him to be semi-conscious?

A: Yes, sir.

BY MR. KOHN: Is there any objection to our seeing the charts, Mr. Waggoner?

BY MR. WAGGONER: No.

(Charts examined by Mr. Kohn and Mr. Adams)

(Resuming before the jury) BY MR. WAGGONER:

Q: Then in your record of his condition on the seventeenth I will ask you whether or not you have this notation: "Conscious—responded to questions with difficulty."

A: Yes, sir. Shall I elaborate on that?

Q: I asked you whether that appeared on your notes.

A: Yes, sir that appeared.

RE-DIRECT EXAMINATION

BY MR. KOHN:

Q: I would like to have you explain that to me, that is, what you wanted to explain to Mr. Waggoner. I would like to hear the explanation.

A: In the course of the bullet, it shot a portion of his tongue away and its base and the difficulty with responding was due to the damage that was done within his throat and tongue.

Q: It had nothing to do with the operation of his mental processes?

A: No sir.

♦

Kohn called court stenographer Agnes Mong as his next witness. Mrs. Mong corroborated previous testimony regarding the questioning of Norman Moon in his hospital room and his signing the two copies of the statement that she had prepared.

Q: Did he sign it in your presence?

A: Yes, he did.

Q: Did he ask for any corrections, additions or subtractions to be made?

A: No, he didn't.

That was the extent of the questioning and there was no cross-examination by Waggoner. Kohn called his next witness, registered nurse Marian Freeborough. He went over the questioning that took place in Moon's room and established that she was present at the interviews and had heard and seen what the other witnesses had testified to—namely that Moon conceived his plan the day before and that he intended to kill Judge Wade and his wife's attorney Harold Hampson. Waggoner's cross-examination was brief and consisted of his going over the previous questions asked by Kohn.

Kohn called his next witness, Sgt. John Mehallick, from the State Police and asked him questions about the hospital interviews and, like Sgt. Naddeo, Mehallick corroborated previous testimony. In a brief cross-examination, Waggoner again went over Sgt. Mehallick's testimony, eliciting the fact that Mehallick, Sgt. Naddeo and Chief Evan all signed the Moon statements as witnesses.

Kohn's next witness was Pvt. Paul Dell of the State Police, who was driving the Sate Police car that was used in the chase and capture of Moon. Pvt. Dell's account was a repeat of Bonavita's and consisted of just a few questions. Waggoner's cross-examination consisted of routine questions regarding the chase and it brought nothing new to light.

◆

Kohn called his next witness, Pvt. John Krupey, a 16-year veteran of the State Police. Pvt. Krupey explained that he had heard a conversation in Moon's hospital room on January 20th between Moon and Warren police officer Willard Zerbe.

Q: What did you hear Zerbe ask him, if anything, with relation to what had happened on January thirteenth, 1954?

A: Well, I walked to the door. Zerbe was in the process of conversation, in conversation with Moon, and then Patrolman Zerbe asked Mr. Moon when he intended to shoot the judge, and specified whether it was the day before, and he replied yes, and there was also a reply where he called the judge a name and said he had no right to try this case.

Q: Suppose you repeat the conversation rather than giving us a paraphrase of it, if you can?

A: Moon said, "The son of a bitch had no right to try this case."

Waggoner cross-examined Pvt. Krupey, asking only a few questions regarding the shift assignments for guarding Moon's room. It was brought out that the State Police and Warren Borough police shared in guard duties. Kohn put on a brief re-direct where he established Moon's hospital routine those first days he was a patient. This prompted Waggoner to offer a re-cross wherein Pvt. Krupey stated that Moon had been able to get out of bed on the 16th with help from a family member.

Kohn's next witness was Zerbe, who testified to hearing Moon say, "The son of a bitch, I had no business being in this court." Zerbe also asked Moon if he had had any experience with a .45, and Moon said he had some in the service. Zerbe then made a report of this conversation and turned it into the police station. Zerbe was asked about other conversations he may have had with Moon.

Q: You may state whether or not during the entire time that you were on guard and had conversations with him if he ever expressed any remorse or sorrow for what he had done.

A: That is the only time that we ever talked about this case.

Q: You mean the time that you have testified to?

A: That is right.

Zerbe's testimony had clearly aggravated Waggoner. After establishing that Zerbe had been Moon's guard for two weeks, he asked him about any other conversations the two may have had.

Q: Were these friendly casual conversations such as would develop between any two people who had a considerable time to spend together?

A: Yes.

Q: I mean you were not trying to see what you could find out from him about the case?

A: No.

Q: But, of course, when something like this turned up you felt it your duty to report it to your superior and that is what you did?

A: That is right.

Q: So that, of course, there wasn't any occasion for any warning that it could be used against him or anything like that?

A: Well, when I asked Norman that question, our conversation up to that time wasn't much of a conversation. We had not done too much talking up to that time.

Q: You were instructed, however, were you not, by the chief of police that anything he might say, and conversation he might relate to you in connection with this case should be reported immediately to the chief?

A: I was.

Q: That is all.

Kohn then recalled Chief Evan and once again went over the sequence of events and the substance of the two interviews that were held with Moon while he was a patient at Warren General. Once again Waggoner, on cross, went over Kohn's testimony without eliciting anything new.

◆

Kohn called Bernice Seavy, who had also been Judge Wade's secretary for the past 12 years. Kohn went over the court setting that morning of the shooting. Mrs. Seavy stated that when Kornreich asked Moon if he was ready to abide by the court order, Moon said, "Absolutely not," and then when Judge Wade asked Moon if he was ready to proceed, Moon answered, "Absolutely."

Mrs. Seavy also cleared up another question—why she walked over to Sire's desk just before the shooting. She explained that she felt that the minutes of the Moon case would be lengthy, that Sires took notes in longhand and that she had gone over to him to ask if she could help him. He did not respond to her question, so she returned to her desk. She recalled that morning in chilling detail.

Q: Were you sitting so that you were facing Mr. Moon or not?

A: No, my back was to Mr. Moon.

Q: What was the next thing that you know of?

A: I saw Mr. Kornreich start to run toward the attorney's room or that way. At the same time there was a shot. I stood up. There was a second shot that was pretty close.

Q: Pretty close to whom?

A: To me.

Kohn tried to structure his questions so that it appeared the shot was fired at Hampson. He had Mrs. Seavy state that Hampson was quite near her when the shot was fired and that she crawled under her desk, into the kneehole.

Q: Did you crawl in headfirst or back in?

A: I crawled in headfirst and turned around so that my head was out.

Q: What happened then?

A: While I was under the desk Mr. Sires dropped to his knees and was, I guess, surprised to find me there and he was in front of me, his face toward mine; there were two shots fired. I don't know where they came from.

Q: When next did you see Judge Wade again?

A: Mr. Sires moved somewhat and I was able to see from under the desk and I saw the legs of a chair. I couldn't see who had it but I more or less stretched my neck, I guess, out from under the desk and I saw Judge Wade lying on his back with his legs in the air.

Q: You say you saw the legs of a chair. Was the chair standing on the floor normally or just describe how the chair was when you saw it.

A: I saw only the legs of the chair. They were in the air.

Q: Which way were the legs facing, towards the floor or towards the ceiling?

A: Towards the ceiling.

Q: You went on and said you stretched your neck out, and what did you see?

A: I saw Judge Wade on his back. His feet were in the air. Norman Moon stood on the end of the dais with a gun pointing toward Judge Wade.

Q: What if anything did you see in Moon's hand?

A: A revolver.

Q: How close would you say this revolver was from Judge Wade's body at the time that you noticed it?

A: Three feet probably.

Q: Where was the gun pointed?

A: Right at Judge Wade.

Q: At that particular time you may state whether or not you recall any conversation.

A: Judge Wade's feet were in the air. His arms were extended, and he was saying, "Don't shoot. Please don't shoot. I won't sentence you."

Q: When you were finally able to see him was the chair to the right of where he was lying on his back?

A: Yes, in an upturned position.

Q: What was Moon's reply, if he made any, to Judge Wade's pleading, "Please don't shoot?"

A: He used some vulgar language and he said, "You will never get the chance to."

Q: I am sorry Mrs. Seavy, but you will have to repeat the exact words. You will have to tell us what he said.

A: He said, "You goddam fucking son of a bitch, you will never get the chance to."

Q: What followed that language?

A: As Moon said that he shot right toward the judge, and the judge's legs straightened out and he rolled over and I don't know anything after that.

Q: Do you recall any shots after that particular one?

A: There was one shot after that but I don't know where it was.

Q: Did you see anything after he shot the judge? What did you do?

A: Stayed right there.

Braemer conducted his cross-examination as he had with all the previous witnesses: he repeated the questions that Kohn had asked and at intervals inserted questions that appeared to add nothing relevant to the proceedings. Nonetheless, he did elicit one surprise from Mrs. Seavy.

Q: And was there anything particular that directed your attention towards Moon?

A: I didn't like his looks. I don't know what there was about it.

Waggoner instantly jumped on the statement in an attempt to suggest Mrs. Seavy may have been a biased against the defendant for some time.

Q: You didn't like his looks. Was your feeling in that respect something of long standing with you?

At this question Kohn jumped up.

MR. KOHN: Object to the question. It is highly improper, irrelevant and immaterial to what was happening that morning.

The Court intervened and a discussion ensued as to what she had said. Braemer stated that she said she had never liked his looks. But when the answer was read by the court stenographer, it was, "I didn't like his looks. I don't know what there was."

Braemer apologized to the court, and then continued asking questions that Kohn had already asked. When he had finished with Mrs. Seavy, Kohn stood and addressed the court.

MR. KOHN: The commonwealth rests its case at this time.

The Commonwealth's case, which began at 10:37 on the morning of Monday, May 17, 1954, ended just two days later at 10:20 on Wednesday morning. The state, with Deputy Attorney General David Kohn as its prosecutor, had called 22 witnesses and had produced more than 300 pages of transcript.

After Kohn announced, "The prosecution rests," a hush fell over the courtroom. Judge Flick banged his gavel and called a 10 minute recess. Hundreds of residents, who sought to get a seat in the courtroom, were turned away and inside the courtroom every seat was taken as spectators sat rapt waiting to hear the sordid details of Norman's marriage and whether the strain of his crumbling marriage could have caused him to commit murder.

◆

When court resumed, Moon's assistant defense counsel, Thomas Waggoner, stood and addressed the jury. First, he thanked the jury, then he stated that in order for them to render a fair verdict, they had to understand Pennsylvania law. Attorney Kohn objected, saying that he didn't feel that a discussion of the law was proper. Judge Flick stated from the bench that he believed Waggoner was only going to give a brief outline of the law and allowed him to continue.

Waggoner continued, "First degree murder in Pennsylvania is defined as a person of sound mind and discretion kills with malice aforethought and premeditation. Second degree murder is malicious with no intent to kill. Another degree which is lesser is that of voluntary manslaughter when the person under the influence of justly provoked passion kills in the heat of such passion. If the Commonwealth has not definitely proven all of the elements, and that the defendant was of sound bearing and discretion at the time the act was committed, if Norman Moon was insane, did not know between right and wrong, then you can give a verdict in his favor."

Kohn objected again. Judge Flick said to Waggoner, "Don't go too far. Tell about the defense and how you intend to prove it."

Waggoner continued, "We will reveal Moon's life as a boy, as a service man, calling relatives and others, and we will call Norman, himself, to tell the history of his marriage to Janet Schwab Moon. We will call a psychiatrist who will tell you what went on in Norman's mind before and during the acts of January 13th

"We want you, when you retire from the Jury Box and begin your deliberations, to bring in what you believe to be a just and true verdict."

Braemer then called the defense team's first witness, Norman's mother, 62-year-old Dolly Moon. Braemer's questions and Dolly's answers informed the jury about Norman's quiet childhood in Connellsville, his enlistment in the U.S. Army during World War II and the fact that he had flown 24 combat missions, as a tail-gunner in a B-17. Dolly Moon stated that when Norman returned from the war, he was moody and depressed. She told of Norman's tumultuous married life with his wife, Janet, and how the subsequent filing for divorce and the support trial had led Norman to the brink of suicide and his behavior on January 13, 1954. Braemer's examination ended with Mrs. Moon stating that Norman had told her that he was going to commit suicide with a pistol he had borrowed from a friend.

When Kohn began his cross-examination, he continued questioning Mrs. Moon about whose pistol it was and how she had taken it from Norman and hidden it in a dining room cupboard. She said she was worried that Norman would use it to kill himself, yet Kohn pointed out that the gun was stored in an unlocked cupboard and that Norman could have found it. Kohn continued to hammer away at Mrs. Moon about the gun and how could she remember certain details and not others. Mrs. Moon stated that she marked important dates on her calendar at home. Kohn then asked her if she remembered when the police came to her home in regard to Norman's actions on January 13th. She said she couldn't recall but that she had noted the event on her calendar. Kohn asked if he could send someone to her home and retrieve the calendar. Dolly answered that she was the only one who could get the calendar.

Kohn then skipped to Norman's activities on the few days prior to January 13th.

Q: Isn't it a fact that your son was out practically all night the Saturday night before going to a hockey game at Pittsburgh?

A: He went to a hockey game.

Q: Isn't it a fact that he was down at the American Legion on Sunday following that hockey game?

A: I think he was there a while.

Q: Isn't it a fact that he was down at the American Legion on the afternoon of January eleven which is the Monday following the hockey game?

A: Well, I couldn't say definitely that he was. He may have been.

Q: What time did he get home that night?

A: I could not say. I was at a meeting at our minister's home that night.

Kohn kept up his rapid-fire questions regarding what time Norman had gotten home that night, until the noon recess. When court resumed at two, Dolly Moon returned to the witness stand and Kohn immediately asked the same questions he had earlier about the calendar she kept notations on, where she had put it, and about when, precisely, the police had come to her home.

Q: Would you tell us where you put it now?

A: (No answer)

Q: Would you tell us where it is?

A: (No answer)

BY THE COURT: Do you understand the question, Mrs. Moon?

A: Yes, sir, and I answered him as far as I can and he keeps repeating it to me so I don't know what more to tell him.

BY MR. KOHN:

Q: Tell us where you put them so I know. Are they in the cupboard, under the sink, in the kitchen, bedroom, where?

A: No.

Q: Where are they?

A: Put away.

MR. KOHN: I insist that this witness answer the question.

THE COURT: Ask her if she knows.

Q: Do you know where they are?

A: I would have to look for them.

This back-and-forth went on for a dozen questions more until finally Kohn gave up and started in with more questions about the pistol that Norman had borrowed from a friend the summer before. He asked where she hid it and where she hid the shells. He even asked her what color the gun was. Once again, Kohn and Mrs. Moon battled each other through a series of questions about the gun and the shells.

Q: Was it loaded?

A: I don't think so.

Q: Was it an automatic or a barrel pistol?

A: I don't know enough about a gun to tell.

Q: How could you tell it was loaded then?

Kohn then brought out the fact that even though Mrs. Moon was afraid that Norman would commit suicide, she did not discuss either or fears or the fact she had discovered the gun with her husband. He asked her if she told her other sons about her concern for Norman.

Q: Did they say anything that would indicate that they thought he was going to commit suicide?

A: I think the whole family was worried about him.

BY THE COURT: Did they say anything?

A: Father several times told me that he looked to find him hanging downstairs and he looked in the clothes cellar for him, that he just thought he'd find him anywhere.

BY MR. KOHN:

Q: When was that said?

A: I believe it was on the twelfth of January whenever he wasn't home in the evening.

Q: On the twelfth of January 1954 your husband said to you that he was worried about him committing suicide. Is that right?

A: He had been worried before.

Q: Just answer the question first, then if you want to, explain. Was that on January twelfth, 1954?

A: Yes, I think.

Q: What did you tell your husband?

A: (No answer)

Q: This is the evening of January twelfth, 1954, that he said that to you. Is that right?

A: Yes, when he came home he asked me if he was there and I told him no.

Q: Where did you tell him Norman had gone?

A: I did not tell him. I did not know.

Q: Mrs. Moon, isn't it a fact that on January twelfth you wakened Norman at seven in the morning to go out to help his brother to fix a compressor?

A: Yes, sir, around seven.

Q: Isn't it a fact that he got up and he got back into bed around nine o'clock?

A: Somewhere in the middle of the forenoon. I do not know the exact time.

When questioned further, Mrs. Moon said that after Norman had left that day, she went in and made his bed and it was then that she saw the letter directing her son to report to the Warren County Courthouse. Kohn next skipped to questions about Norman and Janet's wedding.

Q: Isn't it a fact that you told him she wasn't good enough for him?

A: I did not.

Kohn then started on the calendar issue again. He wanted Mrs. Moon to say why she kept notations of certain events on her calendar and not other events. He noted that she had taken to noting troubling events in Norman's marriage.

Q: What were you looking for?

A: When incidents like that happened why I thought it was a good idea to remember.

Q: For what purpose?

A: If anything ever come up.

Q: You were looking for something to come up, were you?

A: From the way things was going you didn't know what to expect.

Q: So, in spite of the way things were going and in spite of the fact that you testified that while she was in Colorado she took a job as a waitress and enticed men up to her room, you later testified that you tried to get your son to go back and live with her, to be a good girl and go to Sunday School. Is that it?

A: Yes.

Q: I ask you why, if you were making these memoranda of the things she was doing, including that she took a job as a barmaid and that she told you that she enticed men into her room and she had contracted a disease of some kind, did you later around 1951 before they separated, try to explain to her that she ought to go to Sunday School and be a good girl?

A: I had always tried to get her to go to church.

Q: Was it church you were interested in or saving the marriage?

A: I was interested in saving the marriage.

Kohn then brought up the trip that Mrs. Moon and Janet's mother and nieces had made to visit the couple when they were living in a trailer in Colorado in July of 1950. He brought out that there were five people staying in a one-bedroom trailer and during that trip was the time that everyone found out that Janet had contracted a venereal disease and was hospitalized in Denver.

Q: Was it for that?

A: I do not know.

Q: Did you ask her what she had?

A: I did not.

Kohn then questioned her as to why she never told Norman that his wife had contracted a venereal disease and she responded that she believed that Norman knew what was wrong with Janet. Then he jumped back into questions about the borrowed gun that Norman had kept in his room until she found it and hid it in a cupboard. It appears his questions were intended to suggest how dangerous it was for Norman to have access to a gun when he was embroiled in an acrimonious divorce battle.

After a handful of questions on this subject, Kohn jumped back to Norman's childhood and tried to establish that Norman was a normal boy—quiet—but normal. He listed some of Norman's high school test scores and added that Norman had been a member of a number of clubs in high school, including the Camera Club, the Nature Study Club, the Sports Club, and even the Leaders' Club, which was a select group of only twenty in the high school. Then Kohn, once again, made a leap—completely out of the blue—in another direction.

Q: Did you know that Janet Moon's father gave her a thousand dollars which was put into the trailer which you described?

A: Norman gave her a payment to pay.

Q: I asked you about the thousand dollars. Did you mark that on the calendar?

A: No.

Q: That is all.

♦

Mrs. Moon had been on the stand for just about three hours: from about 10:40 in the morning until noon and then from two until 3:30. When she left the stand she was visibly weak and appeared, as would be expected, distraught.

At 3:37 Braemer called his next witness: Norman's brother James Edward Moon and questioned him about Norman's childhood and whether or not he seemed troubled and different even then. James noted that Norman was normal but that he was quiet, tended to stay at home with his parents, and did not—as a child or an adult—ever really share his feelings with him. James described how Norman's performance at work for Moon Construction had gone downhill after his marriage to Janet.

Kohn started his cross by trying to establish that Norman had had a normal childhood. James repeated that Norman was quiet as a child and didn't go out and play like his older brothers. Kohn quizzed James about the quality of Norman's marriage after the couple returned to Connellsville from Colorado. James answered that Norman never shared with him his feelings about his marriage but that it was general knowledge among his family that the marriage was troubled.

Kohn then questioned Norman's work with Moon Construction. He was trying to get James to say how much money Norman had made in 1953, but was having a hard time.

Q: I ask you whether your records show six thousand dollars paid to him in 1953?

A: I don't know how to answer it other than—

Q: Did you report that much income for him in 1953?

A: Could have been that much but he could have put some back in the company.

James stated that Norman had worked for other companies at various times and that Norman had sometimes put part of his pay from Moon Construction back into the company, even though he wasn't a partner. Kohn never did get an answer, so he moved on to the $1,500 Norman had in his possession on January 13th.

Q: Did the fifteenth hundred dollars come from Moon & Sons?

A: We have no way of telling.

Q: Have you had any conversation with your brother since you took that check, and talked to him about it and told him what you did with it?

A: I told him at the hospital it was deposited. He was worrying about hospital bills.

Kohn then led the questioning to January 12th and asked James if he had noticed anything peculiar about Norman's behavior. James stated that Norman came into the shop that morning and then went to a gas station to help his brother Melvin with a compressor and that Norman did not seem any different than any other day.

In order to clear up any confusion about the employees' pay at Moon & Sons, Braemer began a re-direct examination and established that with just a day's notice the accountants for the company could provide all the payroll records to the court.

Q: Do you have any hesitancy in revealing those figures?

A: I have no hesitancy.

Braemer asked James about his visit with Norman in the hospital after the shooting. James stated that Norman couldn't talk very well so he wrote notes to communicate. Kohn started his re-cross examination with questions about the hospital visit, asking whether Norman told him anything about the shooting. James responded that he hadn't. Kohn retraced Braemer's examination about the days prior to the shooting, then he brought out the fact that on the morning of January 13th, Norman mailed him a letter with a $1,500 cashier's check and the title to his trailer. Kohn asked to see the envelope and this prompted a sidebar:

MR. KOHN: We ask for an offer.

(At side bar:) (Defendant was present.)

MR. BRAEMER: We intend to follow this testimony with proof of the actual issuance of the check, and follow it with testimony of the defendant to the effect that the check was purchased for the purpose of giving it to Janet Moon the night before the hearing was had, to negate any possibility that there might be that recently, or as close as the night before, he had any thought or intention of committing any act such as was committed the following morning.

MR. KOHN: We have no objection.

James Moon then testified that he received the cashier's check on January 14th and that it was postmarked Warren, January 13th. He added that on the advice of Mr. Braemer, who was the Moon family attorney for quite some time, he deposited the check in a bank in Warren. The envelope in which the check came was entered in to evidence as Defendant's Exhibit #1.

On re-cross Kohn pummeled James with questions about the check: when it was mailed, when James

received it, and what he did with it. Kohn then brought
up the fact that the trailer title, which Norman had
mailed to James, was in both Norman and Janet's name
and that Norman had signed it but Janet had not.

Then Kohn jumped into a totally unexplored territory
with his next question:

Q: You were familiar with Janet Moon? You knew her?
You had an opportunity to observe her? You had seen
her around the shop?

A: Yes.

Q: She was somewhat mentally deficient, wasn't she?

A: I never said that.

Q: I didn't ask you if you said that. I asked you if she
was or wasn't.

A: I am no doctor. I can't tell.

Q: Did she appear a little dumb to you?

A: She was a long way from being normal.

Q: Did you know that she had been in a mental
hospital?

A: Yes, I did.

Q: So then when Mr. Braemer asked you if there was
anything peculiar you thought it was peculiar when she
came down there to the shop at one time and kicked up a
storm because she wanted Norman to go along some
place they had made arrangements to go? You thought
that was unusual, did you?

A: Yes, sir.

Q: How long have you been married?

A: Eighteen months.

Q: That hasn't happened to you yet, has it?

A: No.

Q: If it did would you think it was unusual?

A: Sure would.

♦

Braemer called his next witness: Robert Moon. At 41
Robert was the eldest Moon brother; he was a postal

worker, had been married 18 years and had three children. Robert stated that he did not meet Janet Schwab until the day of her wedding to Norman. Braemer led Robert through Norman's marriage and asked him if he felt Norman's marriage was in trouble., Robert answered that he and his wife and children always felt that there was a strain in Norman's marriage, but since Norman never shared his problems with them, he and his family avoided visiting Norman and Janet. Braemer's questioning ended with Robert visiting Norman in Warren General Hospital after the shooting.

Kohn began his cross-examination by going over Robert's visits to Norman's hospital room and later visits to him in jail. Robert answered that he did talk with his brother and that Norman was not himself.

Q: Did he talk normally?

A: No sir. He did not talk in the usual manner that he—

Q: You mean he had some physical impediment or some mental impediment?

A: Both.

Q: Has your brother ever expressed to you one iota of regret or remorse over the fact that he killed Judge Wade?

A: I did not press him.

Q: I asked you whether your brother has ever expressed to you one iota of regret or remorse over the killing of Judge Wade?

A: I can't answer that in that manner because he did not.

◆

At 9:30 on Thursday morning, May 20th, 1954 Braemer called his client, Norman Wilford Moon to the stand and began his direct examination. Braemer began with Norman's childhood years and followed his life through his service in World War II, his marriage to Janet

Schwab, their separation, which led to the nonsupport hearings. Those hearings, of course, led eventually to Norman walking into Judge Wade's courtroom with a .45 automatic tucked in his belt (Norman's unabridged testimony of what happened in the courtroom is contained in the earlier chapter titled "Murder in the Courtroom").

The courtroom was packed. And hundreds of residents—those who couldn't wait for the newspaper account—were turned away at the front steps of the courthouse. Norman's life played out like a soap opera. He had loved his unfaithful wife (and as it would come to light later, he still did) and for the three years that he and Janet were together, he had tried to please her. When Janet got bored in Connellsville, he chucked his life and job with the family business and moved her to Colorado. There he discovered her working as a bargirl, hustling drinks and taking men to her room upstairs in the bar.

When Janet felt the heat of his anger, she broke down and hurt herself, and when that didn't calm Norman, she made Norman take her to a mental hospital. In the end, after the separation, Norman sank into a deep depression. Coupled with a homicidal rage against what he felt was unfair treatment from the court, the train of demoralizing events ended just a few feet from where he sat, on the floor of the very courtroom where he sat today trying to explain how his anger built until it just exploded.

Braemer kept Norman on the stand all morning and most of the afternoon and ended his questions at 2:50. Everyone—from Judge Flick to Braemer to the audience to the news reporters—appeared drained. But the day was not over.

♦

There was a 10-minute recess and afterward, at three o'clock, David Kohn began his cross-examination of Norman Moon. Kohn started with questions about the pistol Norman had borrowed from a friend in Connellsville in August of 1953. Then he jumped to the question of whether Norman had called Janet at her job at the Carver House during the evening of January 12th. Norman said he was sure he had not.

Q: As far as you know you didn't call her? Is that right?

A: That is right.

Kohn next jumped into whether or not Norman had complied with the support order. His peripatetic technique seemed an attempt to jar Norman, to catch him off-guard.

Q: How much have you paid on this order?

A: I have not paid anything on it.

Kohn and Norman sparred around about the money that was owed and whether or not Norman had ever intended to pay toward it. Kohn also pointed out that when Norman and his attorney Nicholson and Janet's attorney Hampson argued in his jail cell, it was brought out that in addition to support payments, Janet wanted the $1,000 she had invested in their trailer. Kohn moved on to ask Norman why he had not made arrangements with his attorney to meet in court at two o'clock on January 13th.

Q: I asked you why you didn't notify your attorney any time before January thirteenth that you wanted him in court that day?

A: I had pretty much ceased to care to live, to a certain extent. I didn't do much of anything.

Q: Why didn't you shoot yourself in Pittsburgh instead of waiting to come up here?

A: I had contemplated different times.

Q: What was the matter? Couldn't you pull yourself to it?

A: That is pretty much true.

Q: Then you went out for a nice drive early in the morning contemplating it, did you?

A: Did I say it was a nice drive?

Q: Yes.

A: I went for a drive in the morning.

Q: When did you load the clip?

A: When I was north of Warren, if I remember right.

Q: When you came back and you didn't shoot yourself you went to the post office, didn't you?

A: That is right.

Q: And you sent the fifteen hundred dollar check that would have ended all your troubles back home and addressed it to Norman W. Moon?

A: Did I say it would have ended all my troubles?

Q: You came up with that idea. You said that you would make a settlement.

A: Pretty much ran through my mind, if I may state it. That wouldn't settle any of my troubles.

Q: Why did you get the check? Didn't you say that is what you got it for?

A: The only thing it would have did was brought me up to date on payment.

Q: You wanted to do that? That would have gotten you out of trouble?

A: Would that settle my troubles, sir?

Q: But you brought it along with you for what purpose?

A: I was contemplating walking in, settling up, if possible, or doing something. I also had ideas even before I got here of killing myself.

Kohn went on about the check. Finally he asked Norman how it was that he seemed unable to answer the questions asked, or more to the point, how he seemed to add statements to his answers that had no bearing on the questions asked.

Q: Have you written all this out?

A: Written it out? No. All of this out?

Q: Yes.

A: Man, I couldn't write that much.

Q: Did you write any of it out?

A: What parts?

Q: I don't know. I mean you just seem to answer my questions and you go on telling me about something else.

A: Well, it is only things that are in my mind, that is all I can tell you.

Q: You arrive here at about quarter of ten, you go to the post office after you decided you were not going to commit suicide. Is that right?

A: I didn't say I was deciding not to commit suicide.

Q: Why would you send the check home? You have got a cashier's check so you could come into court and settle up your difficulties and then you go out here and load your clip and come into court and before you come in you send that same check home. Why did you send it home?

A: Because I was contemplating killing myself more or less.

Q: Why didn't you go out and kill yourself then instead of coming into this court?

A: Seemed like I was getting more despondent.

Q: Why didn't you go back out into the country and do what you were contemplating?

A: Maybe I should have but I can't tell you exactly what all my thoughts were.

Q: Isn't it a fact that you didn't intend to use the fifteen hundred dollar check, you intended not to pay anything on the court order and kill Judge Wade?

A: No, I didn't contemplate that.

Q: But you did come into the courtroom with a gun?

A: Yes.

Kohn asked a few questions about the .45 and whether there was a live round in the chamber.

Q: The safety was on but the bullet was in the chamber. All you had to do was pull the trigger?

A: That is right.

Q: Why didn't you unload that gun before you came into the courtroom?

A: Because I contemplated killing myself in this courtroom.

Q: Why did you wait a whole hour sitting here when there was nobody in to bother you?

A: I wished to find out whether it was in this court or not.

Q: You what?

A: May I finish?

Q: I want to hear you.

A: I had read a statement in Pittsburgh in superior court and I partially gathered that it wasn't in this court from the ruling that was down there. I don't know if I misunderstood it or what but I didn't know whether it was or not exactly. I didn't have any, what you would call definite in my mind whether it was in this or out after I read that statement.

Q: Do you have a high school diploma?

A: I have one at mother's I guess. I never received it myself.

Kohn continued, trying to point out that it stated in Norman's letter from Nicholson that he should appear here at the designated time. The match between Kohn and Norman had only been set in motion a few minutes and already their contempt for each other was obvious. Kohn had given Norman a copy of the letter and now wanted it back.

Q: I understand all about the copy, but do you understand what he says about whether your appeal was confirmed or refused? What does he say about that?

A: Who says that?

Q: Mr. Nicholson.

A: He didn't say either way. Wait a minute. May I read it?

Q: You will give it to me. I am running this now.

A: I guess you are.

Q: Suppose you don't get smart.

Kohn kept trying to make the point that Norman knew that the Superior Court had ruled against him and that was why he came to this court with $1,500—in case he decided to make a payment—and with a .45, in case he decided to kill Judge Wade. Norman insisted that neither he nor Nicholson knew what the ruling meant and that he, Norman, was not sure he should have come to the Warren County Court.

Finally, Kohn had Norman read aloud the letter Nicholson had sent him informing him that he had lost his appeal: "This I take to mean that the case was decided against you. I do not have a copy of the opinion. You can secure a copy of the opinion directly from the court by sending one dollar to the Superior Court at Pittsburgh, Pennsylvania and asking for a copy of the opinion in your case, referring to the number and term. I am very much surprised at this result, as I felt that we were covered on the law on all points, and as you will remember the Commonwealth cited very little authority to substantiate its position. I shall be very much interested to read the opinion."

Norman continued to state that he did not know if that letter meant that he had lost his appeal or not. Kohn pointed out that Norman never called his attorney for clarification of the ruling nor did he call him about being in court on January 13th. Exasperated, Kohn summed up what he felt was going on in Norman's mind.

Q: That is the crux of this case as to why you killed Judge Wade, because you decided that you were not going to follow either the Superior Court's or Judge Wade's ruling?

A: No, it wasn't. I can't say yes to that statement. May I make a statement more?

Q: No. You just answer my questions.

Kohn moved on and brought out that the Sunday before the shooting Norman had been to a hockey game in Pittsburgh, and that on the Monday before the shooting Norman had spent the afternoon and part of the evening at the American Legion in Connellsville. He kept hammering at Norman's apparent inconsistencies, which nobody—including Norman—could quite understand. He asked him why, for example, did he get a $1,500 check one day, then a .45 a few days later. Norman stuck with his notion that his mind was muddled and that during this period he had thought of a number of alternatives and may not have known for sure what he was going to do until a split second before he did it. Cross-examining Norman Moon, Kohn quickly found out, would end up being a contentious and frustrating experience.

Q: Now, if you were going to commit suicide why did you load two clips with about fourteen bullets?

A: I don't know I did that, to tell you the truth.

Q: You didn't do it to protect your rear after you killed Judge Wade, did you?

A: You say my ear?

Q: Your rear going out, while you were getting ready to escape, so you would have another clip ready.

A: You mean I meant to escape? Is that what you're trying to say?

Q: Well, you did.

A: I did?

Kohn then wanted to know why, if Norman were going to kill himself, he needed two full clips of bullets with a total of 14 bullets. After an extended go-round wherein Norman's best answer was that he didn't know why, Kohn moved on to questions about the morning of the shooting. But when Kohn asked a question, Norman appeared not to understand him.

A: What's this now?

Q: Can't you hear me?

A: I can't get you all the time. Things are jumbled up. I don't understand you every time.

Q: Me or you jumbled up?

A: Both of us, I believe. May I hear you again?

Apparently frustrated with Norman's answers, Kohn finally asked him if he was insane.

A: I don't know. I am no doctor. Maybe I am.

Q: You think you are?

A: No, I didn't say that, sir. I can't tell.

Q: You think you are?

A: No, I don't know what I am.

Q: Do you know the difference between right and wrong?

A: I can't say. I think I do.

Q: Did you know on the morning of January thirteenth, 1954, when you came into this courtroom?

A: What is this now? Well, to a certain extent I believe I did, not totally.

Q: You knew when you came into the court it would be wrong to shoot anybody?

A: Yes. I know it seemed wrong to shoot myself but I contemplated it.

Q: Did you know on January thirteenth, 1954, when you came into this courtroom at ten minutes of ten in the morning that it would be wrong to kill Judge Wade?

A: Yes.

Q: You did?

A: Yes.

Q: Your mother said you went to church and Sunday school.

A: The early part of my life, sir. I pretty much drifted away from it in the last couple of years.

Kohn talked about Norman's grades in high school then abruptly shifted gears.

Q: Do you believe in telling the truth?

A: I do to the best of my ability.

Q: Would you make a statement for the purpose of misleading anybody?

A: I am not exactly—I don't recall any.

Q: What?

A: What statement?

Q: Any statement that might be material to this case. Would you make a misstatement?

A: Not purposely that I can remember.

Now it was Norman's turn to throw the prosecution a curve. It appeared that Kohn was attempting to get Norman to say that an honest person, such as himself, would never tell an untruth or a statement like the one he signed at the hospital for the police. But Kohn's strategy backfired.

Q: Do you recall signing a statement for the police?

A: Now, when? I can't recall signing any exactly.

Q: At Warren General Hospital?

A: I can't exactly remember that period very much.

Q: You can't remember a thing within that period?

A: No, sir. I can remember officers being in the room at different times but, as I remember, they was a guard duty.

Q: Do you recall reading the statement?

A: The statement?

Q: Yes.

A: What statement?

Q: The statement that you gave. You know what statement. The statement that was testified to here.

A: I can't remember of giving any statement.

Kohn produced the statement and asked Norman if it was his signature on the paper. Kohn called out each page number, and Norman responded that it looked like his signature on each page. Just when it seemed as if Kohn had elicited the answers he wanted, he asked one too many questions and the sing-song questions and answers started all over again.

Q: Do you deny that you told police that you had contemplated killing Judge Wade at least the day before, that is, on January twelfth, when you bought the gun?

A: What is this now? Repeat that again.

Kohn went through the statement calling up question after question, and Norman responded that he didn't recall it or anything else from that period. It looked as though Kohn was giving up and moving on to another subject, but after one question regarding another time period, he returned to the hospital scenario. The testimony became even more tangled when Norman appeared to confuse the name of state trooper Mehallick with that of his psychiatrist, Wollack.

Q: That is your psychiatrist?

A: That is right.

Q: He is the one who had you confused?

A: I—

Q: Wollak had you confused, didn't he? Wollack, your psychiatrist?

A: Maybe so.

Q: Didn't you say to him, "I wonder who is confused, Doctor, you or me"?

A: That could be true. I am a little confused now. Will you ask that question, say who stated it and what I said.

The court called a 10-minute recess.

♦

After the recess Kohn brought out a new plan. He had Norman read the questions and answers that were typed up on the statements that he signed in the hospital. Of course, Norman never admits it's his signature: all through the procedure, when he is asked if it is his signature, he replies, "Yes. Looks like mine." Using this technique Kohn takes Norman through all the pages of the statement and by the time they are finished Norman has answered that some of the signatures—those on non-incriminating questions—are his.

Kohn then handed Norman the murder weapon—and asked him to reenact the crime. Norman's attorneys might well have objected at this point, arguing that the request was overly theatrical or prejudicial to their defendant. Judge Flick might well have over-ruled them, saying that once Norman chose to testify, he could not refuse to answer any germane questions. In any event Norman's attorneys decided not to object. Norman took the Colt .45 in his hand, stepped out of the witness chair—and began to recount the bedlam of January 13th.

Q: Were you standing there at the entry, the banister there?

A: I can't tell you exactly where I was standing.

Q: Is that where you fired the first shot from?

A: As far as I know.

Q: Which direction did you point?

A: If I remember right, it went over there. (indicating)

And so it went while an entire courtroom sat in stunned silence. Kohn led Moon shot-by-shot up to the bench.

Q: Where was the judge then?

A: As far as I can remember, he was behind the bench.

Q: Then where did you go from here?

A: I believe I went to here, stepped up here, and shot a hole in the wall.

Q: You stepped that close and shot a hole in the wall, that close to the platform there, and shot a hole directly in front of you?

A: Do you want this here gun or want me to have it?

Q: Just carry it along with you.

A: It went off when I was going over toward the dais here.

Q: There is a safety on the back of this gun. It won't go off unless you put your finger on this and release this, that trigger won't go off?

A: (No answer)

Q: Aren't you familiar with this gun?

A: I fired it.

Q: Do you recall the judge lying here on the floor? Do you recall him at all? Was he lying on the floor at all?

A: Yes. I believe he was.

Q: Did he have his feet up in the air, his hands up in the air?

A: I can't tell you.

Q: Did you hear him saying, "Please don't shoot. Please don't shoot. I won't sentence you"?

A: I believe, if I remember rightly, that it was in the back of the bench he was saying that, if I remember that.

Q: You heard him say that?

A: Well, it comes back to me I sort of heard him say it.

Q: You didn't fire any more shots after that but you walked out towards the entrance to the bench here, did you?

A: As far as I can remember?

Q: You walked out here with the gun, didn't you?

A: (No answer)

Q: Where did you walk to when you left the dais?

A: I think I walked out here and went out in here.

Q: Did you say the judge got up off his back and you fired two shots?

A: The last shots I remember, I was standing there when I shot them.

Q: Where was the judge at that time?

A: Best I can recollect, I was about to shoot myself and somebody started coming toward me.

Q: Then you turned around and did what?

A: I shot, as far as I can remember.

Q: How many times?

A: Twice, if I remember rightly.

Q: Then what did you do with the gun?

A: I attempted to shoot myself, as far as I can remember.

Kohn, in his attempt to show that Norman wasn't going to kill himself in the courtroom immediately after he shot the judge, questioned him about how there were six shots fired and two live rounds ejected from the gun. In other words, if Moon were going to kill himself after he shot six rounds why did he eject the last two live shells.

Q: Why did you want to shoot yourself then? Did you realize that you had killed Judge Wade?

A: When this was ejected?

Q: Yes. You said you fired two shots when you saw someone coming at you, then you proceeded back towards the courtroom, pulled the trigger intending to shoot yourself. Is that right?

A: Things happened so fast I didn't much realize what I was doing. That is what I intended to do first.

Q: When you saw the person you allege coming towards you, did you intend to shoot at him?

A: I can't say that I intended to shoot at him exactly, I don't know what all my intentions was, it happened so fast.

Kohn, perhaps satisfied that he had elicited all that was necessary from Norman, leapt back to another time and another place.

Q: What time in 1952 was it that you went to the Schwab house with a shotgun and told Mrs. Schwab to put down the phone, that you had come to kill Janet.

A: I didn't make any statement such as that.

[Authors' note: Kohn is apparently referring to a published report in the *Times-Mirror*, attributed to Janet Moon's mother. There is no record of this incident being testified to in court, and if prosecutors actually had any proof that it was true, it's hard to believe they wouldn't have presented testimony to document a previous instance of Norman threatening to kill someone with a gun. In the absence of admissible proof, it's extraordinary that neither Norman's attorneys nor Judge Flick objected to Kohn's introduction of such inflammatory hearsay. As noted earlier, the *Times-Mirror* had received complaints about its story containing the accusation.]

Q: Your wife was somewhat mentally deficient, wasn't she?

A: How am I going to state that?

Q: Was she a little mentally ill?

A: At some times. Some of the time she seemed very good.

Q: You may state whether or not Judge Wade was considerate of you during these nonsupport hearings and allowed you to cross examine.

A: You mean you are stating he was considerate or whether I cross examined?

Q: What do you think I said?

A: I don't quite understand you. It is like the other question. I don't get all of it. Restate it again so I can answer you well.

Q: Don't you understand me?

A: Yes, I understand to a certain extent but it is more than one question in one, as far as I can get it.

With that, Kohn gave up. It was obvious that he'd had enough of Norman Moon and Moon's way of confusing things and confounding people. In the end the jurors would have to decide whether Norman Moon was genuinely befuddled or, as Kohn suggested, was shrewdly trying to confuse the issues.

◆

At this point Waggoner announced to the court that he had brought two defense witnesses from Connellsville. He asked that the court take their brief testimonies so that they could go home and not have to stay overnight in Warren. Judge Flick agreed and there was no objection from Kohn. The first witness, Lawrence Weaver, testified that he was employed by the National Bank and Trust Company in Connellsville. His testimony established that Norman had purchased the $1,500 cashier's check on January 8th, 1954, (which was the Friday before January 13th), and that it was cashed on January 14th.

Waggoner then called Norman back to the stand and questioned him about the pistol he had borrowed from a friend named Milford Shultz the previous summer. Kohn jumped up for a cross-examination and asked a handful of questions regarding the borrowed gun. Then Waggoner called another of Moon's friends from Connellsville, Earl Henry. Henry was a veteran and a captain in the Reserves. Waggoner established that Henry was the actual owner of the gun and that he had loaned the gun to Shultz prior to Shultz loaning it to Moon. Henry said that as soon as he heard that Moon had shot somebody, he went to the Moon residence to see if he had used the borrowed gun. They found the borrowed gun and so knew Norman had used a different weapon.

The day and the testimony had been long and painful to hear, but Moon's time on the stand was not over; there would be one more day of testimony; then there would

be one final day when the animosity between 28-year-old
Norman and one of the state's top legal minds would fill
the courtroom like so much acrid smoke after a half-
failed attempt at a fire. Judge Allison Wade had been
murdered on his watch, and Deputy Attorney General
David Kohn did not like that—he did not like that one
bit.

◆

Court started at 9:30 on the morning of Friday, May
21st, 1954, with Norman Moon on the stand and Deputy
Attorney General Kohn asking the questions. Kohn
started right away wanting Moon to tell about the
borrowed gun and his buying the .45 automatic in
Pittsburgh on his way to Warren. He got Moon to say
that he considered not buying the .45 because the price
was too high.

Q: What was the difference? Why did you buy a new
one instead of the secondhand one if all you were going
to use it for was to commit suicide?

A: I can't say exactly why I did it.

Then it was back to the signed statements that Moon
signed in the hospital but said he didn't remember. Kohn
continued to question him about his signature, and
Moon responded that he didn't know if that was his
signature simply because he could not remember that
time period. Kohn jumped back to when Moon got to
Warren on the evening of the 12th, and Moon said that he
ate dinner and checked into his room at a tourist home.
Moon said he didn't know the name of the home, and
Kohn offered that it was the Annex Tourist Home, run
by Mrs. Schreckengost. Kohn asked again if Moon had
called his wife that night at her job at the Carver House,
and Moon reiterated that he had not.

Kohn then asked Norman, again, was he writing out
the answers he would give beforehand, in his cell. Then
things took a turn toward the bizarre as Moon tried to

say that he had written out two different stories—the one that was not true he had deliberately left in his cell so that the prosecution could find it.

A: What you have wrote down is something my lawyer instructed me to write and—

Q: What I have wrote down where?

A: You must have a copy of it because it was moved around in my cell yesterday and it was left there by me. The lawyer instructed me to write it and that is probably the variation you have.

Q: You mean to tell me that you were writing variations of this story in preparation for this trial and put down a deliberate lie?

A: On the paper for you to find.

Q: For me to find?

A: That is right.

Q: So you were deliberately trying to mislead the Commonwealth, were you?

A: You picked it up yourself.

Q: Did your lawyers direct you to write this variation for me to find?

A: They didn't write it, I wrote it.

Q: Answer the question. Did your lawyers direct you?

A: No, they didn't.

Q: That was your own idea, was it?

A: No.

Q: Whose idea was it?

A: The lawyers'.

Q: You mean your lawyers told you to write different variations for the Commonwealth to find in your cell?

A: That is true.

Q: Is any of this true?

A: Some of it, yes.

Q: Who told you what to write that wasn't true and what was true? Who directed you to do that?

A: The lawyers, I suppose.

Q: What?

A: The lawyers, I suppose.

Q: Did you say "I suppose"?

A: No, I didn't sir.

Q: Is it now your testimony, under oath, that your lawyers directed you to write as follows: "When I got to Warren at the tourist home, I drove to town and stopped at some drugstore and called the Carver Hotel where I thought I could reach her. It was about nine o'clock that night." They told you to write that, did they?

Norman answered in another convoluted response that ended up meaning that Braemer had told him to write down aspects that would be important to his case and that he, Norman, wrote that he had called Janet the night before—so that it would appear that he had not, by the night before, planned to murder Judge Wade but had, in fact, planned to settle the case. And he insisted that Braemer told him to write out different variations of the same story.

Q: You copied a deliberate falsehood, did you?

A: I copied down instructions of my lawyer.

Q: Who were you hoping would get hold of these false statements?

A: I didn't know who would get hold of them, sir. I guess it was anticipated by my lawyer that you would.

When this line of questioning was over, it appears that in the weeks between the murder and the trial, Braemer would meet with Norman in Norman's cell and Braemer would write out variations of what had happened, then he would have Norman copy down these accounts in his own handwriting.

Kohn kept on about these various accounts of the same incidents and asked if Norman had responded the same way when the prosecution psychiatrist examined him. Another confusing question and answer period followed: Norman stated that he was confused the day before when he was on the stand and that after thinking about his answers, he wanted to make a few corrections. Kohn moved on to another subject.

Q: You testified yesterday that you didn't think you were getting a fair deal in this court (during the nonsupport hearings).

A: I said at a later date things come back to me after I was trying to recollect, after I was starting to recover, trying to recollect what all came in. The attorney asked me what caused me to do such things, what actually happened to me. I—

Q: Did you or did you not say yesterday on direct examination that you did not feel you were getting a fair deal in this court (during the support hearings)?   Did you say that or didn't you?

A: At different times I felt that, sir, yes. That is why I—

Q: Did I ask you how you felt?

A: I appealed to the Superior Court.

Q: I don't care what you feel. Did you testify to it?

A: Yes.

Kohn then jumped back to September of 1952 when the support hearings began in Warren and Norman was acting as his own attorney. Kohn's point here was to show that the court had been more than fair with Norman.

Q: Do you recall whether or not the court allowed you, without counsel, to cross-examine your wife?

A: That is right, sir.

Q: Did you cross-examine your wife by asking as follows: "Why did you leave"?

A: That is right.

Q: Do you recall her answer: "You had me locked out"? Do you recall that answer?

A: Yes.

Q: Do you recall asking the question: "I am asking her the reason she left the house. What were the circumstances leading up to your leaving the house; was there any reason"? Do you recall asking that question?

A: Yes.

Q: Do you recall her answer: "Yes, I was afraid of my life"?

A: I recall her answer.

Q: "What was the reason for that"?

A: Yes, I do recall asking the question.

Q: Do you recall her answer: "You threatened to kill me if I didn't give you a divorce"?

A: That was her answer.

Q: Do you recall asking the question: "Were you in any other institutions previous to St. Francis Hospital"?

A: Yes, I remember asking that.

Q: Do you recall her answer: "Yes"?

A: Yes.

Q: Do you recall asking the question: "May I ask you how many"?

A: Yes.

Q: Do you recall her answer: "Several of them, thanks to you "?

A: That was her answer.

Q: Do you recall the court then asking her: "He asked you how many"? Do you recall the court saying that?

A: Yes.

Q: Do you recall her answer: "A private sanitarium in Colorado and I was in the hospital for a few days when he ran off and left me." Do you recall that answer?

A: Yes.

Q: Do you recall the question: "Do you recall a statement you made in the presence of your mother, my mother, and your two nieces that all I was using you for was for a whore"? Do you recall asking that question?

A: I asked her that question.

Q: Do you recall the answer: "No I don't"?

A: That was her answer, yes.

Q: Do you remember the question: "What was some of your activities while they visited you in Colorado"?

A: Yes, sir.

Q: Do you recall the answer: "I remember your mother taking a hand in all my work and she told me I didn't do it correctly and tried to show me up. After all everyone has to learn; she probably did too"? Do you recall that answer?

A: That was her answer, yes.

Q: Do you recall the following question: "What happened the rest of the evening? Did you come back home after you went to Salida"? Do you recall asking her that question?

A: Yes, I remember asking that question.

Q: Do you remember this answer: "We stopped along the road and you came along and jumped out of your car and he ran up and socked the side of the car. There was no reason for it either."

A: That was her answer.

Q: Do you recall the question: "What happened? Did you go home"?

A: Yes

Q: Do you recall the answer: "I went home with you, do you remember, and I got an awful beating for it." Do you recall that was her answer?

A: That was her answer, that is right. That was her answer, yes.

Q: The next question: "You were struck by me?" Do you remember asking that?

A: Yes, I remember that.

Q: And her answer: "Yes, I was."

A: That was her answer, yes.

Q: Do you recall questioning her about a pocketbook she received in Denver? Do you recall questioning her about a pocketbook?

A: Yes, I did.

Q: And do you recall asking her this question in relation to the man who she admitted gave it to her: "Would you say he was rather a fast man?"

Moon hedged here a little, saying that he didn't believe that that was the correct wording of his question. Braemer stood and confirmed that he had a copy of that transcript and that that was the correct wording.

Q: Do you recall an answer: "I wouldn't know anything about it. I was never out with him." Was that her answer?

A: That was her answer, yes.

Q: Do you recall asking your wife this question during the nonsupport hearing: "For what reason did you go to the American Legion"?

A: I remember asking that question, yes.

Q: Do you recall her answer: "I was looking for you"?

A: That was her answer, yes.

Q: Do you recall the next question by yourself: "Where had you previously been"?

A: I asked her that, yes.

Q: Do you recall her answer: "Out to the trailer"?

A: That was her answer, yes.

Q: Do you recall asking her the question: "What prompted my father to buy you a dog"?

A: I did, sir.

Q: Your next question: "Were you on a cordial relationship with him?"

A: Yes, I asked that.

Q: And the answer by your wife: What do you mean?" Is that her answer?

A: That was her answer, yes.

Q: Question: "Was I friendly to my father's activities?"

Norman hedged again about the wording. Kohn produced a copy of the transcript and had Norman read it.

Q: Was her answer as follows to your question, "Was I friendly to my father's activities?" Answer: "No, you weren't; you were never friendly with your father."

A: That was her answer, yes.

Q: "When you had your first upset was it my father who upset you that day?"

A: Repeat the previous question or something. I don't get the full meaning of that.

Q: That is the question. Did you ask that?

A: That is the question you are asking now? May I read that statement?

Q: Are you trying to play games with me?

A: No, I am not trying to play games. I am just trying to get straight answer to the best of my ability.

At this, Judge Flick stepped in. Norman told the judge that when Kohn took a question out of the original order in which he had asked it, he got confused. Flick said it didn't matter in what order the questions were asked, Norman had to answer them.

BY THE COURT: You are now being asked whether you remember asking your wife certain questions on cross-examination (in the nonsupport case). Either you remember asking her or you don't.

A: Yes, I do, but it comes in different phases the way he is presenting it and I can't give it the proper light it should have, the way he is doing it, sir.

BY MR. KOHN: I am not asking you to give anything the proper light. I am asking whether you asked those questions.

A: Ask it again and I will answer it to the best of my ability, sir.

Q: Question: "When you had your first upset was it my father who upset you that day?" Answer: "What first upset?" Do you recall that?

A: I recall the question.

Q: Do you recall this question and answer: Question: "When I lived at 1232 Sycamore Street, Connellsville, was my father the one who upset you that first day? Did you ever go to any night clubs or anything with my father"?

Moon got confused again and this time Kohn handed him his copy of the transcript and had Norman read it aloud.

A: (Norman reading) "I never did. I'll take that back, I did go to a nightclub with him on a friendly basis."

Q: The next question: "Did you ever go to Wilson's dining room with my father?" Answer: "Not with your father."

Q: Did I state that question and answer correctly?

A: That is right.

Q: "Did you ever go to "The Spot" with my father?" Did you ask that question?

A: Yes, I asked that question.

Q: Did you get the answer: "Yes, I stopped there with him."

A: Right.

Q: The next question: "Did you ever go to Alretta with my father?" Is that the next question?

A: Yes.

Q: And the answer being, "Yes"?

A: Yes.

Kohn kept on with the reading of the nonsupport hearing transcript. There were a few questions about who hit whom on the night Janet charged Moon with assault and battery and surety of the peace and who called whom a "vile name." Norman's questions brought out that Janet left their home that night and went to the Club Lido.

Q: Did you ask this question: "Did you leave in company of Bill Dye at the Club Lido?"

A: I asked that question.

Q: Answer: "No, I didn't."

A: That was her answer, yes.

Q: Did you ask: "Is Bill Dye on bond for assault and battery and admitted robbery in Morgantown, West Virginia?"

A: That was the question, yes, sir.

Q: Did she say, "I believe so"?

The next series of questions was about whether or not Janet had stayed out all night that night. Kohn and Moon sparred a bit over this question until it finally came out that Norman saw her car at a neighbor's house at 3:30 in the morning. Janet said that she—and her mother and two nieces—stayed at the neighbor's house because Norman had locked them out.

♦

At 10:30 A.M. there was a 15 minute recess, and when court resumed at 10:45, Kohn began where he had left off: He questioned Norman about the nonsupport case going back to the first hearing held on September 26th, 1952. Kohn's objective was to show that no matter what Norman Moon said or what he thought or how he felt, the court—meaning Judge Wade—had bent over backwards to make sure that Norman's nonsupport case was handled correctly and that Norman was treated fairly. Kohn had done his homework. He had the copies of the transcript of those hearings laid out on his desk and he, of all people, knew the lawyers' adage: "Never ask a question unless you already know the answer."

Kohn brought out the fact that the September 26th hearing was continued to October third and that Moon did not show up in court on October third. Moon testified that he was not notified to be in court that day. Moon then said he received a letter directing him to be in court on October 13th and when he got to court, he was notified that a support order of $30 a week had been lodged against him. Kohn pointed out that October 13th was incorrect, that the date was October 31st, that Norman was in court that day and that the judgment was mailed to his attorney and eventually to him.

Then Kohn jumped to a new subject.

Q: Do you recall calling your wife on September twenty-sixth right after the first hearing and telling her that you were sorry about the lies that you had told about her in court that day?

A: No, sir, I can't say it that way, no. I called her but I didn't make that statement.

[Author's note: At some point in our examination of this trial there is a question that needs to be asked and this seems like the best time to ask it: Why was Janet Schwab Moon never called to testify in Norman's murder trial?

It's obvious by the previous question that the prosecution had been in contact with her and that it planned on using her answers—true or false—to discredit Norman. If Janet had something to say about the nonsupport hearings and her testimony in them, why not bring her in and let her testify in person?]

After much haggling back and forth, Kohn established that Norman had been notified that a judgment of $30 a week had been lodged against him.

Q: Did you make any payments?

A: No, I did not.

Q: Why?

A: I had not had a chance to appear in court for my own defense.

Q: Did you make any payments in Fayette County?

A: No, sir, I wasn't ordered to.

Q: Did you make any payments direct to your wife?

A: No, sir.

Kohn then lead Norman to the crux of his refusal to pay his wife support, in short, that because the case began in Fayette County, it should have remained there.

And that the reason his wife brought the case to Warren County was her presumption that she would be awarded more support in Judge Wade's court.

Q: What would be the difference where the court order was entered if you didn't make any payments?

A: It would be a legal matter, sir. The different places to pay the same payment. If there was a ten dollar order, it would be a hundred dollar order when you finished up.

Then Norman threw something new into the mix.

Q: Why didn't you give her some money voluntarily so she could live?

A: Well, I didn't feel as though she would handle it properly.

This didn't go anywhere, so Kohn got back to the September 26th hearing and how it was continued to October 3rd and how Norman didn't show up. Kohn then established that there were a total of four hearings in Warren regarding Norman's nonsupport case and that at the final one, on December 12th, 1952, Norman—who acted as his own counsel—had been allowed to take the stand.

At 11:30 Kohn asked for a 15-minute recess. When court resumed, he brought out the transcript of the December 12th, 1952, nonsupport hearing where Janet was present and had testified. His first questions concerned the night that Norman testified that he saw Janet and Bill Dye in a car in the Club Lido parking lot. Judge Wade had said that just seeing two people in a car didn't mean anything. Janet's attorney also objected, noting that Norman had not produced any witnesses to corroborate his testimony.

Kohn referred to the transcript detailing the crucial night of August 22nd, 1952, when Janet took money from Norman's wallet and there was a slapping match.

Q: Do you recall giving this answer and it being in the transcript: "She removed fifty-three dollars from my wallet and she wouldn't give it back to me until I had slapped her a couple of times. She had hit me in the bedroom and after that she removed the fifty-three dollars, and when I discovered it, I asked her to return it and she wouldn't. Her niece didn't know where it was."

A: Yes, it's in the transcript.

Kohn read aloud from the transcript regarding other facts Norman presented about that night. In the end, after another statement from Wade that Norman's attempts at being his own lawyer were woefully inept, Norman rested his case opposing support for Janet. Wade immediately ruled against him. "I can only make an order for support. Before I do that I will look the record over and study it." Norman answered: "That's all right by me."

In the murder trial Kohn and Norman continued their contentious back-and-forth. Kohn got Norman to admit that he had received a notice in the mail that he should begin paying the support, but Norman then threw another curve.

Q: Why didn't you pay between December twelfth, 1952 and July first, 1953?

A: I was pretty low on funds.

Kohn pointed out that according to Norman's tax statement, he had earned close to $6,000 for 1953. Kohn added that when Norman turned himself in to the Warren County sheriff, he had $1,000 with him. The sheriff asked why Norman didn't give Janet some of that money for support.

Kohn lead Norman through the entire struggle of his refusal to pay support to Janet Moon, noting that no matter what Norman felt or thought was correct, he had indeed had a fair hearing, had had every chance to defend himself, and that he had been notified about the court's decision each step of the way. Kohn questioned Norman about his learning to shoot a .45 automatic in the service. Then, without skipping a beat, he jumped to the morning Norman shot Judge Wade, stating that Norman had testified previously that at 10:10 he had no intention of killing Judge Wade.

Q: Did you intend to kill him at that time?

A: No, sir.

Q: Did you have any reason for killing him?

A: No, sir.

Q: At that time were you sane?

A: I can't say. I don't know. I had a lot of thoughts running through my mind, thought of going away and killing myself.

Q: Do you think you got a fair trial during all your support proceedings and more consideration than most people would get in a case of that kind with four or five hearings?

A: Am I supposed to enlarge upon that or say yes or no?

Q: You are the judge. You said you had no animosity toward him.

A: I think it was highly irregular in lots of ways.

Q: Were you mad at him?

A: Not especially extremely mad at anyone, but I don't say I liked him. I didn't know him. I didn't especially like him.

The court recessed for lunch and resumed at two. Kohn stepped up and asked probably one of the most bizarre questions ever asked in the Warren County Courthouse. He was referring to the morning of the shooting and he was —somehow—trying to shore up his contention that there was nothing wrong with Norman that day.

Q: Now, there was nothing wrong with you at 10 minutes of ten that morning, outside of the fact that you wanted to commit suicide?

There is no record of Norman giving any answer to the question. Kohn was wrapping up his cross-examination, establishing that Norman had never expressed remorse for shooting Judge Wade to any of the hospital or sheriff's personnel. Norman admitted that he hadn't.

Kohn ended his cross-examination by presenting evidence that neither Norman nor his attorney at the time, Mr. Brown of Connellsville, had received any letter that the court had ruled against Norman.

Court called a 15-minute recess at four o'clock..

♦

When court reconvened at 4:15, Judge Flick explained to the jury that in order to save attorney Brown a trip to Warren to testify, that attorney Braemer called and spoke with Brown and reported that Brown stated that he had not received a letter in October, 1952 stating that Judge Wade had decided the case against Norman and that Norman should start paying $30 a week in support.

Waggoner then asked that the complete record of Norman's nonsupport case be offered into evidence. Kohn objected to a number of points that he referred to as collateral, as well as statements that the defendant may have made that were self-serving. Waggoner stated that the nonsupport proceedings, which he identified as No. 20 November Sessions, 1952, in the Quarter Sessions of Warren County, were critical to Norman's murder trial.

Waggoner addressed the court: "The entire proceedings becomes part and parcel of the background which we claim created a state of mind which led to the particular occurrence on the date of January 13th." In the end there were four items that the attorney's agreed should be omitted.

After that was settled, court adjourned.

◆

Court convened at 10:00 in the morning on Saturday, May 22nd, 1954 with a conference between Kohn and Waggoner. The discussion revolved around Waggoner calling as a witness Dr. Theodore Wollack, a psychiatrist who examined Moon at the defense's request.

Waggoner told Judge Flick that Wollack would testify that in the doctor's opinion that, at the time of the shooting, Norman was suffering from a mental condition which rendered him unable to appreciate the difference between right and wrong or the consequences of his act.

"May I ask," interjected Kohn, "if you are attempting to prove that this defendant was of unsound mind and didn't know the difference between right and wrong prior to January thirteenth, 1954?"

"No," Waggoner replied, "it will be as to his mental condition for a period of a year or two prior to that time. We intend to prove that he was insane and that the condition was not a temporary condition."

Kohn told Judge Flick he would have no objection if he were permitted to cross examine Dr. Wollack regarding his qualifications.

Waggoner then called Wollack as a witness and questioned him about his training, which began when he received his Doctor of Medicine degree from the University of Maryland in 1927. Wollack enumerated his various positions up until 1940 when he took a postgraduate course in nervous and mental diseases at Columbia University before returning to private practice in Scottdale, a small town about 10 miles north of Connellsville.

At this point Kohn was allowed to question Wollack about his qualifications. It was soon apparent that Kohn had already investigated the doctor's background. He asked Wollack if he had ever heard of forensic psychiatry. Wollack responded that he had not. Kohn then produced the listings of the American Psychiatrist Association and showed the court that Wollack was listed as being a doctor qualified in forensic psychiatry.

Q: Is that the listing you have in the society you belong to?

A: Yes.

Q: But you don't know anything about forensic psychiatry?

A: No, I don't.

Q: You don't know what it means, is that right?

A: No, I don't.

Kohn got Wollack to admit that he was not recognized by the American Psychiatry Association; also that Wollack had been called as an expert in a recent murder trial testifying for the defense and that the defendant was convicted.

Waggoner then resumed his direct examination by having Wollack testify that when he was superintendent at Torrance State Hospital, he had been called upon a number of times to testify in criminal cases. Then he brought out that Wollack had examined Moon on April 28th in his cell and that Sheriff Linder was present for the whole exam, which lasted from 1:15 to four o'clock.

Q: Of what did the examination consist, Doctor?

A: Of course I took a complete history of the case and went into his early life and his marital life and his marital difficulties up to and including January thirteenth this year when he suddenly refused to tell me anything after that.

Q: Will you tell us the conclusions to which you came?

A: My feeling is that at least from the diagnosis I made, is that this man is suffering with a paranoid condition.

Q: Now will you just elaborate, Doctor, and tell us what a paranoid condition consists of?

A: A paranoid is an action formation, a mental condition in which there is, over a period of months or years, the formation of a systematizing illusional attitude maintained in the face of contrary evidence.

Q: Will you state, Doctor, whether or not this condition is a temporary one or whether it is a long time in developing?

A: I believe that most of these cases, paranoid conditions, are rather long in coming on, it is not acute in onset.

Q: In this particular case what was your opinion?

A: My feeling is that this man has been sick for probably several years.

Q: Now, Doctor, will you explain to the court and the jury what symptoms you observed and upon what you base your diagnosis?

A: Well, to begin with he was very suspicious, wouldn't give me too much information. In fact I introduced myself—but didn't tell him the purpose of the examination. He seemed very suspicious and questions had to be repeated a number of times. He was very restless. He seemed to be rather flattened emotionally. He didn't seem remorseful at all. His attitude was one of "I don't give a damn." I believe his attitude is still that. He seemed to be rather sensitive about the attitude and behavior of others and he was unwilling to discuss the situation freely. In general conversation that I had with him, it appeared that he seemed to work over his delusional material over and over again in an effort to support his contention that what he had done was right. In other words, to him his conclusions were logically correct.

Wollack went on to say that Norman told him that he felt that quite a bit of political influence had been exerted on this court by his wife's father, and in that respect he couldn't get anywhere with this court. Waggoner tried to get Wollack to summarize the examination.

Wollack answered: "Wait a moment. I have tried to summarize this as best I could. One felt that he had a rather rigid makeup with a tendency of pride and self contained haughtiness and mistrust, a feeling of uneasiness with a tendency to be sensitive about the attitude and behavior of others, misinterpretations, brooding, a long line of set suspicions and fancies with the inability to make concessions and his absolute unwillingness to discuss things either with his family or friend, or with me. As I said I probably made a mistake by not telling him the purpose of the examination. I didn't tell him who I was, I just walked in and talked to him. Now the unusual thing—there is the presence of the ideas of persecution, misinterpretations and urge for vindications and justice in those types of cases. Another thing that happens in these cases is the feeling of an irresistible need for working over the material for evidence to support his dominating actions into working for one thing, an amount of vindication, feeling that he was right in his own mind. He felt that there is no doubt that he was right. This, he accomplished through misinterpretations. One thing very common in this type of case is the fact that they have inter current crises."

Kohn interjected, "Inter what? Crises?"

"Yes," Wollack replied. "Panic states or outbursts, sudden bursts of suspicions. That happens at any time with these patients, these paranoids. They are anti-social and dangerous and have reactions of homicidal intent."

As you can imagine, after all this Kohn was on his feet. He objected saying that the witness was describing a general category of paranoid persons and not limiting his remarks to Norman. Judge Flick advised Wollack to confine his remarks to Norman.

Wollack continued, "My general impression of this man was the fact that in his own mind the homicide was justified—it was a means to an end as far as his difficulties were concerned. From my observations here in court he has a certain kind of arrogance in refusing to take the court's decision against him, which sustains my contention that this man has been, undoubtedly, mentally sick for some time."

Waggoner asked if the panic outbursts or crises were typical in paranoid cases.

"Well, a good number of them don't proceed to that as a good number of them are hospitalized and it never materializes as deterring factor, but in some cases, the first thing that occurs to these patients is to commit homicide. That's when we appreciate the fact that he is mentally sick."

Waggoner then asked Wollack if on the day of the shooting Norman knew the difference between right and wrong. Kohn objected, and there was a discussion with Judge Flick as to what was a medical diagnosis and what was a legal term. Afterward, Waggoner resumed and asked Wollack if, when a paranoid is in a panic state, he knows right from wrong. Wollack said he couldn't answer because that was a legal term. Waggoner tried again.

Q: What would your answer be from a medical standpoint?

A: I don't believe he knew right from wrong from a medical standpoint.

Q: From a medical standpoint would you say he was able, at that time, to appreciate the consequences of his act?

A: Not if he lost all sense of reason.

Q: And would you say that at the time he fired those shots he had lost all sense of reason?

A: I think he went into a panic state at that time.

With that Waggoner ended his direct examination.

Before Kohn could start his cross, Judge Flick cut in:

BY THE COURT: Doctor, it's a little different picture that you have given us of a person in a panic state who couldn't reason and act and a person in a paranoid condition who came into court in order to eliminate all those who are against him. What if the purpose in coming in may have been from illusion—would he have to have any definite purpose or intent to be able to carry it out?

A: He was delusionary. My belief is that this man was delusionary for quite a while. While sitting in the court room he was suddenly called up to the bench for sentence. That's when he probably went into a panic state. That's my feeling.

BY THE COURT: Would that panic state preclude the intent to eliminate all those who are against him?

A: Would it preclude it? No.

♦

Kohn began his cross-examination by referring to a number of insanity defense cases. Then he asked Wollack whether or not he believed Norman knew the difference between right and wrong when he went to the Pittsburgh Hornets hockey game a few nights before the shooting. Wollack replied that Moon probably did know right from wrong on that day. Kohn led him to the next day and the next day, each time asking him if Norman knew right from wrong on that day; and Wollack answered that Norman did know right from wrong on those days. Kohn continued:

Q: Do you have any basis to tell us, from a medical standpoint, whether on the morning of January thirteenth, 1954, prior to ten A.M. this defendant did not know right from wrong?

A: He did know right from wrong.

Kohn summed up this line by asking Wollack if Moon was mentally sick but still knew right from wrong.

A: Yes.

Kohn brought up the term "malingering" which means faking an illness.

Q: Isn't it true from your volume of experience that you have had that almost all persons charged with a crime engage in this pastime of malingering when they are examined either by the police or by a physician?

A: Some do.

Q: What percentage?

A: Oh, probably fifty percent.

Q: And therefore your statement as to his condition is based on what he told you would be on the question of whether or not he told you the truth or was malingering, is that not correct?

[Authors' note: The question is highly confusing. Kohn appears to be suggesting that Wollack took Moon's statements at face value in deciding that Moon was mentally ill and did not attempt to determine whether or not Moon was "malingering," that is, faking mental illness.]

A: That's exactly right.

With this Kohn ended his cross-examination. Waggoner had a one-question re-direct and Kohn objected; this brought on a sidebar with Judge Flick as to whether it was relevant to talk about average or typical cases. Flick said that if Wollack thought Norman was typical he could explain typical situations. Kohn stood and began a re-cross consisting of questions about the onset of paranoia. He referred to a textbook he had in hand and asked Wollack at what age does paranoia typically begin. Wollack said he had seen patients as young as 13.

Q: Isn't it a fact that this type doesn't become paranoid until after forty?

A: No, it isn't a fact.

Kohn and Wallock went round and round. Kohn insisted that Wollack cite an instance from his career where he had seen a paranoid between the ages of 13 and 20. Wollack said that of the thousands of mental cases of all sorts that he had seen over the years, he had seen some paranoids that were between 13 and 20, and he added that even if he could remember the case he wouldn't name the patient.

Judge Flick stepped in once again, having caught an apparent discrepancy in Wollack's testimony.

BY THE COURT: If a psychiatrist referred to one patient as a paranoid and another patient as someone with a paranoid condition, would he be describing two entirely different types of mental illness?

A: Yes.

BY THE COURT: You referred to the defendant as having a paranoid condition?

A: No, I referred to him as a paranoid, not as having a paranoid state or paranoid condition.

BY THE COURT: "Condition" is the word you used.

Kohn stepped up again to finish his cross-examination.

Q: From what you say, will he be liable at some time to become in this condition again?

A: Yes, sir.

Q: Would you say he is committable at the present time?

A: I would commit him, yes sir.

Q: For what?

A: For the fact, first, that he has proven that he is dangerous.

Q: Who hired you for this case?

A: The defense.

Q: How much are you being paid?

A: Two hundred dollars a day.

Q: How many days have you been here?

A: Three.

◆

At this point Norman's attorney, Thomas A. Waggoner, called the following character witnesses for Norman: John J. Brady, Abe I. Daniels, Clarence G. Gallagher, James W. Kennedy, William DeBolt, Mead M. Snyder, and H. Daniel Minerd, and Emory I. Mankaymer. All of these men were from the Connellsville area, and as might be expected, they testified that Norman never seemed to have a temper and that he had never been in trouble. At the end of the first four witness' testimony, Kohn asked, "Did you ever know him to go into a frenzy or become violent?" They each answered no. As for the remaining four witnesses Kohn responded, "No questions."

This marked the end of the defense case—which consisted of testimony from Norman, Dr. Wollack and six character witnesses.

◆

The prosecution started its rebuttal by calling its first witness, Dr. John C. Urbaitis. Urbaitis testified that he had been a doctor since 1931 and had been an assistant physician at Warren State Hospital from 1931 to 1937. He spent two years in the graduate school of medicine at the University of Pennsylvania and in 1938 he was certified in psychiatry and approved by the Board of Psychiatry and Neurology. He then entered the Army and spent two years as a psychiatrist in a maximum security prison where his job was to decide whether or not prisoners who had been sentenced by general court martial were sane. Urbaitis testified that he had examined 900 of these cases. In 1946 he returned to Warren State Hospital and had remained there as assistant superintendent until the present. He was a Fellow of the American Psychiatrist Association, the Pennsylvania Psychiatric Association, the Philadelphia Psychiatric Association and the Buffalo Neuro-Psychiatric Association.

Q: Will you explain to the jury what forensic psychiatry is, as simply as possible?

A: Forensic psychiatry refers to the legal aspects of the study of mental illness, especially such Commonwealth matters as commitment, competence and testamentary capacity, also responsibility.

Urbaitis testified that he had examined Moon on May 7th, 1954 for one-and-one-half hours in his jail cell with Moon's attorney Samuel Braemer present. Urbaitis explained that he had questioned Norman about events in his life up to the day of the shooting but did not ask any questions about the shooting or anytime time since the shooting. This, he stated, was so that Norman would not make any statement that might incriminate himself. Urbaitis said he introduced himself to Norman as a psychiatrist from Warren State Hospital and then asked him questions about his life, about his attitude toward various people, institutions, stresses and illnesses. Norman told him that he had flown 24 combat missions as a tail-gunner in a B-17 during World War II.

KOHN: During that time did he need any medical treatment?

URBAITIS: He needed no treatment for serious illness or mental disease.

Urbaitis testified that he had been present in the courtroom during all of Norman's testimony and based on his examination and observing him as he testified, he found no evidence of mental illness at the time of the shooting.

A: The evidence as I heard it, and from a professional viewpoint, indicate that he was sane and responsible for his acts on January thirteenth, 1954.

Q: You heard Dr. Wollack testify that he went into a panic, I think it was called?

A: Yes.

Q: Is that the correct word he used?

A: That was one of the terms he used, a panic or intercurrent crisis.

Q: Is there any such thing in medical terminology as that situation, panic?

A: I could not find it in my books.

Q: Paranoic is the general state, is it not? That is a medical term for a class of persons? Is that correct?

A: That is a group definition.

Q: A paranoic is an individual of that group?

A: Paranoic, yes, is an individual.

Urbaitis explained that paranoia is a condition and a paranoic is the individual suffering from it. Kohn asked about Wollack's contention that he had seen paranoics between the ages of 13 and 25.

Q: According to the medical textbooks and your professional observation and experience when is that condition first prevalent, at what age?

A: Around fifty.

Urbaitis testified that during his examination of Norman, he was cooperative, answered all of his questions and never mentioned that he intended to commit suicide prior to the day of the shooting. Urbaitis went on to say that during Kohn's cross-examination of Norman in court, he viewed Norman as self-assured, willful and in command of himself even when he was angry. Urbaitis cited Norman's insistence upon giving lengthy answers, even when he was asked to stop, as an example of his willfulness. Then Kohn asked him about Dr. Wollack's characterization of Norman's emotional state during Wollack's jailhouse interview as someone who didn't appear "to give a damn."

Q: I ask you what significance you attach to the fact that the defendant did appear as directed in court on January thirteenth 1954 at ten A.M.?

A: A man who didn't care would wait for the sheriff to get him.

Q: Would he have made the trip from Connellsville to Warren?

A: He would not have made the trip.

Kohn asked Urbaitis what was the significance of Norman withdrawing $2,000 and making the drive to Warren.

A: Certainly it is not an indication of being despondent and hopeless.

Kohn then jumped to the word "panic" as used by Wollack. He ran through all that had happened in the courtroom during the shooting: Moon picking out the judge, Moon making statements to the judge, and what he did after the shooting, such as reloading the .45, getting his hat and coat, threatening Bonavita, driving away on icy roads and knowing which roads to take.

Q: In summation, Doctor, I ask you whether or not from anything that you have heard or observed either during your examination of this defendant previous to this trial, or during the trial, is there anything to indicate to you that he was not sane and that he did not know the difference between right and wrong?

A: There is nothing to indicate that he was not sane and did not know the difference between right and wrong.

With that, Kohn ended his direct examination

♦

Waggoner began his cross-examination with the goal of getting Urbaitis to say whether or not Norman was normal.

Q: Do I understand you to give it as your opinion, doctor, that Norman Moon is perfectly normal mentally?

A: He is not committable and he is not insane.

Q: You mean that knowing as much as you know right now about him, if he were not under indictment and were brought before you for examination, you could not commit him?

A: I could not commit him.

Q: Even knowing the acts he committed?

A: In spite of his having committed the acts?

Q: Then we will go back to my question. Do I understand it to be your opinion that he is perfectly normal?

A: He is not suffering from any mental illness.

Q: Doctor, do I understand it to be your opinion that he is perfectly normal?

A: Do you want to define what you mean by perfectly normal?

Q: I mean as normal as anyone in the courtroom or as the average person.

A: I could not classify him under any abnormal category in psychiatry.

Q: Then I take it that you think he is perfectly normal?

A: By exclusion, yes.

Q: That is because you don't find any category of mental illness to put him under, you therefore say he is normal?

A: There is a category of people who—many people who will have grudges, who will have prejudices, but they are never labeled as mentally ill nor are they considered abnormal.

Q: Then those people are normal?

A: They are part of our normal population, yes.

Q: And you consider Norman Moon to be a normal person in every respect?

A: What do you mean, in every respect?

Q: Well, Doctor, please understand I am not trying to—I just want to get at the facts as to whether he is normal or not and I feel you, as a qualified psychiatrist, should be able to testify to that.

A: We do have normal criminals.

Q: Certainly.

A: Yes, and I would place him in a category of being normal in spite of having committed a crime.

Q: Then you would think he is perfectly normal?

A: He is normal in that respect.

Q: In what respect is he not normal?

A: No respect.

Q: Then I say you consider him perfectly normal?

A: I do.

Q: Then you could have said that right when I first asked you, "Yes, I consider him perfectly normal"?

A: All right, sir.

Q: Do you consider it normal for a person to shoot someone in court, in any open courtroom? Do you consider that normal?

A: From my point of view of some criminals being normal.

Q: Did you ever hear of that act being done before?

A: Well, not in the courtroom, no.

Q: I was talking about shooting a judge in a courtroom while court is on. I never heard of it before and I wondered whether you had.

A: I have not.

Waggoner then tried to get the witness to agree that casually getting a coat and hat and walking out the door as well as driving away at a moderate speed was not acting as a normal person would after shooting someone. Kohn objected that Waggoner's premise was too broad and that what a normal person would do had no probative value. Waggoner said it went to state of mind.

BY THE COURT: In other words, you are comparing certain acts about picking up the coat, walking out, with what other people might do, and I don't think that particularly bears on the state of mind. The Doctor has testified he thought he was normal.

Flick heard objections from Kohn and statements from Urbaitis, then told Waggoner, "I still feel that the comparison of an individual act with other acts of individuals generally is not quite in point but you can pursue it a little and I will see what you have in mind."

Waggoner pressed on, trying to get Urbaitis to concede that Norman's behavior after the shooting was not normal. But the doctor would not agree. He said that Norman's behavior was that of a normal criminal.

Q: And the act of suicide, would you say that was the normal act, or the attempted suicide?

A: That was only after he was cornered.

Q: Would you say that was the act of a normal person?

To this, Urbaitis made statements that are perhaps the second most bizarre statements to come out of the trial.

A: People do commit suicide without being mentally ill or abnormal.

Q: Then you say that normal people do commit suicide?

A: I do.

Q: That is your professional opinion?

A: That is my professional opinion.

Waggoner brought up the panic state again. After a number of questions, he got the doctor to admit there was such a thing but that it would last longer than an instant. The panic state could last a few minutes or over an hour.

Q: You say you couldn't find any reference to a panic state in any textbooks?

A: Not a panic state of this sort.

Q: What do you mean, of this sort?

A: We have seen in other types of mental illness where the mental illness is a continuous one, one which is obvious to other people.

Q: What kind of mental illness do you find panic states in?

A: In neurotics.

Q: How about paranoics?

A: I am not admitting that this man is a paranoic.

Q: You say he is not a paranoic. We can agree on that. But do you find panic states in a paranoic sometimes?

A: There may be.

Q: And is it not true that if a man is a paranoic, understanding that you say Norman is not a paranoic, but if a man is a paranoic, a panic state under circumstance of pressure and tension may develop?

A: In a paranoic there is a possibility of it developing.

Q: Surely you didn't want us to understand you to say, Doctor, that no one under fifty is ever a paranoic?

A: The condition of paranoic is a condition of mid-life. That is correct.

Q: No doubt you have known paranoics younger than fifty?

A: Not much younger, forty to forty-five, perhaps; not under forty.

Q: Did you ever know of a paranoic under forty?

A: I never did.

Q: In all your years of practice?

A: Correct.

Q: Would you say that it would be impossible for someone to be paranoic under forty?

A: It would not be recognizable by even the most astute psychiatrist.

Q: Then what you mean is, because they were under forty, you wouldn't call it paranoia?

Waggoner asked about delusions of persecution, which he suggested Norman suffered from. Weren't these delusions part of being a paranoic? Urbaitis agreed that when a person shows no remorse, that is also a symptom of paranoia. Waggoner asked the doctor whether or not he had talked to Norman about the suicidal thoughts Norman said he'd had before the shooting. Urbaitis stated that he did not ask any questions about suicide.

Waggoner ended his cross-examination.

Kohn opened his redirect by getting the doctor to testify that the panic state was transitory and that a person previous to having a panic state would know right from wrong.

Waggoner began his re-cross by asking Urbaitis questions about paranoic conditions. What were some symptoms that might appear before the full onset of the disease?

A: There would be brusqueness with people around him; there would have been interference with sleep and appetite; there would have been interference with work efficiency so that the individual could not earn a comfortable or more than comfortable living.

Q: Possibly quarreling with your wife and violence on her and things like that?

A: Well, that is something—quarreling with the wife can be a normal marriage.

Waggoner ended his questions and essentially ended the case for the defense of Norman Moon.

Kohn, in his rebuttal, recalled Agnes Mong and State Police Sergeant Charles Naddeo and had them review once again the circumstances surrounding Moon's statement in the hospital the day after he shot himself.

After that, court was adjourned until 9:30 A.M. Monday, May 24th—when summations would be delivered.

◆

Monday morning started out like the previous Monday morning. As if a king-size chess match, all the players were present and in the spots where they were supposed to be. Judge Flick was behind the bench, the jury was in the jury box, Norman Moon and his counsel were at the defense table and the prosecution team was at its table. But all was not well with prosecutor David Kohn, who was feeling a little off in the stomach. Court was held up until 10 A.M. so he could get himself squared away. Afterward, he said it was nothing serious, just a case of nerves.

At ten o'clock Braemer was on his feet and addressing the jury. There were no surprises. He went over Norman's childhood and the fact that Norman felt that he wasn't being treated fairly by the Warren County Court. One of the most important responsibilities they had, Braemer said, was to be certain the Commonwealth had proved beyond a reasonable doubt that Norman Moon was sane the morning of the shooting and that he knew the difference between right and wrong.

Braemer urged them to see that when Moon opened fire, his intention was to kill himself and no one else. For this reason, he added, Norman had not formed an intent to kill and therefore should not be found guilty of first degree murder. Braemer again went over the differences between first and second degree murder.

Braemer ran through the litany of problems that Norman had in his marriage with Janet: her stays at mental institutions, her job in Colorado enticing men, her clawing of Norman's face during an argument and the final showdown when Norman caught her out with Bill Dye in Connellsville. All of these things, Braemer emphasized, drove Norman to do what he did.

Braemer went over the same statements he had made when he began the defense's case. He added that, while Norman was 28, he was still a boy, a confused boy who had delusions of persecution and didn't know right from wrong.

During Braemer's summation many women in the courtroom broke into tears, and one woman in the jury held a handkerchief to her eyes.

Speaking of the manner in which he and his associates chose to handle the defense—allowing Norman to testify unaided, seldom challenging prosecution witnesses—Braemer declared, "We tried to give you everything for one reason: because it has been our contention that while a killing took place and while Norman held the gun, the man behind the gun was not a conscious mind."

He asked the jury to take a mental picture of Norman Moon with them into the jury room and consider what their brother or son might have done under similar circumstances.

"What would have happened if this boy had never met and married Janet Schwab? What if he had met instead some good and loveable girl and had not started on the long trail that brought him here?" Braemer ended with, "The Lord works in mysterious ways, His wonders to perform"

♦

Braemer's closing had run from 10 o'clock to 11:30. There was a recess until 1:30, at which time Kohn began a prosecution summation that lasted an hour and 40 minutes.

Kohn began by going over the main points of Braemer's closing arguments, countering them, point by point, with the prosecution's view. He said that even though the Commonwealth's witnesses varied in their testimony as to some of the specifics of what happened the morning of the shooting, this was to be expected. "With a maniac shooting up a courtroom with hatred and vengeance in his heart, and a method to his madness, what could anyone expect?"

He spoke of the insanity defense: "In the history of a community, very seldom is the defense of insanity used except in murder cases. This state does not recognize temporary insanity as an excuse for crimes of violence."

Kohn told the jury they only had one decision to make: either find Moon was insane or find him guilty of first degree murder and vote for the death penalty. "The defendant not only had malice in his heart, steel in his nerves, cursing in his mouth but death in his hands."

Kohn emphasized many of his remarks by pounding on the speaker's stand. His voice rose to a high pitch at times, at others it would drop so low he was barely audible. He peppered his remarks with quotes ranging from the Bible to Abraham Lincoln.

At one point Kohn told the jury that Moon's parents voluntarily left the hospital room when police obtained Norman's disputed confession. Dolly Moon, was sitting in the second row, shouted at Kohn, "That's a lie!", and a court officer rushed to her seat to quiet her.

In an extraordinary response, Kohn went on to blame Dolly Moon with being the cause of all Norman Moon's marital troubles. "She knew more about the marriage than Norman did," he told the jury, "but what she apparently did not know was that Norman accused his own father of running around with Janet."

Kohn finished, as Braemer had, by asking the jury to take a mental picture into the jury room. Only the image the Deputy Attorney General wanted them to think of was Judge Wade lying on the floor of the courtroom bleeding to death—and Wade's nine-year-old adopted daughter watching her father's body being lowered into the grave.

♦

After a break Judge Flick began his instructions to the jury at 3:50. His instructions consisted of a three-hour, 70-page dissertation. Afterward, at 7:10, Flick released the jury for their dinner. At eight o'clock the jury began its deliberations. At 11 o'clock the jury asked to meet with Flick to clarify certain points of guilt and the sentences involved. Flick informed them he could not tell them ahead of time what sentence he might hand down if they decided on second degree murder or manslaughter.

The jury resumed its deliberations. They returned to the courtroom at 1:30 in the morning to announce that they had reached a verdict. Despite the late hour, Flick asked the defense, prosecution and observers to reassemble in the courtroom. "Before we receive the verdict," Flick announced, "I want to tell all in the audience that the Court will remain in session for 10 minutes after the jury has left the courtroom to give its members a chance to leave the building without molestation.

"I wish to further inform you that I do not want any demonstration of any kind regardless of the verdict. The killing that took place in this courtroom was tragedy enough."

Asked by Judge Flick if the jury had reached a verdict, Dick Curtin rose and said, "We have, Your Honor."

Temporary clerk Don Shuler took the written verdict from Curtin and handed it to Judge Flick. He read it, then passed it to Shuler, who read it aloud: "We the jury find the defendant Norman W. Moon guilty of murder in the first degree and we recommend the death penalty."

In the spectator section Dolly Moon moaned and fainted. The jury was polled. All 12 answered in the affirmative—that was their decision.

◆

# ◆ THE JURORS' TALE

The trial of Norman Moon was over. Right, wrong or indifferent, fair, foul or otherwise, Norman Moon had his day in court and he was to be sentenced to death. The trial—to say the least—was controversial and there are many questions that remain unanswered to this day:

◆ Why didn't Norman's attorneys seek a change of venue?

◆ Why did Norman's attorneys allow him to re-enact the crime?

◆ Why was Norman's wife Janet never called to testify?

◆ Why wasn't Norman's father Fred called to testify?

Norman's trial was over but he was about to embark on a long, strange journey through the state's penal system. Many of those touched by the drama would never forget Norman Moon.

When interviewed some 35 years later, attorney Sam Bonavita felt that Norman's attorneys did indeed have a strategic reason for not asking for a change of venue: "I think Moon's lawyers were counting on Judge Flick to make a lot of errors in law, since this was going to be his first major case, and I think it was a bad choice—rather than going for a change of venue."

As it turned out, Norman's attorneys found no errors susceptible to successful appeal. What's more, the strategy nearly led directly to a poisoned jury, precisely what changes of venue are designed to avoid. Juror Harry Johnson claimed years later that one man initially accepted for the jury let it be known to other jurors that he was there to make sure Moon "fried." Word eventually got back to Court officers, Johnson said, and the man was removed from the panel. According to reports in the *Times-Mirror*, only one man was initially selected as a juror but removed before the start of the trial, and that was a Robert Honhart.

As for Norman Moon's re-enactment of the shooting, Bonavita described it as "a dramatic moment" in the trial. "Because there you were, seeing a re-enactment of the crime right at the scene of the crime."

Dick Curtin was the first juror picked and became the jury foreman. "One of the particular questions I recall during jury selection," recalled Curtin in later years, "was, if you're selected as a juror, do you feel you could give this man a fair trial? And I said I would never convict a man until I'd heard the evidence against him. Because there were a lot of people, of course, willing to try a man on hearsay.

"Members were sequestered on the second floor of the Carver House Hotel. The court tipstaff slept on a cot by the room door with a .45 under his pillow. Jurors were not allowed to discuss the case, listen to the radio, read the newspaper, or watch TV. When we walked through the lobby a sheet covered the rack of newspapers. We walked the four blocks between the courthouse and the hotel and we were not allowed to talk to anyone along the way. We also had no communication with our families.

"I never believed for a moment Norman was insane. But what did bother me was trying to understand what did prompt him to take the law in his own hands. He never gave the indication of being the kind of person who would do such a thing. And we never got an answer to that.

"This thing turned out, unfortunately, to be a premeditated case. The man purchased a gun, a pistol, in Pittsburgh, came up here and target practiced in the old gravel pit where the Jamesway is now in North Warren. He practiced shooting at a target a day or two before the shooting."

[Authors' note: this unsubstantiated accusation was given wide circulation and often accepted as fact, this time by the jury foreman. Evidence was presented at trial that a target was found in Norman Moon's car but no testimony exists in the trial transcript regarding Moon's having taken target practice anywhere at anytime before going to court. Moreover, the owner of the sporting good store who sold the Colt .45 to Norman testified that along with the gun he sold Norman a single box of ammunition containing 50 rounds. Subsequently, Chief Evan in his testimony accounted for all 50 rounds by adding up the shells found in the courtroom and the unspent bullets found in the ammo box inside Norman's Dodge, plus the single bullet Norman fired in his suicide attempt.]

"I believe that attorney Kohn was baiting Norman," Curtin continued, "attempting to show that he had a short fuse. When Kohn was questioning Norman about the relationship between Janet and Norman's father, Norman got flushed and angry.

"That did come out in the previous court hearings— that Norman Moon was very upset with his father in that he had bought a cocker spaniel for Janet and took her out while Norman was out working on some project.

Certainly, I would hope that wasn't true. But there was so much talk about it, I thought it could have been true.

"Always there are rumors that go around—that he wasn't given a fair hearing in the support matter. If I had any sentiments going into the trial, it was that if this man had not been given a fair hearing, I was going to find out why. So I did request all prior information on the non-support that this man had had. So the court did provide us with that information, which we went over very carefully. Of course, if we had found any discrepancies, this could never justify acquitting a man on a charge like murder, but it would have had an effect on us. But from all the evidence I saw, there was nothing to suggest he hadn't been treated fairly."

"We began deliberations in the afternoon. One woman asked if the jury could simply find Moon guilty and leave the penalty to the judge. The answer from Judge Flick was no. The two women on the jury voted against the death penalty on the first ballot. Some of the others got angry. I asked for the two who had voted against the death penalty to identify themselves. The two women spoke, saying they just didn't like sentencing anyone to death. But on the third ballot it was unanimous."

"After the verdict Don (Rice) and I came down the stairs, a couple others behind us. There were two fellows blocking the doorway coming out of the hotel. So I asked them if they would excuse us and let us through. One of them was a reporter for the Pittsburgh *Press*, and he asked me how the polling of the jury had gone, and I told him. So then this other fellow said, 'Hey buddy, do you have any children?' And I said, Yes I have two daughters. And he said, 'I hope they see you hang someday.' I started to set down my suitcase, but my better judgment—I just said, Thanks, buddy, thanks a lot."

Juror Elizabeth Hunter recalled the rumors:

"There was a story going around that he had a reason for what he did. I'd heard the story about Janet and the Judge, but I didn't believe it. I didn't believe Judge Wade was that sort of person.

"The death penalty," Hunter added, "is a hard decision—to condemn to death. I mean, you can say you believe it, but when it comes right down to it, it's hard. I remember that several jurors got phone calls condemning them for the verdict. Well, they didn't hear the testimony we heard or maybe they knew Moon's wife."

Juror Harry Johnson was out buying a newspaper when the police tapped him for jury duty. Harry recalled that everybody had heard rumors and that nobody—including himself—wanted to serve on the jury of this controversial trial.

"Yes, of course the jurors had all heard the rumors about Wade and Janet, it was all over town immediately after the shooting. But nobody knew if it was true. And it didn't matter if it was true—the only thing that mattered was whether or not Moon was the guy that stood up and shot Judge Wade. If he was, he deserved to go to the electric chair.

"I always felt sorry for Dolly Moon," Johnson added, "because her husband had been having an affair with Janet and that poor woman had to bear all that. Janet was a whore, that's all, a whore. She even worked in some nightclub out in Colorado.

"Kohn was cruel, but he apologized saying it was his job. He had a habit of looking at the spectators while questioning witnesses."

Don Rice recalled what he didn't see: "What stuck in my mind more than anything else was, his father never took the stand. Never gave any testimony about his son. Seemed strange to me. If it had been my own son, I think I would have tried to do everything I could to help him.

"Observing Moon during the trial I thought how very disturbed, bitter—bitter against the system and the way he had been treated."

♦

# ◆ GOODBYE JANET MOON

For those of us who sit around and ponder Life's imponderables, the strange, sad life of Janet Moon provides much to ponder. In this book we have not set out to malign Janet and provide yet another juicy story of a fallen woman. We have instead set out to investigate her behavior with the eyes of a journalist and the benefit of modern medicine and science.

In retrospect, it now seems apparent that Janet Schwab suffered from an unrecognized emotional illness. There was widespread awareness of her sexual profligacy, which went far beyond any norms. And we know she was hospitalized briefly several times for what was generally described as a "nervous" condition. But no one apparently diagnosed the depth of her problem.

In 1964 psychiatrists Albert Ellis and Edward Sagarin published a book titled *Nymphomania: A Study of the Oversexed Woman* (Gilbert Press). In it they write that, "A woman may become a nymphomaniac—a compulsive female who indulges in sex—not because she enjoys sex but because she is driven by fears." The authors go on to list a group of characteristics for such women that is virtually a description of Janet Moon.

Ellis and Sagarin note that such women are usually driven by a demand for certainty and therefore frequently become anxious about the smallest things. If so, that would help explain why Janet so often went into what her mother-in-law described as "hysterical fits." Think of the night newlyweds Norman and Janet arrived in Connellsville and Janet became emotionally unstrung because the furniture store wouldn't deliver their furniture that very evening. Think of Janet's irrational demand that Norman not leave her even to go to work and her distress whenever he did not return from work on time. Think of Dolly Moon's description of a day spent with Janet compulsively searching in Colorado from one bar after another for a man she'd apparently had an affair with. During that same visit Dolly observed Janet clawing her arms until they bled, because of her anxiousness. "They get the irrational idea," Ellis and Sagarin write, "that when one doesn't get exactly what one wants in the world (that is to say, when one is frustrated), it is horrible and catastrophic and one cannot possibly be happy."

Ellis and Sagarin observe that many nymphomaniacs fall into one affair after another because it distracts them from the effect of their general disorganization, they win male acceptance at the same time., and at least something is going on.    "This series of sexual relationships gives them something to live for." Those who knew Janet Schwab are uniform in describing her relentless need to be doing something all the time, to in effect escape the general emptiness of her life. And when Norman "abandoned" her to go to work, she found comfort and relief from her feelings of abandonment in the arms of a succession of lovers.

Perhaps most telling, a stepson of Janet's described a middle-aged woman so fearful of germs that she wore a surgical mask around the house and even while driving.

"Many kinds of irrational ideas lead to compulsive behavior," Ellis and Sagarin write. "In the area of sex, these modes may take the form of nymphomania or other closely related, equally uncontrollable drives. For example, an individual may repeatedly wash her hands because she feels guilty about some act. She believes she can 'wash away' the deed. Thus, her guilt leads to compulsiveness."

If in fact Janet Schwab was a sexual compulsive as defined by Ellis and Sagarin, then much of Janet's life becomes more understandable. She also becomes a more sympathetic figure, a troubled woman driven by compulsions not even she understood, as opposed to simply a callous, uncaring human being.

Early on she felt emotionally abandoned by her parents. Her father was always out doing whatever he pleased and her mother was often remote or made harsh demands. But when Janet was 13 or 14 she realized that she could command closeness by using her body and as she got older she went from one conquest to another. She had little else in life—few, if any, friends—no career or overriding interests, and she apparently made few attempts to try to achieve any nonsexual rewards in life. She just couldn't see herself succeeding in life. She gave up on her dream of being an actress almost as soon as she got the notion. Aside from her conquests and affairs, Janet led a dull life. It was her affairs that gave her a reason to live and something to look forward to: she always knew there would be another.

Janet left Warren County right after the shooting and settled in Texas, where she married for a second time. She returned in the 1960s and married twice more, living in a house her father reportedly bought for her on Follet Run Road. By this time her obsessive compulsive behavior included choking sensations which produced a panic attack so severe that she felt like she was going to die on the spot. To counteract these choking fits, she constantly sucked on cough drops to relax her throat; eventually she took to carrying a soft drink in her purse so that if she felt an attack coming on, she could take a drink, again to relax her throat.

In her last years she joined a woman's religious group and did volunteer work. When her brother Joe died, she went to the funeral and sat next to her sister-in-law, Mary, and they talked. "I'd seen Janet occasionally before," recalled Mary, "but we'd just speak—you know, a person didn't want to be seen with her. But at the funeral, she was nice. She had a heart in her. You'd never dream she was capable of the things she did if you didn't know all the stuff.

"She said, 'Mare, can I come up and visit with you sometimes on Sunday?' And I said yes, if you want to. So she came quite a few times. I just thought—if that poor girl had had a decent chance from the start." Even so, Mary Schwab found it hard to forgive. "I don't understand that being born again," she observed. "What's the use of being good all your life, if you can be rotten all your life and be born again and go straight to heaven. I don't understand it at all."

Janet's childhood girlfriend, Phyllis Hunter, also saw Janet in her last years. She remembered one night in particular. The two had been to a meeting of Women Aglow, a spiritual group. Afterward, she and Janet went to Perkins' Restaurant in Warren for soft drinks. "We talked," Phyllis recalled, "and eventually Janet told me her problem had been that she'd never had any luck with men. That was how she saw it—her bad luck." Phyllis found her girlhood friend self-pitying. "She knew she wasn't long for this world, and I don't know whether she felt she owed me an explanation or what."

Janet Schwab Moon died in Buffalo General Hospital in New York state on Oct. 18th, 1985 after a 10-month struggle with cancer. She was survived by her fourth husband, Paul F. Moore and one son, Freddie Marmolejo.

♦

# ◆ END OF THE JOURNEY

Before the ink was dry on Norman's verdict, his attorney Samuel Braemer filed a motion asking for a new trial. In his motion Braemer listed nine reasons where the court had failed to provide a fair trial. On the face of it, these nine points were legal issues that only a lawyer or a judge could comprehend. In addition to these, Braemer requested leave to file even more objections up to 30 days after the trial transcripts were made available to him.

Meanwhile Norman was held in the county jail where he was placed under 24-hour suicide watch. By July it appeared to Sheriff Larry Linder that Moon's mental condition had deteriorated to the point where he felt that Moon should be taken to Warren State Hospital to see what was wrong. He petitioned Judge Flick to authorize Norman's transfer, and Moon was sent to the hospital on July 31st. Flick also appointed a sanity commission made up of Dr. Robert Israel, superintendent at the hospital, Dr. William Walters and attorney R. Pierson Eaton to determine what was going on inside Norman's head. That examination took place at two o'clock on Thursday, August 5th, 1954.

The Sanity Commission filed its report, which included the following statements: (a) Norman W. Moon is in fact mentally ill. (b) Norman W. Moon's mental illness is that of dementia praecox of the paranoid type (c) This illness is chronic and continuing (d) Norman W. Moon is a proper subject for commitment to a mental institution.

But, in answer to a question by Judge Flick as to whether Moon "has the sufficient intelligence or mental ability to comprehend that by generally accepted standards an unjustifiable and inexcusable killing is to be wrong and considered a crime?" The commission Answered: "Yes, except during the two periods of acute mental disturbance he has exhibited."

The commission said that Norman was okay until a few weeks before the examination and at that point he started acting strange. "He had outbursts of anger particularly after visits from his attorney and his family, refusal to keep clean and shaved, insistence on leaving the lights on all night, sitting around in the nude, playing with his food, writing indecipherably on the walls of the cell, indulging for the first time in filthy language, physical self abuse, irritation for the first time with the guards, carelessness of personal possessions, and from a statement from the guards, a changed man from the person they knew as of May 25th, 1954.

"On July 31st Moon created a disturbance in the jail. He piled furniture on the table and was sitting on top of the pile with a book or a magazine for almost three hours waving at a light and babbling. His conversation at this time was not understandable. Shortly thereafter he was taken to Warren State Hospital under Order of the Court."

The following are excerpts from the Sanity Commission hearing:

Q: In your conversation with one of the guards, do you recall saying something about the "the triangle of life"? What did you mean by that?

A: The triangle of life. Naturally as you start to get older you start contemplating things, more or less trying to think yourself out every once in a while, but it's a very hard thing to do. I have to try to remember my life as best as I can, try to think out where I have been and what I have done and everything in my past history.

Norman seemed to talk crazy at times. Yet, in answering other questions he seemed sane.

Q: It is my understanding that the Superior court had made a decision?

A: I thought it was going to be interpreted there (on the morning of January 13th) more or less. I had no notice from the Superior Court as to what the decision was or anything, I only had a copy of what the Superior Court's proceedings were, not a direct order of their outcome. That was what I was called there for, to have the interpretation of the Superior Court's ruling. The first thing I knew I was called forth for sentence and I blew my stack more or less.

Judge Flick's ruling, issued on October 21st, 1954, stated that while Norman may be medically insane now and may have been medically insane on January 13th, 1954, he was legally sane enough to know what he was doing was wrong and he knew what the outcome of killing someone could be.

On December 2nd, 1954 Braemer and Waggoner appeared before Judge Flick and presented their case and filed their brief objecting to Judge Flick's findings. Braemer, who spoke for an hour, raised the following objection:

"Our objection is based on the contentions that the Court had made an error in law in using the wrong standards of interpretation of the Public Health Act of

1951, and that the Court had acted arbitrarily in not accepting the findings of the Sanity Commission."

Flick responded from the bench: "The court appreciates your argument and agrees with you that something fundamental is involved, but I do not agree that the Public Health Act of 1951 controls this case. The Court will study your brief and write an opinion."

While nearly every aspect of Norman's life in jail was under scrutiny, there was one happening that went unnoticed by everyone but Norman's family. On November 3rd, 1954 Norman spent his 29th birthday—the first of many to come—behind bars. By Christmas Norman had been locked up in the county jail and under the watchful eyes of his guards for 347 days.

On January 4th, 1955 Norman's chief counsel attorney Samuel D. Braemer was sworn in as judge of Fayette County Common Pleas Court. He would no longer be part of Norman's defense team.

On Thursday, February 10th, 1955 Judge Alexander Flick officially dismissed the exception to the Court of last October 31st finding Moon to be legally insane. He announced that the proceedings in his case would continue. In other words, Flick said that Moon was legally sane and that the Court would proceed to sentence him to death. If Moon's attorneys could come up with any other objections, they would have 30 days to respond.

Flick's decision began: "This Court cannot agree that the Legislature intended, by the Mental Health Act of 1951, as amended, to abandon the common law concept of legal insanity in determining whether proceedings should be stayed in the case of a defendant convicted of first degree murder by a jury which set the death penalty and to replace the common law concept with a medical or psychiatric concept of mental illness regardless of how such illness affected his understanding.

"The common law does not and never has prohibited the trial, sentence or execution of all persons suffering from mental diseases or disorders. It is only when mental illness affects the mind to a certain degree that proceedings are stayed—that trial, sentence or execution is postponed. It is only when the defendant's mind is affected to the extent that such illness made him unaware of the charge against him and was incapable of defending himself."

Flick went on to say that after reviewing the Sanity Commission's report and some of the answers Moon was able to make, he felt that there was no basis for his attorneys to say Moon could not participate in his own defense.

Years later Dr. Robert Israel, superintendent of the Warren State Hospital and one of the three sanity commission members, reflected on the issue of Moon's sanity: "I had some doubts about whether Norman was psychotic or not," Israel admitted. "Because on the surface, he looked pretty well mentally integrated. But I was talking to him one time, in interview—see if I can get this straight now after all these years—and he started questioning me. He said, 'What's your work here?' I said, well, it's working primarily with mental patients and my work is to a considerable extent in administration.' And his immediate response was, just like a flash, 'So you're accusing me of being a woman!'

"Now, do you follow his thinking? Schizophrenics may show a corruption of the use of words, and I was used to this, so I could follow his thinking. Administration— menstruation. You are accusing me of being a woman. And that was the final evidence for me. To make connections of this sort instantaneously, it's hardly possible to fake that."

By March 17th, 1955 Judge Flick was tired of keeping Moon in the Warren County Jail and having the county pick up the tab for Moon's extra living expenses, such as 24-hour guard and necessary medical care. Flick drew up a measure that stated in cases such as Moon's, smaller counties would seek to have defendants convicted of first degree murder transferred to a state prison, where the care and guarding would be less expensive. The smaller counties would still have to pay for the prisoner's maintenance, but that cost would be considerably reduced.

Meanwhile, Moon's attorneys appealed Flick's ruling to the Supreme Court of Pennsylvania, where it was hoped that the justices would reverse Flick's order and have Moon committed to an institution for the criminally insane. Their hearing was scheduled for April 18th, 1955, and the date was changed to May 23rd, 1955 in the Supreme Court at Harrisburg.

On May 11th, 1955 Judge Flick received word that his measure to have smaller counties, with populations under 40,000, transfer their prisoners to state prisons made it through the Senate and was on its way to Pennsylvania Governor George Leader.

On Monday, May 23rd, 1955 Moon's attorney, Thomas Waggoner, appeared before the State Supreme Court and stated his position that the question was whether or not Norman Moon was insane. Waggoner's opponent, Deputy Attorney General Frank Lawley, said that Moon "has given no hint of mental illness since May 25th, 1954, when he was convicted of first degree murder with the death penalty, for the murder of Judge Wade."

Lawley said, "Moon is smart and is making his own defense. He was perfectly sane at the time of his trial. After the verdict he embarked on a campaign to avoid the penalty."

Chief Justice Horace Stern presided over the case and said that if it can be found that Moon is truly mentally ill, "that would be the end of it."

On July 7th, 1955, Flick's measure to have prisoners who are convicted of murder housed in a state prison as opposed to county jails was signed into law and Moon was transferred to Western Penitentiary in Pittsburgh.

In October of 1955 the Pennsylvania Supreme Court handed down a decision that ordered the sentencing process to continue. Although both courts agreed with the jury's verdict of murder in the first degree, the Supreme Court ruled that Flick should reconsider his ruling in light of the fact that prior to 1951 his ruling would stand, but after the Mental Health Act of 1951, the language had changed and Flick should reexamine his ruling as it was defined by the new language.

On January 28th, 1956 Judge Flick announced that he had ended his reconsideration of the Moon case, as directed to do by the Supreme Court. Flick said he reviewed Moon's case once again and even interviewed guards at Western Penn who agreed that they had not noticed anything unusual or abnormal in Norman's behavior. Flick was standing by his decision that Norman Moon was legally sane.

Two months later, on March 29th, Flick announced that he had finished considering the 22 exceptions to his January ruling brought to the Court by Moon's attorneys and that these had not changed his position that Moon was legally sane. Flick said the objections were denied and the proceedings could continue; he added that if Moon's attorneys had any additional or new reasons for appeal, they could file those with the Court.

On April 10th, Moon's attorneys filed another appeal in Warren County. They also filed another appeal with the Supreme Court, which then ruled that the Court would once again review the matter and that all the paperwork of the case was to be in its possession by June 12th, 1956.

At the June Supreme Court hearing Moon's new attorney, Edward Dumbauld, told the Court that Judge Flick "acted beyond judicial reasonableness in discussing a sanity plea." Answering for the majority opinion, Justice T. McKeen Chidsey wrote that Flick had interpreted the law correctly and that sentencing should occur. In a dissenting opinion, Justice Musmanno wrote that what Judge Flick did was to "call in experts to solve a problem and then discard their conclusions for the opinions of passersby."

By November of 1956 the case was still being argued in Warren County. This latest appeal was based on the claim that the there were four prospective jurors who clearly showed bias, but the Court found no bias and forced the defense to use up its preemptory challenges. In other words, if the Court had ruled out these four prospective jurors because they were biased, the defense wouldn't have had to use its challenges. Furthermore, if they had used these challenges elsewhere, it may have altered the makeup of the jury.

In January of 1957 Norman Moon was back on page one of the local newspapers. Reporters filed their stories as to whether or not this would be Judge Flick's final ruling on Moon's appeal. If so, Moon's appeals would be exhausted and he would be sentenced to death immediately.

Moon would have to be picked up at Western Penn, where he had been incarcerated since July of 1955, and brought to the Warren County Courthouse. Sheriff Linder would need the assistance of three deputies to form a two-car procession to Pittsburgh and drive Moon to Warren. If Moon were sentenced to death—as many who were following this case expected—Linder would then have to transport Moon to Rockview in Centre County.

Moon would then be escorted to death row, a series of one-man cells just a few yards from the electric chair. Since 1914 when Rockview was built to ease overcrowding at Western Penn, all executions in the state had taken place in Rockview. Before 1914 prisoners sentenced to death were hanged in the county in which they had committed their crime.

Norman's appeal for a new trial was denied and on April 27th, 1957 Moon's attorneys once again appealed to the State Supreme Court. A month later this latest appeal was denied and it looked like Moon was out of options.

But then something happened in Harrisburg by way of Allegheny County that would change not only Norman's life but the life of any defendant who found himself in Norman's predicament. In June of 1957 Senator Theodore Schmidt from Allegheny County introduced a bill in Harrisburg that would force the courts to accept the decision of sanity commissions. The bill was not voted upon in that session.

But the wheels of justice continued to turn and on June 1st Governor Leader set September 30th, 1957 as the date for Norman's execution. Chances are even if Schmidt's bill did pass, it would be too late for Norman.

On September 17th, 1957, Moon's attorneys pleaded his case before the State Board of Pardons. Meanwhile, in order for Moon's appeals to be considered, Governor Leader extended Moon's life to December 2nd, 1957.

On November 15th the Board of Pardons requested that three Pittsburgh psychiatrists—Doctor Henry Brosin, James Henninger and Robert Hidson—examine Norman Moon. They did and they found him mentally ill and reported to the Board that Norman had a disorder commonly known as "schizophrenia, paranoid type."

Based on these findings the Board of Pardons recommended to Governor Leader that he commute

Moon's death sentence to life imprisonment in an institution for the criminally insane. After consulting with Attorney General Thomas D. McBride, Leader held a press conference.

Leader stated, "Moon committed a brutal crime for which he must pay the penalty; certainly in killing a judge he assaulted the very foundations upon which justice is based. Two groups of respected and qualified psychiatrists have found Moon to be mentally ill. The Board of Pardons could not in conscience ignore the considered judgment of these psychiatrists, nor could I."

Norman's commutation was announced just two weeks before he was scheduled to be electrocuted. In an ironic twist—in an already ironic and twisted life—Norman did not jump for joy.

Moon attorney Thomas Waggoner told reporters Moon was "anxious to get it over with"—meaning his execution. Waggoner added that he was the only one of Norman's attorneys left and that over the years he'd had to argue with Norman to fight for his life. Waggoner also admitted to reporters that Moon's case had been a charity case and for the last two years the money he received from the Moon family wouldn't cover his printing costs.

On November 21st, 1957 Governor George Leader sentenced Moon to life in the Fairview Hospital for the Criminally Insane at Waymart in Wayne County, near Scranton.

Prior to this announcement Waggoner had taken Moon's appeal all the way to the U.S. Supreme Court but he withdrew the case after the commutation was announced. Now all that was left was for Judge Flick to appoint a local Lunacy Commission to examine Moon. This was a legal technicality that had to be done so that it could be stated that a Warren entity had found Moon insane. Flick appointed two physicians—Dr. W. Glenn

Srodes and Dr. Raymond L. Raw—to the task. The following is an excerpt from their findings:

"The patient is shallow and superficial; he expresses bizarre physical complaints, and delusions regarding Judge Wade; and has no feelings of remorse or guilt about killing the judge. He showed poor judgment in that he insisted on going ahead with the court hearing in the absence of his lawyer. He gives a history of confusion and said he would rather be dead than continue in his present state of health. At times he was irrelevant. Diagnosis: schizophrenia, paranoid type."

♦

At six o'clock in the evening of Tuesday, April 15th, 1958. 32-year-old Norman Wilfrid Moon was led into the "D" Ward of Fairview Hospital for the Criminally Insane at Waymart in Wayne County, northeast of Scranton.

Moon's journey had begun nine hours earlier at 9:00 that morning when Sheriff Larry Linder and his chief deputy Don Allen arrived at Western Penitentiary in Pittsburgh to deliver Moon from the maximum security prison to his new home in northeastern Pennsylvania.

When the officers arrived they were directed to the office of Deputy Warden McCune, where Moon sat in his brown denim prison suit waiting for them. The redheaded Moon had gained weight and his complexion had gone pasty from endless hours indoors. When the officers greeted Moon, he responded by raising and lowering his eyebrows ala Groucho Marx. The officers handcuffed him and shackled the handcuffs to an eyelet on his belt. As he left McCune's office, the deputy warden shook Norman's hand warmly then said, "Behave yourself down there, Norman, and pretty soon you can come back here with us. You've got to serve your time."

Norman was well liked by the prison guards and on his way out they playfully punched his arm and gave him understanding pats—almost as if they were sorry to see him go.

Many in Warren felt that Moon's insanity was no more than an elaborate charade on his part to avoid the death penalty. But that day he seemed crazy enough to the sheriffs as he sat the entire trip without moving, took no bathroom breaks and refused food and water. As soon as the sheriffs got on the road in Pittsburgh Norman said that he hadn't eaten for two days and would not be eating that day. He added that while the food at Western was good, he knew that spring was coming and that he would be doing considerable sweating lying around as he was—so he had decided not to eat for a few days.

"I even had a ticket to his execution," former Sheriff Don Allen recalled in later years. "I'd just gotten out of the army, and I thought, well, this isn't something you get to see very often. So one time I was driving Norman somewhere, from one hospital to another, and I said to him, Jeez, Norman, I had a ticket to your execution," Allen recalls, laughing. "He didn't say a word after that. Guess he didn't take it too well."

On the trip from Western Penitentiary to Fairview, the only time Norman seemed normal and alert was when the deputies were discussing women and their foibles. One of them had said you could not use women and sanity in the same sentence, and Norman clapped his hands and said, "Troubles! I've got them."

If Norman Moon's insanity was an act, he was going to have a hard time at Fairview. The institution was a maximum security facility holding 1,334 wards of the state, all of whom had committed acts of violence and were declared insane. What's more, they had to stay crazy in order to remain in the hospital and not be transferred to prison, or even death row. The entire facility was governed by a strict regimen of control where officers met force with force, and Ward "D,"

Norman's new home, was where they put the worst of the worst.

♦

Nobody in Warren County heard anything from Norman Moon for eight months and it seemed to many that the story of Norman Moon had played itself out. Moon was stuck in Fairview, an iron-fisted institution in one of the most remote sites in the state. But in December of 1958, Prothonotary Ralph Sires received word from the Pittsburgh Veterans' Administration asking for a certified copy of the Lunacy Commission report to determine if Moon was eligible for a lifetime pension.

Nothing was ever heard back from the Veteran's Administration, and once again Moon's face and his enigmatic saga slipped from the front page and into the obscurity of one who is out of sight and, presumably, out of the minds of the good folks of Warren County.

But 14 years and 10 months later, Norman Moon was back in Warren. As what can only be labeled one more in a long line of ironic twists, Moon was transferred from Fairview to Warren State Hospital. At this point in October of 1973, the authorities at Fairview ruled that Norman was no longer dangerous and that he and another seven inmates should be transferred to the newly constructed Mitchell Unit of the Warren facility. At the time of the transfer, the Unit was not completed and Superintendent Dr. Harold Rhinehard said that these prisoners would be housed temporarily in Forensic Section 314 of the center building.

Rhinehard added that more inmates would be arriving when the security unit was completed. The transfers were part of a new state policy to house patients closer to their homes and a need to cut the costs of operating Fairview. Rates at Fairview were $41.22 a day and per diem rates at Warren State were $27.61, a difference of almost $14 a day or approximately $5,000 per year per patient.

Once Moon's name was back in print, it wasn't long until it was reported that just weeks before he left Fairview, Moon had filed a writ of habeas corpus in the U.S. District Court, middle district of Pennsylvania. His plea was that he did not commit murder in the first degree because he had not planned his crime, and second, that his trial should have been heard in federal court.

Warren County District Attorney William Morgan replied to the federal writ stating that Moon had also appealed to the Supreme Court of Pennsylvania citing charges unrelated to the murder charge but failed in that case to file a writ of habeas corpus. Morgan requested that the federal court dismiss Moon's petition.

Moon's stay in Warren State Hospital lasted only weeks before he was transferred to Somerset State Hospital, which was even closer to Connellsville, his home. But his brief stay in Warren put his name back in the newspapers once more as county commissioners sought to ease Moon's financial burden on the county by transferring his costs—$45 a day—to the state. Commissioner Thomas Donnelly outlined his thinking, saying that if Norman Moon was no longer insane, then he should be transferred to a state prison and the state would then pick up his tab.

Donnelly may be the first—and last—county commissioner to have psychic powers. Six months after his pronouncement, Dr. William Ryan, Norman's psychiatrist at Somerset, declared, "I found no current evidence of any significant psychiatric disturbance and considered Moon as not requiring psychiatric hospitalization. The patient is competent."

Moon's long, strange journey took yet another twist when Warren County Judge Robert Wolfe stated that once he received the proper certification, he would execute the appropriate order to have Moon returned to prison. He added that if Moon had no attorney, he would name Public Defender Joseph Massa, Jr. as his private counsel.

Norman Moon was sent to Rockview Penitentiary, outside Bellefonte in 1975.

◆

Once Norman Moon was once again deep in the bowels of the state's Department of Corrections in Rockview, his name and his story slipped off the radar screen. In 1978, it had been 23 years since that fateful day in 1954 when he shot Judge Wade to death in his courtroom. In the Warren County judicial community there was by now a whole new cast of players—some of whom were not even born when the shooting took place. Nevertheless, in the summer of 1987, Moon was back in the press.

That year 53-year-old Moon once again petitioned the state board of pardons for a hearing to ask that his life sentence be commuted. Warren County District Attorney Richard Hernan wrote to the Board that in his opinion Moon should never be released. Just as it had on three previous occasions—in 1973, 1979 and 1983—the board denied Norman's request for a hearing.

Once again Norman Moon slipped out of the public's memory and returned to his life as just another inmate doing his time at one of the state's toughest prisons.

◆

# ♦ AFTERWORD
by Lyle James Slack

B y April of 1991 I had spent nearly three years researching the circumstances surrounding the shooting death of Judge Allison Wade. I had spoken with dozens of people with first-hand knowledge of the case. Nearly all of them, along with many who had written to me, felt the shooting had been a crime of understandable momentary passion full of circumstances which mitigated his guilt. I had sat with Norman Moon himself half a dozen times in the visitor's center of Rockview state penitentiary. In our very first meeting, he had told me he had only one wish left: "I don't want to die in prison." I found him to be a gentle man and couldn't believe he would ever again be a threat to anyone. Then in mid-1990 Norman was diagnosed as suffering from throat cancer. He was refusing treatment, preferring to die rather than spend the remainder of his life in prison.

Inevitably, I had come to my own conclusions about the events which precipitated the shooting of Judge Wade. I felt the evidence was overwhelming that Norman had not planned to deliberately kill Judge Wade. Violence was totally out of character for Norman, as virtually everyone who knew him understood

"I talked to a lot of people in Tidioute about Norman," Sam Notoro told me one day. For many years Notoro was police chief for the village of Clarendon, just east of Warren. "And they had nothing but good to say about the guy. He was quiet, minded his own business. But these are the kind of guys who break," Notoro added. "You see, it's only no-good guys, they don't break. Life to them is just a big joke. But you take an honest, conscientious guy, he'll break. Because he just can't believe these bad things are happening to him. And he just can't take it."

Beginning on the day Janet Moon filed for support in Warren County court, Norman was caught in a judicial vice grip that, over a period of 18 months, crushed him emotionally. He was not in great shape to begin with. He'd endured three years of a marriage in which he was confronted, month after month, with his wife's sexual affairs. Anyone who has experienced that kind of betrayal knows how deeply destructive it can be.

Finally unable to bear the emotional agony any longer, he ended the marriage—only to find himself dragged into court and ordered to pay support to the woman who had hurt him so deeply. Not only that, he was ordered to pay her an indefensible amount of money, by the standards of the time. Not only that, the order came from a Judge Norman knew very well was supported politically by his wife's father. Not only that, the order came from a judge who insisted on claiming jurisdiction in the case even though the suit had been initiated earlier in another court and was still proceeding.

This, to me, is the heart of the case against Allison Wade and why the title of this book accuses him of judicial misconduct, a serious charge. He was not only wrong in our view in taking these actions but arrogantly wrong. Add to this eyewitness testimony that Wade at times had drinks with Janet Moon in the lounge of the

Carver House Hotel while Norman's case was still before him in court, clearly unethical behavior.

Additionally there is the possibility Wade may have been having a sexual affair with Janet Moon. In all the years I investigated this case, I could find no hard evidence to prove this accusation, despite a widespread belief that Wade and Janet were involved. Given the contradictions in Wade's character, I confess I can't even make an educated guess about whether or not the accusation is true.

Norman told me during my prison visits that he learned of the rumors about Wade and Janet only later, after the shooting. So that possibility played no role in the emotional breakdown which led to the shooting. What eventually drove Norman over the brink, I'm convinced, was his belief that the officers of the Warren Court—Wade, Kornreich, Hampson—were violating a bedrock of American justice. Norman always referred to it as the Constitutional prohibition against "double jeopardy," which bars the government from trying a person a second time for a crime he has been acquitted of. Norman wasn't quite accurate in that, since what was going on in his case was more a jurisdictional dispute. But that was how he perceived it, with some reason, and that belief just confirmed in his mind that he was being railroaded.

He was convinced an appeals court, outside the influence of local Warren politics, would reverse Judge Wade. But when the ruling came, it was unclear, at least to Norman, and for good reason. His own attorney, Henry Nicholson, wrote to him saying that he couldn't believe the court had ruled in favor of Judge Wade and that he, Nicholson, was waiting to see a copy of the decision. To Norman, a somewhat simple and unsophisticated soul, that meant the issue hadn't yet been settled.

That is why I believe Norman was telling the truth during his testimony in the murder trial when he said he came into court on the morning of January 13th, 1954 to find out whether or not the Appeals Court had ruled in his favor. And what did he discover when he got to court? That Judge Wade had ordered his $500 bond forfeited—that would be equivalent to $3,600 in 2005 dollars—and that Judge Wade was going to sentence him to prison.

At this point in his life, it's clear Norman was consumed by two emotions: depression and anger. Depression led to his taking the gun into the courtroom because, as he told me at Rockview, if Wade were going to sentence him to prison, he couldn't see any life ahead of him. He no longer had the girl he once adored, the court was taking all his money, and now he was facing indefinite imprisonment. Who wouldn't have been suicidal?

But anger led to his opening fire. There was the unexpected, last-minute blow of learning the Court had taken his bond. After which he had to sit and listen to Meyer Kornreich and Harold Hampson explain to Judge Wade how the Court had bent over backwards to be fair to Norman and that Norman had been irresponsible in failing to support his poor wife. Who in his position wouldn't have been angry?

Beyond all this, a verdict of premeditated murder makes no logical sense. I sat with juror Don Rice years after the trial and asked him if he thought it made any sense that someone would plan to murder a judge over $30 a week.

"No," Rice agreed.

I said, if in fact Norman had decided to commit premeditated murder—which Rice and all the other jurors decided he had—couldn't he have found a more clever way to do it?

Rice couldn't help but laugh and add, "Than in the middle of a courtroom with a bunch of witnesses!"

I noted that Norman had no organized escape plan.

"No," Rice agreed.

He just walked out, got in his car and drove out of town at the speed limit. And when the police caught up with him, he shot himself.

"Right," Rice agreed.

Did any of this behavior, all of which suggests a lack of planning, trouble Rice at the time he was on the jury?

"Gee, I don't know if I thought too much about it," Rice replied. "It never made any sense to me."

Dick Curtin, the jury foreman, had much the same reaction when I talked to him.

"You know, I could understand becoming irritated," Curtin told me, "and just doing something on the spur of the moment. But I just can't understand what in Norman's background would ever cause an intelligent, law-abiding man, as I guess he was, to attempt to take the law into his own hands. I just can't understand."

Finally, Chuck Sellin, who was a friend of both Allison Wade and court clerk Ralph Sires, related to me a conversation he'd had with Sires. Sires, of course, was one of the handful of people in the courtroom when the shooting occurred, and what he told Sellin seems to me probably the closest we'll ever get to the truth.

"As Ralph Sires told me," Sellin recalled, "Allie wanted to take the gun away from Moon but fell over backwards to the floor. And that kind of a move is what triggered Moon to shoot Allie.

"There was no great reason for him to shoot Allie," Sellin continued, relating what Ralph Sires had told him. "You know, a man so totally upset, as people get, some unusual happening physically can set the person off, and he can do something he never intended to do... I think it was just a queer happening that he shot Allison. So the guy, it's a great tragedy for him, too.

"This was Ralph Sires' story to me," Sellin continued, "that that's what happened. ... As I understand what Ralph said, Allie tried to quiet him down and take the gun away from him."

If, in fact, Sires was right, then as attorney Sam Bonavita suggested earlier, a charge of voluntary manslaughter would have been the appropriate charge—that is, murder committed because of "a sudden and intense passion resulting from serious provocation," as the Pennsylvania crimes code has it. That would certainly have spared Norman from the death penalty and undoubtedly from a life sentence as well.

♦

For all these reasons I decided to try and obtain Norman Moon's release. I didn't really believe anything I did would make any difference. On four previous occasions over two decades, attorneys hired by Norman had attempted to obtain a hearing before the state Board of Pardons and had been turned down each time. But I felt I had to try.

In 1957 Norman's death sentence was commuted to life in prison by then Governor George Leader. Under Pennsylvania law, a life sentence is just that, imprisonment until you die. The only way to obtain release is through commutation of your sentence by the governor. And the only way to obtain a commutation is on the recommendation of the state Board of Pardons. By statute the board is composed of the lieutenant governor, the state attorney general and three others appointed by the governor. Application to the board is a two-stage process. You ask for a hearing, laying out the reasons you believe a hearing is justified. If the board turns you down, that's the end of it. If the members agree to hear a petition, a representative is given a chance to appear before the board and make a personal appeal. Those opposed to granting the petition are also given a chance to be heard. If the members vote to turn down the appeal, that's the end of it. If the board votes in favor of commutation, its recommendation is forwarded to the governor, who can either accept or reject it.

So in the fall of 1991, I worked closely with Norman's brother, Melvin, to file a clemency application with the pardon board. We forwarded the required nine copies together with supporting material concerning Norman's medical condition. Melvin wrote a letter confirming his willingness to take Norman in and give him a place to live. He ended his letter by saying, "May God's hand guide you as you decide my Brother's future." Afterwards I visited Norman at Rockview and convinced him to allow doctors to treat his cancerous tumor at least until we got an answer from the Board of Pardons.

I had learned that it was standard procedure for the board to inform the district attorney in the jurisdiction where the crime took place of the clemency hearing and offer the DA an opportunity to oppose clemency. So on October 5th, 1991, I wrote to Joseph Massa, who was then Warren County's district attorney. In my letter I reviewed very briefly the research I had conducted into Moon's case, told him I had now filed an application for clemency and asked to meet with Massa to explain in detail my reasons for doing so. Massa agreed to see me at the end of October.

We met in his office at the Courthouse. It turned out we had grown up a few streets and a few years apart in the West End of Warren and that his father had been one of my high school teachers. I laid out the whole tragic story for the DA. My principal arguments were, first, that I didn't believe the shooting was premeditated and, second, that if in fact Norman were indeed guilty of unpremeditated second degree murder, he had probably already served far more than the maximum penalty for that crime.

Massa listened intently for about 40 minutes, asking a few questions along the way. He didn't seem to know much about the case, as it turned out, and he appeared to accept without argument the facts I presented. I left with the impression that he was sympathetic to my views, and I followed up with another letter to him. In it I told him I had found almost universal sentiment in Warren County for Moon's release. Perhaps the most important of those favoring parole, I told him, was Elizabeth Hunter, a member of the jury which had convicted Norman in 1954. I had found Elizabeth, a tiny, soft-spoken woman, at her small farmhouse on the outskirts of town. When I told her Moon had been denied a clemency hearing by the Board of Pardons on several previous occasions, she had said, "I think that's rather sad. I don't think he'd hurt anybody." I also mentioned to Massa that Sam Bonavita had told me that, if we believe in the concept of parole, then by any reasonable standard Moon deserved to be released.

I concluded my letter to Massa by relating an incident that occurred when I had last visited Norman at Rockview on September 27th, 1991. When I entered, the prison guard monitoring the visitation room saw that I had an application to the pardon board for Norman to sign. The guard looked at me and asked, "So are you going to get Norman out of here?" I said I was going to try. "Good," he replied. "Long overdue."

That took me by surprise. In the years I'd been visiting the prison, the guard had been clinically professional. Prison operations are governed, almost minute by minute, by rules and regulations, both for the prisoners and the guards, and this was the first instance in which a guard had said anything personal to me. "I've known

Norman for 10 years," he added, "and I don't think I've heard him say a mean word to anyone. I don't think there's a mean bone in his body." The guard went on to say that he believed in the concept of a life sentence but that in Norman's case, he thought continued imprisonment was a waste of taxpayer money. He thought the state could put Norman's cell to much better use by getting someone genuinely dangerous off the street.

Early in November of 1991, I flew to Los Angeles to meet with my literary agent and discuss the screenplay I was writing about the shooting of Judge Wade. I rented a car while there and drove to Phoenix where I met with and interviewed Norman's oldest brother, Robert. That December I got a Christmas card from Norman addressed to "Lyle and Family," and signed, "Norman W. Moon, AC-4664."

The last week of January, 1992 I received a letter from the secretary of the Board of Pardons informing me that the board had granted a public hearing for Norman Moon. The hearing had been tentatively scheduled for 9 AM, February 27th, 1992. Again I was taken aback. It was the first time in 38 years the board had agreed to hear an appeal of his sentence.

On February 11th I spoke with Frank Stover, Norman's counselor at Rockview. I wanted to confirm what Norman had told me, namely, that in his 17 years at Rockview he had never received a misconduct report. Stover said that was true. And then he informed me that, in response to a standard inquiry from the Board of Pardons, the state Department of Corrections had decided not to oppose Norman's release. I was told later, by the secretary of the board that Joseph Massa had not responded to the board's similar inquiry.

I drove from Toronto where I was living to Harrisburg the day before the pardon board hearing. I knew nothing about the board's hearing procedures but imagined a conversational setting, behind closed doors, all of us sitting at a big table, talking like reasonable people. So I was shocked when I walked into the Heritage Room of the Harristown II at 9 the next morning. It was a very large room, with probably a hundred folding chairs lined up facing a long dais. On the dais was a long conference table with name plates and microphones for each of the board members. The audience seats were probably half-full with what appeared to be attorneys, family members and interested parties of the convicted men whose appeals were to be heard. Norman's appeal was one of 14 to be heard that day, and I was scheduled to speak 10th.

The members of the board soon filed out of an anteroom to the left of the dais and took their seats. Lieutenant Governor Mark Singel presided. One by one the speakers for the other appeals, mostly attorneys, approached a tall microphone set up in front of the dais and stood to plead his case. In several of the cases, an assistant DA spoke in opposition to clemency. Many of the attorneys and board members knew one another and exchanged friendly or humorous remarks. I got the feeling there was a kind of club, one of which I obviously wasn't a member. Three of the other 14 appellants seeking parole had, like Norman, been convicted of first degree murder. They had served, respectively, 14, 21 and 22 years and had now been granted a clemency hearing. Norman had served 38 years before finally being granted a hearing.

When Norman's appeal was called, I walked to the microphone with my prepared remarks. I thanked the board for granting Norman a hearing and for allowing me to appear on his behalf. I told them I was not a lawyer and could not speak to the legalities of the case.

"My attempt," I told them, "has been to understand Norman Moon's case in simple human terms."

I reviewed briefly Norman's early years, his service in World War II and his return to civilian life. I then recreated, as succinctly as I could, the painful history of his marriage to an unfaithful wife, the filing of her suit against him in Fayette County, Judge Wade's irregular decision to hear the support case in Warren County court, and the events of January 13th, 1954, ending with Wade's death and Norman's attempted suicide.

I then went on to point out the discrepancy between the facts of the shooting, as laid out in sworn testimony, and the inflammatory—and erroneous—version of the shooting that at least three jurors subscribed to. I drew the obvious parallels between the juror's erroneous beliefs and the overheated accounts of the shooting which ran in the *Times-Mirror* and other local newspapers. The conclusion, I argued, was inescapable: the jury's perception of the shooting had been fatally tainted by inflammatory news reports and thus their verdict had been based on misinformation. I told them what juror Elizabeth Hunter had told me, that she was "relieved" when Norman Moon's death sentence was commuted to life in prison; as well as how she had originally voted against the death penalty but was coerced by the other, male members of the jury into voting in favor of electrocution.

I told the board about the dozens of Warren County citizens who had written to me in support of Norman Moon. "I must add, in all honesty," I told the Board in my prepared statement, "that eventually almost everyone I've interviewed has gotten around to saying the same thing to me, namely, that the only reason they believe Norman Moon has not been paroled after all this time is that he shot a judge. And many are frankly incensed about that."

Before driving to Harrisburg I had wrestled a long time with this issue, wondering whether I'd do Norman's case more harm than good by raising it. A few months earlier Sam Bonavita, a supporter of the death penalty, had told me that he felt Norman was entitled to have his parole considered by the pardon board. "But his sentence was commuted to life by Governor Leader," Bonavita observed. "And once you've served 15 years, you can apply for parole." At the time we spoke, Norman had been eligible for parole for 17 years. "Here was an individual," Sam added, "who had an exemplary background. He came from a good family. He never had a previous record. He was in World War Two like the rest of us. But unfortunately, he never has had his parole considered, mostly—it's my opinion—because the person he shot was a judge. And he shot him in court at the seat of his authority."

Finally, I decided it was too important a point not to argue. "Many are incensed," I continued in my remarks to the pardon board, "because it says to them that the judicial system considers the life of one of its own more important than the life of ordinary citizens. And these people believe that is wrong. If it is true that Norman has been kept in prison longer because he shot a judge, I presume the reasoning is to send a message—that flouting high legal authority will not be tolerated. And yet, ironically, treating this crime differently only seems to have increased disrespect for the legal system."

I reviewed Norman's medical condition, which was serious.

Finally, I told them what I had come to believe, that 38 years earlier, in a moment of anger and despair, Norman Moon had made a single, tragic mistake. He had paid for that mistake with the great bulk of his life. He was 28 when he went to prison. He was then 66. Nothing could excuse what he did, I wrote. But we could recognize that the shooting was not the calculated act of a hard-hearted man with a violent history. It was the act of an ordinary man driven to an emotional breakdown.

"Norman Moon may only have a few months to live," I said. "Whatever time he has left, many of us hope you will allow him to live it as a free man. And allow him to die with some dignity."

I sat down and waited as the last four appeals were made. Then Lt. Governor Singel declared a recess. The Board would return, he said, in approximately a half hour and announce its decisions. The members then filed out, back into the left side anteroom.

I sat stunned by Singel's announcement. I had expected it would be weeks if not months before a decision was rendered. Now suddenly I had to prepare myself for the board's verdict. While waiting, several others from the audience came up to introduce themselves and talk, curious about Norman's case and about my decision to champion his release.

Thirty-five minutes after leaving the dais, the board members filed back in and took their seats. The board secretary called the cases one by one. One by one each member voted yes or no on each case. When finally Norman's appeal was called, one after another each member called out "Yes," and the vote was recorded as unanimous in favor of a recommendation of clemency.

It's hard to express my emotion at that moment. I've been all too selfish too often in my life. Which perhaps helps explain why at that moment I felt the elation that comes from doing something entirely selfless, something exceptionally important to someone else.

I drove directly to Rockview after the hearing, passing endless rolling, snow-covered farmland. At Rockview Norman came into the visitors' room, escorted as always by a guard. He came across the large visitors' room in his characteristically awkward, loping gait, and asked me, even before sitting down, "Well, how'd it go in Harrisburg?"

I told him it went pretty well—that the board had voted unanimously to recommend his release. Norman stared at me with a blank look of disbelief. Then he grinned and scratched his head and looked around, embarrassed, and his face turned red. We sat for half an hour, Norman grinning the whole time. We talked about the first things he would do when he got out. He wanted to ride a horse, don't ask me why. He wanted to go to McDonald's. The board still had to file its recommendation with Governor Robert Casey, and there was no set time frame for the Governor to approve the board's decision. But Norman's eventual release seemed a foregone conclusion.

Afterward, I drove to Warren, stopping only when I passed a phone booth to call Norman's brother, Melvin, and tell him the news. Melvin wasn't home but his wife answered. When I told her how the pardon board had voted, she responded without emotion, saying matter-of-factly that she would give Melvin the message. Driving on, I tried to make sense of her obvious displeasure and finally guessed I could understand. A brother-in-law she hardly knew, who had spent the bulk of his life in a mental institution or prison, would be coming to live with her and her husband.

In Warren I drove directly to the *Times Observer* office on Pennsylvania Avenue where I found reporter Rory Pollard. Having been a reporter myself, I knew the *Times Observer* would run the story as soon as they heard the news, and I wanted to do whatever I could to put Norman's imminent release in a positive light. Pollard was enthusiastic, taking me into a small room and scribbling notes as I answered his questions.

His story, headlined JUDGE'S KILLER MAY BE FREED, was the lead the next day. The Associated Press picked it up, and the story ran in a number of other newspapers around the state. Besides quoting me in the piece, Pollard included comments from District Attorney Massa, who confirmed that he had not appeared at the hearing to oppose Moon's release and said he would wait to receive official word from the board before deciding whether or not to make a recommendation to Governor Casey.

Two days later the *Times Observer* ran a follow-up story on the front page based on Rory Pollard's initial interview with me. That piece focused on my motivations for investigating the shooting of Judge Wade and for filing the clemency appeal on behalf of Moon. Pollard quoted me, accurately, as saying I thought the crime was the result of the emotional breakdown of a normal man, not the act of a cold-hearted criminal. "Once you meet Norman and find out what a gentle, sympathetic man he is," I had told him, "and once you understand the circumstances that led up to the shooting in the courtroom, you can't help but feel sad at the waste of life, Judge Wade's as well as Norman's." I was pleased at the coverage the newspaper afforded me, because I knew Norman's cause would need as much momentum as possible to ensure his release.

The following week I wrote to Massa. I knew that as the county prosecutor he would be tempted to take a hard line, to demonstrate to voters that he was not soft on crime. In my letter I pointed out that the Corrections Department had chosen not to oppose Norman's application and I wanted Massa to know "that many of us appreciate your decision not to oppose Norman's release."

Opposition, as I expected, didn't take long to materialize. On March 2nd the lead story in the *Times Observer* was DAUGHTER: NO FREEDOM FOR KILLER. Rory Pollard's report began, "The daughter of the man

Norman Moon killed not only doesn't want Moon released from prison, she wants to see him die by lethal injection." The story went to say that Wade's adopted daughter claimed the man who killed her father had no right to freedom.

Allison Wade's adopted daughter was nine years old at the time Wade was killed. Thirty-eight years later she appeared to relish the sudden attention. She lambasted the Board of Pardons for not giving her a chance to appear in opposition to Moon's clemency application. "I was upset and appalled that they would even consider letting him out," Pollard quoted her as saying. "I live with it every day, knowing he killed my dad, and he did it in cold blood. It was premeditated."

In the same story Attorney Sam Bonavita was quoted as saying he had no opinion about Moon's possible release. That wasn't exactly the case when I had interviewed Bonavita two years earlier. I had come away from that meeting with the clear impression that Bonavita felt Moon was no threat to anyone and had paid his debt to society. Now, however, Bonavita was quoted in Pollard's story as saying, "The way I feel, after all this time, these are matters left up to the parole board and governor." Still, for a member of Warren's establishment, that passed for courage.

On March 6th the *Times Observer* ran a short piece announcing that Massa had written to Governor Casey— opposing Moon's release. "In a letter sent by Massa to the governor on Tuesday," reporter Chuck Hayes wrote, "the district attorney said he cited the seriousness of the crime committed by Moon and the fact that Wade's family has considerable concern and anxiety about the possible release of Moon."

Two weeks later the *Times Observer* ran a story saying Judge Wade's daughter was still waiting to receive a reply to a letter she sent Governor Casey opposing

Moon's release. "When she didn't hear anything from the governor by last week," reporter Eric Paddock wrote, "she called the governor's Hot Line. She was told by that operator that it takes up to three weeks to process the governor's mail." The story noted that, contrary to the daughter's earlier accusations, the pardon board had, in fact, attempted to notify her of Moon's clemency hearing but the only address they had was a Titusville address where she had not lived for the past 10 years. Paddock's story also revealed that a local attorney, Robert Hampson, had also written to the board to oppose Moon's release. Hampson's father, had, of course, represented Janet Schwab in 1954 and was among those Norman shot at in the courtroom.

In May I wrote a letter to the editor of the *Times Observer*, which it published in full. "Since last February," I began, "the *Times Observer* has run a number of reports concerning the recommendation by the state Board of Pardons that Norman Moon be paroled. As a journalist and screenwriter who has spent the last four years investigating Moon's 1954 shooting of Warren County Judge Allison Wade, your coverage has struck me as quite thorough and fair.

"However, these stories may have inadvertently left two false impressions in the minds of some readers.

"First, recent stories have noted repeatedly that three county people have written to Governor Robert Casey to oppose Moon's release," and I cited Allison Wade's adopted daughter, District Attorney Massa and attorney Robert Hampson.

"I think it equally important, however, that your readers know that many others in the county favor Moon's release. I have interviewed dozens of residents connected with the case, and a number of them have expressed great sympathy for Moon. Among them is one of the jurors from Moon's murder trial who expressly favors his parole."

I was referring, of course, to Elizabeth Hunter.

"I have also received, over the period of the last year, dozens of letters from county residents concerning the Moon case; all of those letters except one were sympathetic to Norman Moon. Several of those people have since indicated to me that they have written Governor Casey supporting the pardon board's decision.

"The second matter which I think requires comment is District Attorney Massa's professed reasons for opposing Moon's release. Your March 6 story noted that Massa's letter to Governor Casey alluded to the 'anxiety' Judge Wade's family feels about Moon's possible release. Whether or not Norman Moon would be a danger to society or to Judge Wade's daughter specifically is, of course, a legitimate concern.

"The fact is, however, that neither Mr. Massa nor Judge Wade's daughter has ever met Norman Moon and therefore has no personal knowledge of what kind of man he is. The people who do have detailed knowledge of Norman Moon's character are the officials at Rockview state prison, and their judgment, expressed to the pardon board, is that Moon no longer presents any danger to society.

"More specifically, I have spoken with perhaps half a dozen guards at Rockview, as recently as last week, in the course of visiting Norman Moon. These guards have uniformly expressed to me what can only be described as fondness for Moon. 'I've know Norman for 10 years,' one of them told me, 'and I don't think I've heard him say a mean word to anyone. I don't think there's a mean bone in his body.'

"All of us can sympathize with the emotions Judge Wade's daughter and Mr. Hampson naturally feel. But mercy does have a place in our system of justice, and after 38 years, the state pardon board, corrections officials and many Warren county residents believe Norman Moon deserves our mercy."

During the spring of 1992, I was concerned not only about maintaining some sort of public support for the Board of Pardons clemency recommendation but also about Norman's health. True to his word, he had permitted doctors at Rockview to arrange for treatment of his cancerous throat tumor at an outside clinic, The Boalsburg Group. I was in contact with them as well as Norman's counselor at the prison and with Norman's brother, Melvin. The last time I had seen Norman he was thin but seemed reasonably well. He was regularly consuming a protein-rich drink, the easiest thing for him to swallow. During that same visit I had asked him in passing what he was reading, since he was always reading something, a book or magazine article. He grinned, flushed and said, *The Dark of Norman Moon*, the title of the four-hour miniseries screenplay I had written and given to him to read.

So on the evening of June 5th, when I got a call in Toronto from Melvin Moon, I wasn't surprised, since we'd been in regular contact. Melvin began by telling me Norman had taken a turn for the worse the day before and began having great difficulty breathing. His doctors scheduled emergency surgery, to try and relieve the pressure the tumor was placing on his trachea. "So how's he doing," I asked. "Well," Melvin replied, "he was pretty weak, you know and—well, he didn't make it."

I sat speechless for a moment. It had never occurred to me Norman would die before we could get him out of prison. Melvin filled the silence with a few details about the surgery. Finally, when I could speak, I asked Melvin when the funeral would be. "Well, we're not going to have anything," Melvin replied. "Norman didn't want any kind of ceremony. He told me he just wanted to be cremated and have his ashes scattered on our mother's grave."

With that phone call, my four year odyssey was suddenly over. Or almost anyway. I phoned Rory Pollard at the *Times Observer*, to tell him the news. Rory and the paper had been honest, comprehensive and neutral reporters of the facts concerning my research and the Board of Pardons action. I felt I owed it to them to make sure they had the news first.

And then it really was over. In the years immediately following, I moved to Los Angeles, optioned my screenplay to NBC briefly and reworked the script a number of times for different producers in an effort to make it fit the TV formula of the moment and see it produced.

But I never again felt the emotion I had felt during the years I saw and spoke with Norman and the scores of others who had briefly crossed paths 30-some years earlier and were permanently touched by sudden death.

♦ ♦

JOHN L. YOUNG grew up in Altoona, PA and has a degree in Journalism from Empire State College. He is a former reporter and columnist for the Jamestown, NY *Post-Journal*. He is a contributing writer for *Pennsylvania Magazine* and *Ohio Magazine* and his travel articles have appeared in *Pursuits*, a publication of the Pennsylvania Tourism Office. His books include *Unemployed No More*, a self-help book that grew out of his own search for a more satisfying occupation; the outdoor guide *Hike*  *Pennsylvania*; and *Murder at the Airport Inn*, the true story of a 1936 murder-for-hire. He lives on three acres just outside Russell, PA, with his wife Debra, an elementary school principal, and has a 23-year-old son, Aaron. His hobbies include hiking and outdoor photography.

 LYLE JAMES SLACK grew up in Warren, PA and received an M.A. in political science from Allegheny College and a B.A. in English from Bloomsburg University. He spent 10 years as a reporter for the Hamilton, Ontario *Spectator* before turning to freelance writing and authoring numerous articles for most of the national magazines in Canada. In 1986 he began writing for television, scripting episodes of various series for CBS, Fox, the Disney Channel and the USA Network. In 1993 he moved to Los Angeles to write and produce television movies. His full-length TV dramas include, for NBC, *The Sleepwalker Killing* starring Oscar-winner Hilary Swank; and for CBS *Another Woman*, based on a popular Harlequin novel. He lives in Los Angeles with his wife Jane, a print production manager, and their seven-year-old daughter, Brett.